ROUTLEDGE LIBRARY EDITIONS:
GERMAN HISTORY

Volume 26

THE POLITICAL ECONOMY OF GERMANY, 1815–1914

THE POLITICAL ECONOMY OF GERMANY, 1815–1914

MARTIN KITCHEN

Routledge
Taylor & Francis Group
NEW YORK AND LONDON

First published in English in 1978 by Croom Helm Ltd.

This edition first published in 2020
by Routledge
52 Vanderbilt Avenue, New York, NY 10017

and by Routledge
2 Park Square, Milton Park, Abingdon, Oxon OX14 4RN

Routledge is an imprint of the Taylor & Francis Group, an informa business

British Library Cataloguing in Publication Data
A catalogue record for this book is available from the British Library

ISBN: 978-0-367-02813-8 (Set)
ISBN: 978-0-429-27806-8 (Set) (ebk)
ISBN: 978-0-367-24641-9 (Volume 26) (hbk)
ISBN: 978-0-429-28365-9 (Volume 26) (ebk)

Publisher's Note
The publisher has gone to great lengths to ensure the quality of this reprint but points out that some imperfections in the original copies may be apparent.

THE POLITICAL ECONOMY OF GERMANY 1815-1914

MARTIN KITCHEN

CROOM HELM LONDON

McGILL-QUEEN'S UNIVERSITY PRESS
Montreal 1978

Croom Helm Ltd, 2–10 St John's Road, London SW11

British Library Cataloguing in Publication Data

Kitchen, Martin
The politicial economy of Germany, 1815–1914.
1. Germany – Economic conditions 2. Germany – Politics and Government – 19th century
3. Germany – Politics and government – 1888–1918
I. Title
330.9'43'07 HC285

ISBN 0-85664-610-5

McGill Queen's University Press
1020 Pine Avenue West, Montreal H3A 1A2

ISBN 0–7735–0501–6

Legal deposit second quarter 1978
Bibliothèque Nationale du Québec

CONTENTS

To Dick, Katharine and Emily

PREFACE

Writing an introduction to the Political Economy of Germany in the nineteenth century has proved to be both challenging and frustrating. The opportunity to organise and discuss in greater detail some of the major themes of my earlier work has proved immensely rewarding, but in the process of attempting to cover such a wide field I have become increasingly aware of the problems of writing such a book. Apart from my own shortcomings there is the lack of much basic empirical research on some of the key issues of the economic development of Germany in this period, an obsession by many historians with economic theories which border on the theological, and a serious lack of coherent and consistent statistical data, particularly for the earlier part of the century. In a book of this size there are perhaps too many opinions that are inadequately substantiated owing to lack of space or inadequate evidence, a certain simplification of complex issues, and an underemphasis of regional disparities. Hopefully, the more polemical passages will be seen as hypotheses designed to stimulate debate rather than over-confident and dogmatic statements of fact, and the book will be of use to a wide audience of all those who are interested in the debate on the question of why German society evolved in its own particular and unique manner.

The theme of this book is the interaction between economic development and social structure. Relationships between economic, technological, social and political developments are examined in an attempt to delineate the history of economic social formations seen as a totality. My main concern in writing this book was to try to discover why German society developed in such a distinct manner and why economic modernisation did not lead to social modernisation. The peculiarities of German industrial capitalism cannot be examined simply in terms of business history, the history of technology, agricultural history or the statistical sophistication of the 'new economic history'. This is partly because to so many economic historians 'capitalism' is a slightly embarrassing word which smacks of a political orientation which is not their own, and partly because capitalism, like all economic activity, is also a social formation. Without an examination of the social dimension of economic activity, economic history all too easily becomes bloodless and abstract, or is one-sided and thus distorted. Social activity is not simply a direct result of the development of the material forces of production, for economic activity is in turn decisively affected by the conscious activity of men and by the social formations within which it develops. I have tried where possible to discuss this interaction of the social and the economic in terms of a reciprocal relationship so that political decisions can be seen as having been determined by economic developments and yet having profound economic consequences.

The process of industrialisation is immensely complex and its consequences are felt throughout a society. In a book of this length I have only been able to discuss some of the factors which made an industrial revolution possible, and to suggest some of the effects of exceptional economic growth in a society that refused to adapt itself to lessen the resulting social and political conflicts. Such an approach will not please many economic historians, but hopefully it will offer suggestions to students of German history who wish to study the relationship between economic, social and political change.

Many shortcomings in the original draft have been at least partially overcome thanks to the incisive and constructive criticism of an economic historian whose desire for anonymity is due less to his becoming modesty than to a profound methodological disagreement over the foundations and principles on which this book is based. To him I owe a great debt of gratitude for his encouragement, scholarly detachment and enduring friendship. I would equally like to thank Peter Weber, whose remarkable knowledge of the period and exceptional bibliographical expertise has saved me from many errors. I should also like to express my thanks to Professor Fritz Fischer, whose work has been a constant inspiration and who in private conversation has provided more guidance and help than he would be willing to admit.

To Sheila Roberts who came to my aid at a critical time in the writing of this book I am deeply grateful. Pearl Sirkia, Elsie Trott and Phyllis Hawkins typed a difficult manuscript with great skill and were unfailingly co-operative and cheerful.

1 GERMANY IN 1815

Abolition of Serfdom

In 1815 Germany was an agricultural society. The population of the German states, excluding that part of Austria which belonged to the German Confederation, amounted to approximately 23 million, of whom 10.5 million lived in Prussia. Of this total population three-quarters lived in rural areas. Apart from the Rhineland provinces and south-western Germany, where much of the land was owned by small farmers, most of the agricultural land was the property of the aristocracy, a class which included a large number of impoverished petty aristocrats, whose estates were still organised on traditional semi-feudal lines. The Napoleonic wars resulted in a serious reduction of the number of farm animals. The crop failure of 1816 caused the most serious famine for almost half a century, a situation which was made even more acute by the outbreak of an epidemic which decimated the seriously inadequate stock of cattle. Widespread suffering and misery among the common people were coupled with a political reaction which threatened to destroy the all too modest advances which had been made since 1806 towards the creation of a less autocratic and hidebound society. Yet although Germany in 1815 seemed poor, backward and reactionary, significant changes had been made, particularly after the crushing defeat of Prussia by the French in 1806, which were to have a profound effect in the years to come by providing the basis for modernisation and economic growth. The most important of these measures was the Prussian edict of 14 September 1811 which revised the relationship between landlord and peasant and which called for the liberation of the serfs.

The feudal order on the land was the corner-stone of Prussian society in the eighteenth century. For this reason it was fiercely defended by those who profited from the system, who feared the consequences of dramatic change or who argued that the preservation of traditional society was the only alternative to a bloody revolution on the French model. Conversely, no aspect of Prussian life was more fiercely attacked by the liberal bourgeoisie, who used the arguments of the British classical economists about the harmful effects of privilege and traditional rights and obligations on the economic life of the nation, which they combined with older arguments from the physiocrats on the importance of agriculture to point out the evil social and economic consequences of serfdom. Thus on both sides there was agreement that the abolition of serfdom would have far-reaching consequences. The aristocracy feared, and the liberal bourgeoisie hoped, that agriculture would be based on free wage labour and the introduction of the capitalist mode of production to the rural economy.

Whereas in France the feudal system had been destroyed in the revolutionary edicts of August 1789, August 1792 and July 1793 and confirmed in the Code Napoleon of 1804, the system remained virtually intact in Prussia. Peasants lived in a condition of hereditary serfdom, the forms of that serfdom differing in various areas. They were unable to move, or to marry, without the permission of the lord to whose estates or person they were bound. Their children were obliged to work on those estates. Even those peasants who owned land were forced to provide labour service on the aristocratic (*Junker*) estates, and such peasants were also bound to the land, for their ownership depended on the performance of feudal duties. Harsh punishments were meted out to those who failed to meet their obligations, frequently involving brutal floggings, from which women were not excluded. The hunting rights of the aristocracy were a particular hardship which excited the indignation of the reformers.

There were many compelling arguments in favour of the liberation of the serfs. Reformers like Stein felt that free wage labour was far more efficient and productive than forced labour service. The great architects of the new Prussian army, Scharnhorst and Gneisenau, were convinced that only free men would be prepared to fight and to die for the liberation of their country. Humanitarians were outraged at the primitive conditions on the land which were so harsh a contrast to their ideal of the basic human right to a dignified life and to opportunities for self-betterment. Others argued that without a 'revolution from above', involving measured and cautious steps towards economic, social and political reform, Prussia could well fall prey to a social revolution 'from below'.

The French Revolution thus provided an important external stimulus to reforms which were long overdue. Some of the peasants on the royal estates in Prussia were freed from feudal obligations, but as these obligations were commuted, the King made a handsome profit from this enlightened reform. The suggestion that a similar reform could be carried out on the estates of the nobility was greeted with the outraged indignation of the majority of Junkers, who were unwilling to abandon their old way of life whatever the immediate economic advantages of such a move. The defeat of Prussia at the twin battles of Jena and Auerstädt in 1806 was so crushing that even many of the most extreme conservatives realised that drastic changes were necessary if Prussia were ever to regain her status as an independent state. The abolition of serfdom in the Grand Duchy of Warsaw and in Westphalia gave the Prussian aristocracy further cause for alarm, for they feared that either there would be a mass emigration to these freer areas by peasants who found the oppressive Prussian régime intolerable, or that there might be a growing demand for reform inspired by events in the neighbouring states.

The first major step towards the liberation of the Prussian serfs was taken with the edict of 9 October 1807, in which the King announced that 'from Saint Martin's day 1810 all states of subjection (*Guts- und Untertänigkeit*) will cease in all our states. From Saint Martin's day 1810 there will only be free men.' In return for the loss of absolute control over the peasantry the Prussian aristocracy was granted free disposition over the land. Thus the abolition of serfdom also involved the abolition of the *Bauernschutz*, the laws which had given the peasant security of tenure over his own holdings, which protected him against unfair competition, and which gave him a relatively secure position in an increasingly hostile economic environment. Feudal land ownership was thus to be replaced by completely free ownership, and the aristocracy would be able to buy and sell land without interference from the state authorities. The elaborate eighteenth-century system of land tenure, which was designed to preserve the social order, was abolished, and capitalist property relationships were to take the place of feudalism. The free peasants no longer needed the consent of the landlord before they could marry, their children were no longer required to perform compulsory service for the landlord. They were free to determine their heirs. Perhaps most important of all, they could change their domicile without prior permission from the landlord. Yet even these freedoms were not absolute; the landlord had police rights over his estates and no one could leave without a certificate from him that he was not suspected of any misdemeanour, and labour relations between lord and peasant were still governed by the 'regulations for servants' (*Gesindeordnung*) which restricted the freedom of the labour market.

The implementation of the October edict proved to be exceedingly difficult, for practices were widely different in the various Prussian provinces and the whole question of feudal obligations and duties was thus immensely complex. The central question was to decide which feudal duties were to be abolished, which were to remain, and whether or not compensation should be provided for the loss of customary privileges. On 14 September 1811 a further edict announced that peasants who had hereditary tenure were obliged to give one-third of their land to the lord as compensation for the abolition of feudal obligations. Those who had no hereditary rights had to give up half their land. Hardenberg's edict was opposed by the aristocracy, who felt that the compensation was inadequate, or who opposed the abolition of feudal obligations altogether. The landlords thus set about sabotaging the edict by raising endless objections and postponing any effective action as long as possible. A further edict in 1816 excluded all small peasant holdings from the reform as well as any land that was not entered in the provincial tax rolls, or which had become peasant property after the land reform of Frederick the Great at the time of the Seven Years War. As a result of these changes only a minority of the peasantry were affected by the reform. The majority continued in a state of semi-feudal dependence and were at the mercy of the aristocracy. These feudal obligations were not abolished until after the revolution of 1848, and the process was not finally completed until 1865. By this time very few peasants were still in a state of dependence as a result of their land holdings. Without the protection of the *Bauernschutz* their land had mostly been absorbed into the large estates of the nobility and they had become landless labourers. The obligations which remained after 1848 were of a minor nature, such as the duty to pluck geese for bedding on the occasion of a wedding or baptism in the landlord's family.

The liberation of the serfs, although incomplete and one-sided, was nevertheless a major step towards the economic and social modernisation of Prussia. The feudal mode of production now belonged to the past and it remained to be seen how the new class of free and equal peasants would survive in a harshly competitive economic system without the support and protection which had been given them in the past. Those liberal reformers, who had hoped to create a class of fiercely independent yeomen farmers from a servile peasantry, were soon to be disappointed. The free peasant was unable to compete in a free market economy. His land was seriously reduced by the provisions of the edicts of 1811 and 1816, and his remaining holdings were often too small to support a family adequately. He had no capital, and no credit was available to him without resorting to usurers, who usually proved to be his downfall. By contrast, the aristocracy had their own credit institutions which provided them with much of the capital required for expansion and for investment in modern techniques. Most of the Prussian Junkers were quick to adapt their way of thinking to the new situation, and as often as not objections to the proposed reforms, particularly in the later stages, were not over matters of principle, but rather in order to extract the highest possible benefit from any changes.

The result of these reforms was an increase in the size of aristocratic holdings and a diminution of the amount of land owned by the peasantry. The Junkers gained land through compensation for the abolition of feudal obligations and duties, they speculated in land on the free market, and they bought up the holdings of peasants ruined in the agricultural crisis of the 1820s. The precise amount of land lost by the peasantry cannot be measured with absolute accuracy, but most historians agree that it was about 2.5 million acres, or about 45 per cent of all peasant land. This increase in the size of aristocratic estates would have been even greater were it not for the fact that the nobility made a brisk trade of selling land to the wealthy bourgeoisie, who were now no longer restricted from purchasing the lands of the aristocracy, and once the rising bourgeoisie began to ape the behaviour of the aristocracy, the position of the latter was further strengthened. The large estates of the Junkers were the product of feudalism, but they grew larger as a result of the reforms of Stein and Hardenberg. Unlike France, they were not divided up among the peasantry, and unlike England, they were not leased out to enterprising farmers. The large feudal estates became large capitalist concerns. Such was the unique 'Prussian way' to the modernisation of agriculture which was to have such a tremendous impact on the future economic, social and political development of Prussia and of Germany.

The peasants were now mostly free wage-earners. They had either commuted their obligation to labour service by handing over part of their land, or, in the case of the smaller peasants, by losing their land altogether they were no longer obliged to perform the duties which ownership of that land entailed. Yet, as Max Weber has pointed out, the distinction between serfs (*Fröner*) and day-labourers (*Insten*) was not so very great. Day-labourers were paid in large part by grants of land, and the serfs had been given money for service. Without the protection of the *Bauernschutz*, and with the relationship between lord and master now based on a mainly economic tie, the position of the peasant might have been freer, but it was also more uncertain and insecure. With the agricultural depression after the wars of liberation there begins a movement of population away from the land to the urban areas, which was to become even more pronounced in the railway age. Until the time of German unification in 1871 this loss of rural population was still relative, and was more than offset by the increase in population, but it was important in that the displaced peasants and artisans provided the manpower for the new industrial enterprises. Thus the liberation of the peasants from the bonds of feudalism was an important precondition for the industrialisation of Germany by creating the necessary mobility of labour.

These reforms affected Prussia east of the Elbe and they had such a profound influence because of the unique position of the land-owning aristocracy in Prussia, and later of Prussia within a united Germany. In other parts of Germany the situation was very different. In the Rhineland and the Kingdom of Westphalia feudal obligations were abolished, usually without compensation, by the French before the reforms in Prussia. In Westphalia the old system was restored after the defeat of the French in 1813 with the somewhat perverse argument that it is better to restore the old, even if it is bad, and then reform it yourself. In fact it needed the revolutionary upheavals of 1830 before the aristocracy would agree to the commutation of feudal obligations. In Schleswig and Holstein serfdom was abolished in 1804, and the big landowners were quick to see the advantages of wage labour and leasehold farming. Bavaria abolished the remnants of serfdom and ground rents in 1808, but the liberation of the peasants was made dependent on the agreement of both parties. The resulting confusion was not settled until 1848, when the old system was finally abolished, as it was in this revolutionary year in Austria and in Saxony. Serfdom had been abolished in Baden as early as 1783, largely because of the influence of physiocratic teaching, but some remnants of the feudal system remained to be swept away in 1848. In north-west Germany, Thuringia and Bavaria, serfdom had played a minor role and the effects of these reforms were less dramatic than in Prussia east of the Elbe.

Although serfdom had been virtually abolished by 1815 throughout Germany and rural labour was almost free, elements of the old system still remained. Thus the landed aristocracy retained jurisdiction over the peasantry, a right which seriously restricted the freedom of the peasants and which remained in force until the revolutions of 1848, in some instances to be reimposed in the 1850s. Freedom of movement was also constrained by governments who feared that their states would be overrun by undesirable elements from other parts of Germany and who imposed stringent immigration regulations. Thus the reform was still incomplete. Conditions in various parts of Germany differed widely and much remained to be done before agriculture was free from the last remnants of a system which had hampered its growth. The question of the compensation to be given for the loss of feudal service was not to be settled in some instances until the unification of Germany in 1871. The change from a feudal to a capitalist mode of production was thus a long and difficult process which caused much disruption and hardship. In some areas, such as the Rhineland and Schleswig-Holstein, the transition was much smoother, but mostly the old order gave way to the new reluctantly, and reform was woefully incomplete.

Agriculture

Throughout most of Germany the old three-field system with summer crops, winter crops and fallow was still used. Yet with primitive farming methods, the shortage of cattle, and consequently of natural fertiliser, and inadequate supplies of winter feed, usually more than one-third of the land lay fallow. The steadily increasing population and the growth of the towns increased the demand for agricultural produce, particularly dairy products and beef. This in turn emphasised the need for more efficient feeding methods and underlined the backwardness of German methods when compared to British agriculture.

Attempts had been made to improve productivity. Frederick the Great had used the fallow lands of some of his estates to produce feed crops, and tried to introduce English methods of farming, but his example was not widely followed. The most influential figure in the movement for the improvement and modernisation of agriculture was undoubtedly Albrecht von Thaer, whose four-volume study, *The Principles of Rational Agriculture*, was published between 1809 and 1812. As the title of his book suggests, Thaer was very much a man of the Enlightenment who wished to break with outmoded traditions from the past and start afresh with a new science of agriculture that would be logical, reasonable and fully scientific. But he was also very much a man of the nineteenth century. Thus at the beginning of his book he defines agriculture as 'a profession the purpose of which is to make a profit or to earn money by the production, and sometimes by the processing of, vegetable and animal substances'. Thus Thaer called for the complete abolition of all feudal residues on the land, and the introduction of a thorough-going scientific and capitalist agriculture.

Thaer was an enthusiastic supporter of the intensified three-field system which used the fallow for crops like potatoes or clover, but he also wanted to go beyond these improvements and introduce a system of crop rotation that would greatly increase the intensity of agriculture and cause a dramatic rise in output. Under the intensified three-field system there was also a rotation of crops, usually two different forms of grain followed by the fallow crop. With Thaer's system every corn crop was followed immediately by a fallow crop, thus the ground was better worked over, better weeded, and because of the increase in fodder, better dunged. Crops tended to be of better quality with a higher return per acre. The disadvantage of the system was that it made much greater demands on the land and on the farmer, so that the initial outlay both in money and in labour was greater. Marginal farms were unlikely to risk such a major departure from traditional methods, and in many cases were lacking the reserves to take such a step. As the land was mainly of poor quality and as the landowners were mainly concerned to produce for the grain market, a more complex rotation system was hardly possible or desirable.

In some parts of Germany these English methods of crop rotation had already been introduced, but only on a very small scale. Thaer was thus not the first to bring these ideas to Germany, but he was the first systematically to introduce his countrymen to them and he did so at a time when the improvement of agricultural production was essential if Germany were to develop economically. Thaer also insisted that such an improvement was not possible on the basis of crop rotation alone, but improvements in agricultural machinery and in the fertilisation of the land were also imperative. On the subject of fertilisation, Thaer adhered to the erroneous but widely held humus theory, by which it was believed that plants were fed solely by rotting vegetable or animal materials, a theory which was not to be displaced until 1840 with the publication of Justus von Liebig's work on the use of organic chemistry in agriculture.

Although by profession a doctor and by birth a Hanoverian, Thaer played an important role as adviser to the Prussian government at the time of the reforms of Stein and Hardenberg. He founded the first agricultural academy in Germany at Moglin near Berlin in 1806, the first of a series of similar state-financed institutions which were to play an enormously important role as research centres and which were to make Germany one of the leading countries in the field of agricultural research.

Agricultural progress was not only the result of the abolition of feudalism and the work of reformers like Thaer, it was also a consequence of political exigencies, of which the most significant was Napoleon's Continental System. The wool export market was destroyed, and farmers were forced by economic necessity to turn sheep farms into dairy farms, thus increasing the need for fodder and giving further impetus to an intensified crop rotation. The Continental System also acted as an incentive to the suger-beet industry. As early as 1747 Andreas Sigismund Marggraf of the Berlin Academy of Sciences had argued that a viable alternative to sugar-cane could be grown in Prussia, but it was not until 1801 that his pupil, Franz Karl Achard, grew the first sugar-beet crop on an estate that had been granted to him by the Prussian King, Frederick William III, in an attempt to make Prussia independent from the importation of sugar. In 1809 Achard published his treatise on the sugar-beet which covers all aspects of the production of sugar.

At first the attempts to create a sugar industry in Prussia were bitterly disappointing. Only 3 per cent of the gross weight of the beets could be converted into sugar, which made the whole enterprise uneconomic. Achard was ruined when in 1810 the Prussian state decided that it could no longer afford to subsidise his estate, and he died in 1821 in abject poverty. The Continental System saved the industry, although it was only able to survive by the ruthless exploitation of labour. With the defeat of Napoleon, the market was flooded with sugar which had been stockpiled in England, and it was not until the 1820s that the German sugar-beet industry revived somewhat, but in the meantime the French had moved far ahead in the field. By 1850 Prussian output had increased to 53,000 tons, using 7.2 per cent of the beet. The industry was to expand dramatically in the second half of the century, so that by 1909 over two million tons of sugar were produced, and extraction methods had improved to the point that nearly 16 per cent of the beet could be used.

Although improvements had been made in animal-breeding, particularly in sheep with the introduction of the merino, the over-all standard was very low. Average weights were about half those reached by the end of the nineteenth century and milk production per cow also doubled in the course of the century. Animals took longer to mature and herds were thus less efficient, for farmers had to keep more animals, thus placing a greater strain on their limited resources.

A knowledgeable observer of contemporary conditions on the land, I.G. Koppe, noted in 1839 that definite progress had been made since the beginning of the century. Techniques had improved, and animal stocks had grown larger. Horses had largely replaced oxen as draught animals, which resulted in improved productivity. But he also admitted that much was still to be done, and many areas seemed hardly affected by the changes. Thus, although much production still took place on virtually self-supporting estates which only sent a small surplus for exchange on the market-place, and allotments and kitchen gardens played an enormously important role, even in large cities such as Berlin where much of the population also kept a pig or a cow in the backyard, the productive forces of agriculture were moving slowly but noticeably forward. Agriculture was the leading sector of the economy, not only in relative importance, but also in terms of the improvement of productivity.

The Guilds

At the beginning of the nineteenth century, life and labour on the land were determined by the still feudal relationships between lord and peasant. In the towns it was determined by the guild system, which dated back to the Middle Ages. The monopolistic rights of the guilds had long been regarded by reformers as a major obstacle to economic progress. The very existence of such organisations was contrary to the basic principles of economic liberalism, which were beginning to take hold in Germany thanks to the efforts of economists such as C.J. Kraus, H.L. von Jacob, J.F.E. Lotz and G. Sartorius. More obvious, perhaps, were the restrictive rights of the guilds which were able to forbid the formation of companies, limit the number of apprentices, stop the introduction of new and improved machinery and techniques, and fix prices. These rights were bitterly resented by those who did not enjoy the protection of the guilds, and were rightly seen as serious barriers to economic progress. Governments had attempted to circumvent the rights of the guilds by creating 'free masters' – master craftsmen who were licensed by the state and not by the guilds – and had usually managed to exclude the guilds from the state-controlled manufactories. Neither course was particularly successful. The free masters were deeply resented by the guild masters, were unable to take on apprentices, and were subjected to all manner of harassment. The state manufactories mostly failed as a result of the upheavals of the Napoleonic wars. It now became clear that if more advanced methods of production were to be used, if industry were to flourish, if trade were to expand and the ideas of economic liberalism triumph, then the privileges of the guilds and state monopolies would have to be ended. Every man should have the right to pursue the trade of his choice and the restrictions on the employment of labour, the use of machinery, privileges and support from the state would be abolished. Careers would be open to the talents, success and failure determined solely by market forces.

This spirit behind the reforms can be clearly seen in the instructions given to the provincial governments in Prussia in 1808 which read in part: 'everyone must be allowed to develop their inclinations, abilities and powers as freely as possible, and all existing obstructions to this must be removed as soon as possible in a legal manner.' Thus with the trade tax edict of November 1810, and the law on the policing of the trades of September 1811, the Prussian guilds lost their privileges. It was no longer necessary to be a guild member in order to practise a trade, it was sufficient to be a citizen in good standing and to pay a trade tax. The guilds were not forbidden, they continued as free private associations for the mutual benefit and support of their members, but they were no longer obligatory. Thus an important barrier to the development of industrial capitalism was removed, for previously a factory owner had either to be a member of a guild and abide by the regulations of that guild or, as was more often the case, seek a concession from the state. These requirements no longer applied, manufacturers were not obliged to employ guild members and could recruit labour on the free market. Conversely, labour no longer enjoyed the protection of the guilds and was abandoned to the tender mercies of the employers.

The effect of the freedom of trades (*Gewerbefreiheit*) on the development of industry was very long-term, the immediate effects being less dramatic. Any artisan could now open a workshop without being a member of a guild, but few took advantage of this new freedom. In some less skilled trades such as dairyman, innkeeper or showman, there was a marked increase as a result of the reforms. In the more skilled trades there was an increase which quickly tapered off after the first two years, and the number of new workshops reverted to the average of the period before the reforms. Part of the reason for the rather modest effect of the reforms was that the old guild system had already lost much of its power and influence. The exclusion of craftsmen from the area surrounding the towns, and the *numerus clausus* within the guilds, both of which had been major factors in restricting the number of craftsmen, had long since been abandoned, prompting one historian to argue that the reform did little more than legalise an already existing situation. Nor were all the old restrictions abolished at one fell swoop. Even in Prussia many trades were excluded from the provisions of the law, the application of the law was often postponed, and the guilds were still able to exercise considerable influence even though they had lost most of their formal authority. In south Germany it was not until the 1860s that full freedom for the trades was achieved. In some areas, among them the Hansa towns, Hanover and Electoral Hesse, the political reaction after 1815 also saw the reimposition of the old restrictions on craftsmen and artisans and the affirmation of the authority of the guilds to control the trades. Areas which had been occupied by the French, such as the

Rhineland and Westphalia, were completely free, whereas in Saxony the guild system was untouched by reform.

The situation of the German artisans and craftsmen in 1815 is thus just as difficult a subject for generalisation as are conditions on the land. Conditions differed widely, not only in the different states, but also in the provinces of the larger states, such as Prussia. The old ideal division of labour between the towns (manufacture and trade) and the country (agriculture) had long since disappeared. Complete freedom no more existed after the reforms than complete control had existed beforehand. There was probably less general enthusiasm for the reform of the handicraft system among the bourgeoisie than there was for the liberation of the peasants. The artisans resisted change, fearing the loss of the security of the guilds, the competition of a freer economic system, and the challenge of mass-produced industrial goods. The reform was the work of liberal civil servants who were fully committed to the ideas of economic liberalism. Men of property were uncertain in their attitude towards the artisans, just as they were suspicious of the new age which seemed to be dawning. They welcomed the new freedoms and opportunities and the diminution of the importance of birth and privilege, but they also feared that the changes were too abrupt, that society would be prey to new and more violent tensions, and that freedom also involved uncertainty and risk. In influential circles the optimism and enthusiasm of the age of enlightenment gave way to scepticism and a weary nostalgia for the 'good old days'. Artisans who opposed the new economic order thus could win the support of conservative aristocrats who feared the social and political consequences of a liberal economic policy and of those sections of the bourgeoisie who felt that the changes had been too abrupt. All those who saw industrial society as a threat to their economic well-being and their social status began to demand the reintroduction of controls and restraints. These opponents of the liberal economic order found no difficulty in producing telling arguments against the system. Full economic freedom meant freedom to the economically strong, but disaster to the weak and the poor. Conservatives contrasted a grossly sentimentalised picture of a patriarchal and ordered society in which everyone had his place and was protected against hardship by collective responsibility, to a new society where the industrial capitalist, red in tooth and claw, was free to exploit and swindle the weak and pile up vast wealth at the expense of others, and society dissolved in struggle and bitterness.

Although the statistical evidence is scanty, it would seem that between 1800 and 1843 there was only a slight decline in the percentage of the total population employed in handicrafts: 14–15 per cent in 1800; 12.8 per cent in 1843. The figures for 1843 show a slight increase over those for 1816 when the percentage was 11.6. The interpretation of the significance of these figures differs widely. Some historians argue that they indicate that the artisans were able to keep pace with industrialisation and that in spite of the customs union (*Zollverein*) and the railway boom, the handicraft industries continued to play an important role in the economic life of Germany. Others argue that the freedom from the old guild restrictions resulted in many trades being overmanned, consequently depressing the standard of living of the artisans. Thus, although there was a steady influx into some handicraft trades, many artisans became proletarianised and were obliged to find work in the new factories, where they worked alongside recent migrants from the rural areas.

A large number of the artisans lived a marginal existence in wretched and overcrowded houses with little hope for the improvement of their condition. Many were forced to send their wives and their children to work in workshops and factories where they competed with labour from the rural areas, thus forcing down wage levels and contributing to the very evil which by their labour they hoped to overcome. This situation was further exacerbated by the increase of population. Population growth, coupled with the increasing use of women and children, resulted in a larger work-force which was not compensated by increases of output and productivity. The resulting growth in poverty was a matter of widespread concern. Contemporary writers were almost unanimous that the standard of living of the working population declined between 1800 and the 1840s, and most historians accept this verdict. Unemployment and poverty became pressing social problems and the fear of being forced to join the ranks of industrial labour became all the more intense. This harsh new relationship between employer and employee, unmediated by the ties and obligations of traditional society, was used by conservatives as further evidence of the evils and perils of liberal society, and their demands for a return to the certainties and the order of the past found wider support.

Some trades were able to maintain their position, or even to thrive, in these changed circumstances. With the process of industrialisation there was a decline in the amount and the variety of things produced in the home. Less bread was baked at home, and thus the baker's trade was able to expand. Much the same was true of butchers, tailors and the building trade. Yet although the handicrafts survived, and some even flourished, most artisans felt that they were doomed. Unable or unwilling to learn new trades, or to specialise in the production of commodities which as yet were not suited to industrial production, the artisans faced the destruction of their way of life and a loss of their independence. The result was a growing frustration and hostility among the artisans, which was to find expression in artisans' riots and later in the revolution of 1848, in which the artisans played such an important role.

The Development of the Capitalist Mode of Production

Freeing the trades from the restrictions of the guilds and the abolition of feudalism on the land was not enough to create a modern industrial society. There can be no doubt, however, that both were significant preconditions for such a development and a clear recognition and affirmation of social and economic changes which had taken place. Germany was neither an industrial state in the sense that industry played a more significant role in the economic life of the country than did agriculture, nor were most manufactured goods produced by industrial enterprises. Cottage industry, putting-out work (the system of the *Verlag*) and the countless workshops of the artisans accounted for the bulk of manufactured goods. The individual worker often owned the means of production and frequently worked for more than one employer. Usually he spent part of his time working his modest holding and was thus closer to the peasantry than to the modern industrial proletariat. Industrial enterprises were thus somewhat exotic exceptions to urban handicrafts and rural cottage industry. Even as late as 1815 it was difficult to say whether the existence of modern industrial enterprises in Germany were to remain the exception or to become the rule. It took far longer in Germany than in England to lay the groundwork for industrialisation. It is possible to discern the beginnings of this process in the 1780s, but it is hardly possible to talk of industrialisation in Germany until the mid-1830s. Social formations which had been incompletely changed during the reform period still acted as a brake on economic development.

A further serious hindrance to the development of industrial capitalism in Germany came from the difficulties and shortcomings of agriculture. In the late eighteenth century agriculture had thrived. The increased demand for agricultural produce by a rapidly industrialising Britain resulted in a healthy export market, particularly for wool and corn. This demand increased still further in the early stages of the

French revolutionary wars, with the result that enterprising landowners were able to make substantial profits, the value of agricultural land increased markedly and many aristocratic landowners began to dance around the golden calf of land speculation. Napoleon's Continental System caused a serious disruption of the export trade, and the invading armies slaughtered animals and plundered stocks. Some landowners were able to make handsome profits by providing supplies to the army, but in general agriculture suffered badly from the results of the war. This had the effect of negating some of the positive effects of the reforms and, faced with such uncertainty, farmers were reluctant to invest more than they deemed absolutely essential, and agricultural production was often kept at a minimum.

This cutback in agricultural production during the war made it all the more difficult to expand after 1815. The exceptionally cold and wet summer of 1816 caused a disastrous crop failure. When agricultural production began a marked improvement in the following years, partly as a result of excellent weather conditions, and partly because of an increase in investment in the land, often by the new bourgeois landowners, it became increasingly difficult to find markets. Lower wages depressed domestic demand and the enormous increase in the productivity of British agriculture achieved during the Napoleonic wars made it difficult for German producers to regain their position in the British market; it became almost impossible with the passage of the Corn Laws. Sweden, Spain, Holland and Italy had all improved their agricultural output during the period of the imposition of the Continental System, and both France and the Netherlands soon followed the British example of imposing import duties on corn, so that it was almost impossible for German grain producers to find alternative markets. As a consequence, grain exports from the most important Prussian ports, Danzig and Elbing, fell by 1825 to one-seventh of the average between 1801 and 1805.

One important branch of agriculture managed to expand during the agricultural crisis. British demand for German wool increased after the Napoleonic wars, so that exports trebled between 1815 and 1818 and increased more than five times between 1820 and 1825. Throughout this period Germany supplied about half of Britain's requirements for wool. Wool prices remained high at a time when corn prices fell disastrously. By 1825 corn prices were about 25 per cent of the 1817 average, when prices were highly inflated by shortages, and by 1830 were still only half the immediate post-war level, although there was a marked upward trend in agricultural prices after 1825.

In such a situation many farmers switched to sheep-farming. This was particularly pronounced in Brandenburg-Prussia, Mecklenburgh and Saxony, but only the larger landowners had sufficient capital to buy flocks of the improved breeds of sheep. In the long run the change to sheep-farming was self-defeating, for it resulted in an over-production of wool and a consequent fall in prices after 1825, although the collapse of the wool market never reached the catastrophic levels of the corn market.

Other landowners who were unable to sell their corn distilled it into *Schnaps*, but once again the building of a distillery demanded a considerable amount of capital and the end effect was an over-production of spirits which could no more be sold than the corn from which it was made. The only positive effect of this change-over to wool and *Schnaps* was that corn prices began to rise slightly, thus helping to offset the fall in the prices of wool and spirits, but the change was not enough to pull Germany out of the agricultural crisis.

Some of the Junkers were only able to survive the crisis by the generous intervention of the Prussian state which provided some 3 million thalers of aid in order to preserve the aristocracy from ruin. Yet in spite of these measures, 230 estates had to declare bankruptcy between 1824 and 1834 in the homeland of the Junkers, Prussia east of the Elbe. Many estates were sold to the bourgeoisie, which in many instances brought a much-needed influx of capital to the agricultural sector and a consequent improvement of techniques and stocks.

Although these 'bourgeois Junkers', to use Hans Rosenberg's phrase, bought the semi-feudal privileges of police and court rights along with their estates, and although they were quick to copy the mannerisms and attitudes of the aristocracy, they were not accepted as social equals by the aristocracy and were unable to share their status and influence. These new landowners set an example of entrepreneurial farming which forced the Junkers to use modern methods of estate management. In spite of the protection afforded by their legal and fiscal privileges and their easier access to credit, and the exemption of their estates from taxation, the Junkers were only able to survive by paying close attention to the profitability of their estates. The introduction of modern agricultural methods and close attention to book-keeping were the only ways that the Junkers could keep their heads above water. Thus changes in land ownership coupled with the harsh effects of the agricultural depression, which lasted from 1806 to 1837, resulted in a distinct modernisation and rationalisation of the larger estates. The old feudal mode of production vanished, now only profit and loss determined the fortunes of the landowners. By and large, aristocratic landowners were very successful in meeting the challenge of these changed conditions, and they seldom allowed snobbery or a distaste for the vulgarity of a competitive world to distract them from the single-minded pursuit of profit. Yet with few exceptions, notably in Silesia, the aristocracy remained aloof from the world of industry and trade, looking down on the mere 'tradesmen' (*Koofmich*) as an inferior class, even though their business methods on their estates differed little from those of the industrialists and merchants whom they despised.

Industrial development lagged far behind that of agriculture, and this is particularly true of the textile industry, which had played such a vital part in the Industrial Revolution in England. The leading sector of the textile industry was the cotton industry, an industry which found it exceedingly hard to compete with the superior British techniques, and whose export markets were seriously disrupted by the war. The imposition of a heavy import duty on raw cotton entering Germany by Napoleon was a further blow to the industry. Cotton weaving in Berlin, which produced mainly for the domestic market and had thus not been as badly hurt as the Saxon mills whose markets were mainly abroad, was crippled by this measure. The number of looms in Berlin that were in active use declined from 4,216 in 1806 to only 1,029 in 1808. There was, however, a steady increase in cotton manufacture in the years after the defeat of Napoleon.

Cotton manufacture was mostly carried out in the old manner of simple commodity production by cottage industry and putting-out using handlooms. Spinning was also done at home, usually as part-time labour in the rural areas, using hand-operated machinery. The German cotton industry in the late eighteenth century suffered from much the same difficulties as the English cotton industry. Primitive spinning methods were unable to produce sufficient yarn to meet the increased demand of the weavers. It was not until 1783 that Brüggelman introduced the first water-driven spinning machine at his factory in Ratingen near Düsseldorf. Although he had managed to get hold of an English spinning machine, it was not until he was able to hire an English mechanic that he was able to get it to work. The Ratingen factory was the first spinning factory in Continental Europe, built some ten years after Arkwright's first mill. Brüggelmann was a prosperous merchant with sufficient capital, and the Düsseldorf area was relatively free from traditional restrictions on trade and industry. He took advantage of the remaining privileges of the old system by securing a monopoly from the

Margrave Theodor, but this potentate's authority did not command automatic respect, and the monopoly could not be enforced.

The introduction of spinning machinery in Saxony was somewhat later, beginning in the mid-1780s with locally produced copies of hand-operated spinning jennies. The Saxon government provided funds to craftsmen like Mathias Frey, who appears to have built the first such machine, to encourage production. The Prussian government also encouraged technological innovation, giving the Swiss cotton merchant Hotho the princely sum of 10,000 thalers to improve his factory in Berlin, and also helping him to smuggle machinery from England, which still refused to export machinery.

These modest beginnings in the 1780s in Saxony and in Prussia, due in large part to the initiative of the state, were unable to flourish in the following years owing to the importation of English yarn when, by the early 1790s, English spinners were producing greatly in excess of the amount that could be absorbed by the domestic market. Investment in cotton mills in Germany was therefore hardly an attractive proposition, and only modest progress was made in the following years. Most of the improved machinery was still used at home, factory production being a somewhat exotic exception often viewed by the authorities with misgivings, for they feared that factory production would lead to unemployment and to the loss of tax revenue. The Napoleonic invasion and the Continental System caused further disruptions, but the exclusion of British yarn from Germany offered an opportunity to German spinners, so that in Saxony the number of spindles increased from 13,200 in 1806 to 255,904 in 1812. This expansion occurred under very unusual circumstances, and although there was an impressive increase in the amount of yarn produced, the methods used were not the most efficient and modern, and the yarn was not always of the highest quality. It was not possible for Germany to use this brief period when British goods were excluded from the domestic market to reorganise production so as to be able to compete with England when the restrictions on trade were removed. Thus after 1815 the hand-spinners, who had done relatively well during the blockade, were destroyed by the competition of English yarn and by the new German factories. These factories, which tended to use water power rather than steam engines, began to dominate the spinning industry in the 1820s in a manner which is characteristic of the early stages of industrialisation. Yet because of the slump, the cotton industry was unable to make the dramatic increases in production without which industrialisation and modernisation cannot become an irreversible process. The abundance of cheap labour and the high cost of fuel were further disincentives to modernisation. Thus in the 1820s much of the groundwork for an Industrial Revolution was laid, but the decisive stage had yet to be reached.

The development of the woollen industry was similar to that of cotton, although technological progress was much slower and the industry tended to stagnate throughout the period. Unlike the cotton industry, the woollen industry declined as a direct result of the Continental System and was unable to recover in the post-war years. Wool was still a luxury material for which there was only a modest demand, with the majority of the population suffering from the consequences of the agricultural crisis and the industrial slump. The German wool trade was unable to match the quality of English wool, and there was thus little opportunity for selling abroad. Technical advances were made during the post-war years, although hand-operated machinery was still the rule, but there was little incentive to invest in a stagnating and demoralised industry. A more specialised luxury trade, the silk industry, which had prospered in Berlin in the years before the Napoleonic invasion, was destroyed by the French in 1806, was revived after 1815, and prospered in the 1820s. Although the Jacquard loom, invented in 1804, was introduced in Berlin, the industry by and large stuck to old methods and techniques, so that although the silk industry was a modest success it was not a significant force for innovation and change.

Although Germany was to become one of the very greatest heavy industrial powers, there was little sign in the early part of the century that heavy industry and mining would one day thrive. In the iron and steel industry traditional methods were still used, and German industrialists were slow to introduce the more modern methods which had been developed in England. Charcoal rather than coal was used as a fuel for the furnaces, and it was not until the 1850s that coke was used in the west in the iron and steel industries. In Silesia the iron and steel industry had made greater advances in circumstances which were somewhat unusual for Germany. Some of the great landowners followed the example of Count Reden and built ironworks on their estates and exploited the coal and ore deposits of the region. These Silesian magnates had no concerns about the loss of caste by entering trade and industry. They had access to sufficient sources of capital so that their works were the most up-to-date in Germany. They were also able to apply the feudal relationship of landlord and peasant to industrial relations, so that the workers in their mines and forges were in a state of dependence upon them. A significant part of Silesian industry, particularly the coal mines, was under state control and this sector was the most technically advanced. A coke-fired furnace was built in Gleiwitz in 1796 under Reden's supervision for a state-owned ironworks. Yet the puddling process, which was in wide use in England since the 1780s, was not introduced in Silesia until 1828. Even the efforts of the great Silesian nobles, Henckel, Thiele-Winckler, Pless, Ratibor, Colonna and Renard were not enough to meet even the modest domestic demand for iron, and the German market offered further opportunities for the more forward-looking Belgian industry, which in turn was to become both a challenge and a threat to Germany and a stimulus to renewed effort.

Although the iron and steel industry had been badly hit by the Continental System, and domestic demand remained low, the machinery industry was in its infancy, iron was not yet used in construction and the railway boom had yet to begin, and although growth was severely restricted by poor transportation facilities and the distances between sources of ore and sources of coal, modest progress was made in the early part of the century, even though the starting-point was very low. Iron production rose by 62 per cent from 1822 to 1834 when Germany produced 110,106 tons compared to 678,417 tons in England. By 1830 Germany was producing just under 1.5 million tons of coal, when England was producing 22.4 million tons.

One of the essential preconditions for the Industrial Revolution was the widespread introduction of the steam engine. A steam engine based on the improved Watt model was first used in Germany on 23 August 1785. The story behind this engine is instructive. The Prussian government sent a civil servant, Bückling, to England to spy on the Watt engine, and as a result of this industrial espionage the government built the engine in its own factory in Berlin. The first model failed to work, and it was not until the inevitable English mechanic could be brought over from England that the engine could be used. The mechanic, Mr Richards, then took over the direction of the Berlin works.

These early German engines were used mainly for pumping out mine shafts. The mines of Upper Silesia provided a healthy market and encouraged an indigenous machine-building industry, of which the most notable was H.F. Holtzhausen's factory at Gleiwitz. Bückling built the first steam engine in the Ruhr for a state-owned mine in 1789. Another artisan, Dinnendahl, started the production of steam engines in the Ruhr, but his enterprise rested on very shaky financial foundations, as he was forced to rely on the credit of his clients as a source of capital. As a result he soon went under.

These early steam engines were used almost exclusively in the mines, and were seldom harnessed to machinery. The steam engines used in the Berlin cotton mills and porcelain factory were exceptions to this rule, and it is not until the mid-1830s that modern machinery driven by steam power was used to any great extent.

As can be seen from the example of Dinnendahl, investment capital was in short supply. Part of the problem was that government securities were an attractive investment. Interest rates ran as high as 6 per cent, and with the introduction of the new consolidated loans in the place of the personal loans of the sovereign, or of a government agency, these loans were very secure. It was thus a much more attractive prospect to invest in government loans than in risky business ventures which, given the depressed state of the economy, were unlikely to offer as high a return even when successful. The new private banks and the stock exchanges in Berlin, Hamburg and Frankfurt-am-Main were very much preoccupied with government securities – the Frankfurt exchange dates from 1818 when the Austrian government floated a loan, part of which was placed abroad. In Hamburg the Parish bank handled Austrian and Russian loans, and Rothschild and Bethmann dealt in Spanish and Dutch paper as well as the Austrian loans. Berlin began to deal in Russian and Polish loans towards the end of the 1820s. The banks were also involved in commodity speculation and in business and trade ventures. As very few people dealt with the banks their business was less specialised than it was soon to become, and they were all too prone to indulge in wildly speculative ventures.

The banks were also involved in currency speculation. In many of the German states, including Prussia, there was a shortage of coin, so that a great deal of foreign coin was in circulation. Exchange rates between the various currencies fluctuated widely. The interest-bearing debentures of the Prussian *Landschaften* was a profitable alternative to the paper money which had been introduced at the time of the wars of liberation, and the aristocracy was loath to see this valuable source of capital for their estates replaced by a paper currency. This attitude was shared by the bankers and many businessmen who profited from interest-bearing loans and debentures. Bills of exchange were also widely used as a money surrogate and German bankers handled them in much the same manner as Scottish and English bankers issued bank notes. Interest rates remained high until the mid-1820s as states were still recovering from the war and resistance to paper money was still strong, but then they began to drop as there was insufficient demand from a docile economy to keep interest levels high.

Free Trade or Protection?

During the period when the foundations for a German Industrial Revolution were being laid, mercantilist ideas of the protection of native industry and the prohibition of the export of raw materials were gradually abandoned. As the land-owning aristocracy was exporting the produce of their estates they had little interest in protectionism, and the merchants and traders were also anxious that the old restrictions on trade and commerce should be removed. The industrial bourgeoisie was as yet not strong enough to protect the interests of their fledgeling concerns against foreign competition.

The French occupation did much to destroy the mercantilist system. Although the Continental System ended trade with Britain, the French reduced the tariffs on French goods which in turn triggered off a series of tariff reductions in Prussia. In 1807 the complex system of regulations and prohibitions was replaced by a simple $8^1/_3$ per cent tax on the value of imported goods for the province of Prussia, a tax which was soon applied to the other Prussian provinces. After the Congress of Vienna, the Prussian government imposed an even lower tax of 6 per cent on goods entering the new provinces such as the Rhineland.

The demand for an end to the protective system was due in part to the shortage of manufactured goods during the period of the French occupation, but after 1815 the German market became saturated with British goods. To the Germans it seemed that the British government was deliberately trying to destroy foreign industry by an aggressive trade policy which involved export premiums and dumping. The German states, small, economically backward and divided among themselves, seemed helpless against the overpowering strength of British industry. Manufacturing interests, particularly in the textile industry, began to demand protective tariffs against British goods, a demand which became more insistent as the German economy failed to recover from the post-war slump. A government commission was formed to examine the whole question of Prussian trade policy and reported in favour of those who argued for protection. But there were powerful interests which wished to retain free trade and which included the Junkers and some sectors of the Rhenish bourgeoisie. These men were interested in the export market, they wanted to keep the price of manufactured goods as low as possible, and they had little desire to further a policy which would benefit the manufacturers and industrialists, for whom they had little sympathy. Thus the landed aristocracy and the commercial bourgeoisie espoused the cause of economic liberalism and, armed with the arguments of the political economists of Königsberg University, they used it as a weapon to attack the manufacturers. In government circles a powerful argument was that high tariffs simply encouraged smugglers which, combined with a sharp reduction in the volume of imports, would lead to a fall in revenue from the customs.

The debate in the Prussian government between the protectionists, whose main spokesman was the President of the government of Brandenburg, von Heydebreck, and the free-traders, led by Kunth and Maassen, resulted in a victory for the latter with the Prussian customs law of May 1818. Customs duties were on the whole slightly raised but did not exceed 10 per cent, and thus were much lower than any of Prussia's major competitors. Only luxury goods such as wines were subject to a heavy duty of up to 30 per cent, but raw materials were duty-free. Although these duties were higher than those in most of the German states, including Bavaria, Hanover and Baden, they were certainly not enough to protect the German manufacturing industries against British competition. The industrialists complained bitterly but the *Smithianer* in the Prussian civil service argued that it was futile for German industry to compete with English quality goods, and that industrialists should concentrate on the manufacture of ordinary goods for daily use. Another very important aspect of the law was that it created within Prussia a free market by destroying the last remaining internal customs and restrictions. It is perhaps this aspect of the 1818 law that most captured the imagination of contemporaries and was to lead historians like Treitschke to claim that it was the first step towards the unification of Germany. Certainly the example of the Prussian customs law of 1818 inspired groups such as the Association of German Industrialists (*Deutsche Fabrikantenverein*) and the German Association of Trade and Industry (*Deutsche Handels- und Gewerbeverein*) to press for an extension of the free-trade zone so that eventually all of Germany could be economically united. As such the law was an important stage in the creation of the customs union (*Zollverein*).

Transportation

It was not merely political divisions and customs barriers which hindered the development of trade and industry within the German confederation; the appalling state of transportation was equally important. Roads were so poor that thirty miles was regarded as a good average day's journey for a stage-coach. Roads built on hardcore (*Chausseestrassen*) were few and far between, even as late as 1815. The great rivers such as the Rhine, Danube, Main, Elbe and Weser had not been made fully navigable and were hardly economical given the exceptional number of customs stations. Thus when the French occupied the Rhineland there were thirty customs stations on the short stretch of the Rhine from Bingen to Coblenz. Johann Gottfried Tulla was not able to begin his great work on the correction of the upper Rhine until the 1820s which, in one of the great engineering works of the century, improved the stretch from Basel to the Hesse border, controlled the flooding and won back valuable agricultural land.

Trade and industry could thus only be established in towns close to navigable water, of which Berlin is a notable example. Transportation problems made it virtually impossible to produce certain commodities on a large scale. Shoes were made by the local cobbler, and high transportation costs insured him against the competition of industrial production.

In 1816 two English steamboats were used in the Rhine and the Elbe, but failure to secure a monopoly and the lack of freight and passengers soon put an end to these ventures. At about the same time, German-built steamships with English engines were used in Bremen and Berlin, but this was also unprofitable and their example discouraged any further growth of steam shipping on the German rivers. In 1822 Dutch interests combined with a group of Cologne businessmen to form a company which owned and operated steamers on the Rhine. The success of this venture encouraged the Cologne chamber of commerce to found a company, the Rhineland-Prussian Steamship Company (*Rheinisch-Preussische Dampfschiffahrtsgellschaft*), which was the first large joint-stock company in the transport industry. By 1830 there were twelve steamships in regular use on the Rhine. Such was the beginning of the large transportation companies which alone had sufficient capital to finance expensive modern means of transportation and which spelt the ruin of the small boatsmen who had dominated the industry. These new companies were quick to exploit the possibilities for expansion offered by the establishment of virtually free traffic on the Rhine in the convention of 1831, the Elbe in 1821, and the Weser in 1823.

A canal linking the Elbe to the Oder was built in the eighteenth century and played a vital role in the water-transport system which served Berlin. The Ruhr Canal enabled the export of Ruhr coal to Rotterdam in the late eighteenth century. Yet these examples were not followed in other parts of Germany where canal-building was sadly neglected. Similarly, only modest distances of Macadamised road were built in the period after 1815. The revolution in German transport was thus not to come until the railway age, which began in Germany in the late 1830s.

In terms of industrial development Germany lagged some fifty years behind England. Although many technical innovations were introduced fairly soon after they were first used in England, they took much longer to take root. Thus, although the beginnings of industrialisation can be seen as early as the 1780s, even as late as the 1830s it is too early to speak of an Industrial Revolution in Germany. At a time when England was almost at the peak of her economic power German economic development was retarded by the remnants of an outmoded social order. A landed aristocracy and a large class of artisans and craftsmen bitterly resented and resisted the new industrial age which threatened their status and their livelihood. Industrialisation arrived late in Germany, and it came to a country in which old social forms were still firmly entrenched, having made tactical concessions to the modern age. From the outset of the Industrial Revolution in Germany, economic and social forces were unevenly developed, which in turn gave rise to severe contradictions and tensions. A restorative political order, dominated by aristocratic agrarian interests and supported by the threatened class of artisans and craftsmen, came in conflict with the forces of technical and economic progress. By 1830 it was still uncertain whether the political reaction would triumph and Germany would turn its back on the modern world, or whether the advocates of industrialisation and economic liberalism would triumph. No one could foresee that the eventual result would be a unique compromise between the two.

2 TOWARDS ECONOMIC UNIFICATION

The Zollverein

In the Europe of the Holy Alliance and the Carlsbad decrees, demands for far-reaching political reforms and the unification of Germany had been silenced. The days of the wars of liberation, of the festival at the Wartburg and the radical students of the *Burschenschaften* seemed long gone and the hopes of the liberal nationalists were dashed. Yet in spite of this oppressive and restorative political climate, demands for the economic unification of Germany were growing. In most instances the arguments for economic unification were of a strictly practical nature. The transportation of goods was made even slower and more expensive by the endless series of customs barriers through which they had to pass. The little German states fought fierce battles with one another over customs duties, and they were totally incapable of agreeing upon a common strategy against the influx of English manufactured goods. Thus many businessmen were frustrated by the inefficiency of the system and fearful that, without concerted action, the German market would become totally swamped with English goods.

In October 1814 Johann Friedrich Benzenberg, the owner of one of the first sugar-beet refineries in the Rhineland and thus a man with special interests to protect, wrote an article in the *Rheinische Merkur* calling for the abolition of all internal customs barriers and the creation of a German customs at the borders of the confederation. This view was shared by none other than Freiherr vom Stein who cried: 'Abolish all internal customs! Customs on the borders of the confederation!'

At the Congress of Vienna it had been agreed that the German confederation should agree upon a common policy for trade, transportation and customs duties, but little was done in the following years. Many factors stood in the way of economic unification. States were jealous of their sovereignty and often suspicious of German nationalism with its dangerous political overtones. Customs duties and taxes on certain commodities formed the major part of the revenues of the larger states, so that the abolition of customs duties would have had profound fiscal consequences and, as far as the governments were concerned, these financial aspects often weighed more heavily than the question of trade policy. For the forty sovereign states of the

German confederation to agree on a common customs policy, many difficult problems would have to be overcome.

First steps towards the economic unification of Germany were taken in the individual states. The Prussian customs law of 1818 is the most dramatic case in point, not only because it created a free market for 10.5 million Germans, but also because after 1815 the Prussian provinces were scattered even more widely than before. Prussia was not one continuous territory, the Rhineland provinces being some considerable distance from Brandenburg, and there were a number of enclaves within the state which posed additional problems. Some of the other important German states had already removed internal customs barriers, so in this sense Prussia was hardly a leader in the forefront of reform. Customs barriers had been removed in Bavaria as early as 1807, in Württemberg in 1808 and in Baden in 1812.

Although the Prussian law of 1818 created a large and viable domestic market, it was resented by other German states because it resulted in higher tariffs and a tax on goods that were in transit through Prussian territory. As Prussia straddled many of the major trade routes, this latter tax was a particular burden. States which were completely surrounded by Prussian territory not unnaturally resented the transit tax, which affected all their trade with states other than Prussia. Such states were, however, very small; the largest, Anhalt Dessau, only had a population of 50,000. The small states which bordered on Prussia had two alternatives: either to join the Prussian customs union or to band together with other states to form an alternative customs area which might be able to compete with Prussia.

In April 1819 many prominent manufacturers and traders were assembled at the spring fair in Frankfurt-am-Main. The German economy was in a depressed state and there was anxiety that Germany might well become divided up into a series of competing customs areas which would further hamper industry and commerce. On 14 April the *Allgemeiner deutscher Handels- und Gewerbeverein* (General German Association for Trade and Industry) was formed at the fair in order to examine ways in which trade and industry could be encouraged and stimulated. The outstanding figure in this group was Friedrich List. Born in Reutlingen in Swabia in 1789, the son of a tawer, he had become professor of political science at the University of Tübingen. List believed passionately in the need for a united German market, in which all customs and trade barriers between the member states of the German confederation should be removed and German industry protected against foreign competition by a national tariff. List was a compelling propagandist, and his ideas had a great appeal to those manufacturers and traders who were desperately searching for a solution to their immediate problems and who looked across the Rhine through rose-tinted spectacles to a France without customs barriers to internal trade, or nostalgically back to the glorious days of the German Hansa which, List told them, had been destroyed by customs barriers. Thirty-eight customs systems seemed to stand between Germany and prosperity.

The Association for Trade and Industry was an immediate success. By the time of the Leipzig fair, held only a few weeks after the Frankfurt fair, it was reported that 800 industrialists had joined, and the activities of the association attracted the interest of a large number of businessmen throughout the country. List immediately drafted a memorandum for the Bundestag in which he argued the case for the economic unification of Germany and the abolition of internal customs. List wrote:

> Thirty-eight customs and toll barriers in Germany cripple internal commerce and have much the same result as if one placed a tourniquet on every part of the human body so that the blood would not flow from one part to another.

This rousing appeal was signed by seventy businessmen from various parts of the country and handed to the federal Parliament (Bundestag). The Bundestag rejected the petition, sternly warning each of the signatories that they had no right to appeal directly to the Bundestag, and that they should address their complaints to their own governments. Thus in the next few months the association sent deputations to almost all the German governments to urge a reform of the customs system and the creation of free trade within Germany. The association's journal, the *Organ für den deutschen Handels- und Fabrikantenstand*, whose editor was List, was a powerful voice in favour of fundamental reform of customs and trade policy, and was widely read and discussed in business circles.

The activities of the association were somewhat alarming to the authorities. Metternich warned of the revolutionary implications of any move towards the unification of Germany. Gentz warned Metternich that the association was 'highly dangerous'. At the ministerial conference in Vienna in May 1820, at which representatives of the fourteen major German states discussed ways and means of combating liberal and democratic movements, it was agreed that List's organisation should not be given any encouragement or recognition. From the outset many people associated customs union with political union.

In spite of this initial negative reaction from official quarters, List was determined to continue the struggle. In September 1820 the south German states held a conference in Darmstadt to discuss mutual problems of trade and commerce. The association decided to lobby the Ministers attending the conference in the hopes that a south German customs union might be formed which would have been an important step towards their goal of the unification of the whole of Germany. Metternich used his influence to ensure that the delegation was not received by any of the governments participating in the conference. The conference itself was a failure owing to differences between the states, of which the most serious was the dispute between Bavaria and Baden over the future of the Palatinate. The association did not survive this rebuttal. Moderates began to attack List as a fanatic and extremist and demanded that all efforts should be concentrated on modest short-term reforms. List decided to concentrate on the political struggle, entering the Württemberg Parliament in December 1820 as the representative of his home town. The association gradually dissolved.

Although the association had little direct influence and was seriously divided between moderates and radicals, and between those who emphasised free trade and those who were primarily concerned with protection against foreign manufactured goods, it was none the less extremely significant. It was the first important organisation of the middle class in Germany. Its activities had done much to heighten the political and economic awareness of the manufacturers and businessmen, many of whom for the first time became aware of the wider implications of their individual efforts. The association had brought the attention of the German governments to the problem of customs and trade, and although the initial reaction was negative, the arguments were not forgotten. A question had been raised which no longer could be ignored.

As soon as List joined the Württemberg Parliament he brought up the question of means to promote trade and industry, thus triggering off one of the most lively debates that the chamber had seen for a long time. His political activities soon involved more direct issues than questions of tariff reform. In 1821 he proposed democratic reforms in the government of the Württemberg towns, a suggestion which earned him a ten-month jail term for insulting the state and its servants. List fled to Strasbourg to avoid arrest. Returning briefly to Württemberg in 1824 he was arrested, but set free on condition that he would leave the country. He promptly left for North America, where he lived for the next seven years.

Although List was enormously important in that he articulated the desires and the needs of a rising commercial and industrial middle class, the movement towards the economic unification of Germany continued during his absence. It was now no longer carried out by protest meetings, deputations and rousing pamphlets, but by sober civil servants and cautious diplomats. The movement thus lost much of its democratic overtone and was less alarming to the German governments, who saw in List's own career confirmation of their worst fears that free trade and democracy were necessarily connected.

The catastrophic crop failure of 1816 had provided a vivid example of the evils of economic particularism. Austria had forbidden the export of corn as soon as the price began to rise, and refused to listen to the pleas of the German states to remove the ban, which was not lifted until the autumn of 1817, when a good crop brought the price of corn down closer to old levels. The customs war which had raged in 1816 was largely confined to the south German states. Prussia pursued a more moderate policy. The Prussian law of 1818 was thus in part a reaction to the experiences of 1816, but it was also the first major step of a policy designed to unite all the states north of the river Main into one customs area. The small states had very mixed feelings about the thrust of Prussian policy. On the one hand their small customs services were inefficient, expensive and often corrupt. Smuggling was rife and income from customs was often insufficient to pay for the service. On the other hand, they were suspicious of Prussian motives, fearful that they would lose the last vestiges of their sovereign independence, and uncertain as to the economic consequences of so radical a break with the traditions of the past. The Prussian statesmen responsible for the negotiations, Eichhorn, Motz and Maassen, acted with great tact and discretion and overcame many of these fears, but they were also negotiating from a position of considerable strength. None of the bordering states could match the economic and financial power of Prussia.

The first of the agreements between Prussia and her neighbours was in 1819 with Schwarzburg-Sonderhausen, followed by Schwarzburg-Rudolstadt in 1822 and Lippe in 1826. The extension of the Prussian customs system, which soon included a number of other small states, was most alarming to many of the central German states who disliked and mistrusted Prussia but who also had no desire to join the customs union between Bavaria and Württemberg which had been formed in January 1828. The central German states were encouraged in their anti-Prussian stance by Metternich, who wished to contain Prussia and who resisted the movement towards economic unification as the first dangerous step towards political unification. The British government also supported the central German states in the fear that a Germany dominated by the Prussian customs system might one day challenge the economic might of Britain, and in the short run would probably place higher tariffs on British goods. Yet in spite of support from outside, there was little besides a fear of Prussia which could keep the central German customs union together. The central German customs union was formed in August 1828, but the signatories frequently ignored the stipulations of the treaty and began negotiations with the rival Prussian and south German unions.

At first Prussia was absorbed with her own immediate concerns to create an economically unified state, to abolish the enclaves, and to secure unhindered access to all her provinces. There was thus no long-range plan for the economic unification of Germany under Prussian leadership. The negotiations between Prussia and Hesse led to a new and more aggressive stage in Prussian policy, in which for the first time much broader aims were pursued. The two Hesses, Electoral Hesse and Hesse-Darmstadt, were an important link between Prussia and the markets of the west, even though the common border between Hesse and Prussia was very short. The Elector of Hesse was a short-sighted and stubborn man who refused to co-operate with either the Prussian or the Bavarian unions. Since 1819 he had carried on a customs war with Prussia and hoped that he could maintain his independence with the support of those forces which were resisting any extension of the Prussian system. Hesse-Darmstadt, however, began negotiations with Prussia in 1825, and in February 1828 entered a customs union (*Zollverein*) with Prussia on the basis of the Prussian tariff of 1818. This treaty was greeted with great alarm by the Bavarians and the Austrians, and was viewed with considerable concern by those west European nations, principally England, who feared that this was the beginning of a united Germany. Of the German states only Württemberg and Baden greeted the move as a positive and encouraging sign of co-operation and as a stimulus to trade and commerce between north and south Germany.

The immediate barriers to the expansion of Prussia's customs system were Hanover and Electoral Hesse. Hanover would have to be included in the system to facilitate trade in northern Germany, and Electoral Hesse blocked part of the area between Prussia's eastern and western provinces. Motz began negotiations for a trade agreement with Hanover but they were not successful. Although tempted with the prospect of joining a vigorous and expanding trade area, the Hanoverians were alarmed that the Prussians might bestride northern Germany and act like robber barons disguised as progressive political economists. Hanover was also concerned that its trade with England might well be adversely affected by joining the Prussian customs union.

Thus by 1828 there were three customs areas in Germany, of which the south German and the Prussian customs unions were the only really viable organisations. In 1828 negotiations began between these two unions, but they were unable to make much progress, as the central German union controlled all the lines of communication between the two. Prussia was able to persuade two Thuringian states, Meiningen and Coburg, that if they would allow Prussia to provide the credit to build a road through their territories, they would join either the Prussian or the south German customs union not later than 1835. The two unions now had a route through Thuringia which was not subject to any transit tax, and the central German union had few defences left against its rivals to the north and to the south.

Two further obstacles were removed as a result of the revolutions of 1830. In both Saxony and Electoral Hesse the reactionary regimes were swept aside and modest liberal reforms were made. In both states questions of customs and tariffs had played a major part in the revolutions. In Hesse the customs houses had been stormed by the crowd, and there had been loud demands for a customs union with Prussia. In Saxony there were similar demands for a reform of the customs and for joining the Prussian union. This marked the end of the central German union and nothing stood in the way of the Prussian advance.

By now it was quite clear to men like Motz that the extension of the Prussian customs area was much more than a matter of tariffs and trade and would involve far-reaching questions of German national policy, of the role of Austria within the confederation, and of reform of the confederation itself. The Prussian Minister, Count Bernstorff, wrote in 1831 that a liberal trade policy which would embrace all of Germany was the best possible insurance against the recurrence of the kind of alarming events of the previous year and at the same time greatly enhance the power and prestige of Prussia. The Rhenish industrialist David Hansemann told Maassen that the customs agreements had done much to strengthen Prussia and would lead eventually to a real German confederation which as yet only existed in theory.

After the revolutions of 1830 events moved very swiftly. The customs union between Prussia and Electoral Hesse was signed in August 1831. This was followed by further negotiations between Prussia, Bavaria and Württemberg, and then the central German states. On 1 January 1834 customs barriers within Germany were removed, creating a free-trade area of 18 states and 23.5 million inhabitants. Hanover, Oldenburg, Schleswig-Holstein, Mecklenburg and the Hanseatic cities were not members of the *Zollverein* and Austria remained aloof. Thus the problem of enclaves remained, and the *Zollverein* did not have easy access to the coast. Many of these problems were to be overcome in the course of negotiations in the following years. By the 1860s all but the Hanseatic cities had joined the *Zollverein*.

The immediate effect of the *Zollverein* was that the Prussian tariff applied to most of Germany. The system was admirably simple. Customs officers were provided with an alphabetical list of commodities, giving the rate of duty which was levied according to weight. Most raw materials and basic foodstuffs were duty-free. The duty on semi-luxury goods such as coffee, tea, wines and spirits, tobacco and gourmet foods and spices accounted for the major part of the income from the customs. By 1871 three-quarters of the income came from these sources, and one-third from coffee alone. Income from the *Zollverein* duties was divided up among the member states on a *per capita* basis and proved to be an essential source of revenue. The *per capita* income of the south German union had been about 9.5 Groschen, that of the *Zollverein* about 24 Groschen.

The original *Zollverein* treaty was to run for eight years, although it was somewhat modified due to the arrival of the new member states during that period. A yearly congress was held for several months every summer at one of the capital cities. All decisions had to be unanimous, and even the smallest states had a veto right. This system remained in force until 1866, when the north German confederation created a 'Customs Parliament' (*Zollparlament*) with legislative powers.

Member states retained the right to tax commodities, but they were not allowed to exceed the Prussian tax on wines, spirits and tobacco, nor the Bavarian tax on beer and malt. This created a severe problem of price differentials due to taxation within a free-trade area, a problem that was only partially overcome with a complex system of compensation payments and transit taxes. Salt smuggling was still a thriving business due to the refusal of the Prussian government to give up its monopoly on salt.

Trade agreements with foreign countries also presented difficulties.

Bavaria and Württemberg had reserved the right to negotiate trade agreements with other states, but in practice made little use of this privilege. Normally negotiations were carried out by the Prussians on behalf of the *Zollverein* on the basis of conditions which had been unanimously accepted by the congress. The veto right of the *Zollverein* states made any complex negotiation extremely difficult and time-consuming, because approval of all the members was required if conditions were changed. It took three years and some very hard bargaining indeed for the states to accept the 1862 trade agreement which Prussia had negotiated with France, and which changed the *Zollverein* tariff in 161 instances. Prussia's strongest weapon in this, and in other similar instances, was to threaten to refuse to renew the *Zollverein* agreements. This threat was highly alarming to the other states because they had made a handsome profit from the *Zollverein*. Bavaria's income from customs duties doubled in the first year of membership, whereas Prussia's income had dropped by 25 per cent in the same period. Prussia thus had a powerful financial hold over the member states, and was always prepared to make financial concessions in order to retain political control over the *Zollverein*. Nevertheless Prussia had to tread carefully. As the treaty was renewed for a twelve-year period, the threat to dissolve the treaty could only be used in dire emergency and was without much effect unless it was made towards the end of the renewal period.

There can be no doubt that the *Zollverein* was a significant step forward in the economic history of Germany. It opened up the large Prussian market to the other German states, it acted as a stimulus to commerce and industry, and offered fresh opportunities to the rising middle class. These factors cannot be exactly quantified, but it is obvious that they encouraged the development of the productive forces by removing many of the old barriers, by encouraging competition in the domestic market and by stimulating the growth of a modern transportation system. Yet it would be a mistake to see the *Zollverein* exclusively in terms of a major stage in the process of industrialisation and modernisation or, as so many nationalist historians insist, as the first major step towards the unification of Germany.

Fiscal considerations always took precedence over concern for domestic industry. Prussian officials did nothing to encourage the native sugar-beet industry on the grounds that if it were successful the state would lose the profitable income from the duty of cane-sugar. Similarly, nothing was done to protect the Silesian linen weavers, the tragic yet inspiring revolutionaries of 1844, against deprivation and ruin by foreign competition. Low wages and a dramatic population increase probably did as much, if not more, for industrialisation as the efforts of the *Zollverein*.

Prussia used the *Zollverein* to enhance her power, prestige and influence both in Germany and in Europe, but she certainly did not see the *Zollverein* as a step towards the unification of Germany under Prussian leadership. German nationalism was still a suspect and dangerous liberal cause, and Frederick William turned down the offer of the German crown in 1848 not only because it was offered to him by liberals and Jews, but because he felt that his cousin in Vienna had a better claim. It was not until the late 1850s that Prussia began to use the low *Zollverein* tariffs as a weapon against Austria.

The *Zollverein* countries agreed on fixed exchange rates for their currencies, and a new south German florin was created. Customs duty could only be paid in florins or in Prussian thalers. Both coins were on the silver standard. Again, it was not until a later period that the rivalry, which was to be an important factor in the wars of German unification, began between the florin and the thaler.

Attempts to introduce a common commercial law for the *Zollverein* states were also a failure. Württemberg made the suggestion in 1836, but particularist concerns were hard to overcome, and it was not until after 1848 that some degree of uniformity was achieved by the gradual adoption of the Prussian commercial law. Most significant of all was the fact that the German states looked to Berlin rather than Vienna for leadership in economic affairs. In the early years of the *Zollverein* Prussia did not use her economic strength to pursue German national ends. Indeed it looked very much as if Count Bernstorff had been correct in his assessment of the political effects of the *Zollverein*. The German bourgeoisie was too busy in the counting-house to be active on the hustings. Economics seemed to take the place of politics in the dreary and repressive years between 1830 and 1848. The political liberalism of the early protagonists of free trade in Germany was quietened and deflected; with Bismarck's policy of unification with 'iron and blood' it was silenced.

With the creation of the *Zollverein* the question of tariffs was by no means settled. The Junkers of East Prussia were delighted with the low tariffs, for they could freely export their wood, wool and corn and import the machinery they needed. Merchants in the great trading centres were also satisfied with the *Zollverein* tariffs. The manufacturers, however, many of whom had sympathised with the aims of the Association for Trade and Industry, felt that the new tariffs left them defenceless against the competition of English industry. Rhineland industrialists looked enviously across the border to France and were convinced that the relative stability and prosperity of the French economy was due in large measure to the high tariffs. They were hardly placated by assurances that the vast new German market would offer them ample opportunity for expansion, and they continued to bombard the local *Landtag* with demands for protective tariffs.

Industry was unable to unite on the question of tariffs. Cotton spinners wanted protection against English yarn, but cotton weavers wanted an ample supply of cheap high-quality yarns from abroad. Similarly, iron and steel manufacturers called for protection, while engineering works hoped to get their raw materials as cheaply as possible. The Prussian civil servants who drafted the treaties which created the *Zollverein* were convinced that low tariffs were desirable not only because they were in the interests of the Junkers but, more importantly, because they had learnt from the classical political economists that free trade and competition were invigorating and stimulating to industry. Protective tariffs were associated with mercantilism and the absolutist state, and they protected the backward and the inefficient and hindered the full development of a country's economic potential. They were not totally indifferent to the pleas of the industrialists and there were increases in the duties on textiles, iron, yarn and linen in the 1840s, but they were convinced that in the long run free trade would lead to prosperity for everyone, and that the hardships of the moment were but temporary.

Friedrich List

In 1832 the greatest champion of protective tariffs, Friedrich List, returned to Germany as United States consul in Leipzig. List's experiences in America reinforced his conviction that a country on the verge of industrialisation needed protective tariffs. The United States was the perfect example of a country that had prospered by cutting off its ties with England and by protecting its native industry by high tariffs. List argued that Adam Smith's ideas had been deliberately used by British governments from Pitt to Melbourne to 'throw sand in the eyes of other nations for the benefit of England'. Free trade as a universal principle benefited the strong and spelt disaster to the weak, given that states were at an uneven level of development. Thus the question of free trade or protection was one of expediency rather than a law of nature. This expediency was in turn historically determined. Adam Smith and the classical political economists saw human beings as abstractions, and the economy as behaving according to its own absolute laws governed and directed by the invisible hand of supply and demand. List used arguments from the German political romantics – Adam Müller, Justus Möser and Herder – that the activities of man, and particularly of the *homo faber*, were directed and influenced by a multiplicity of historical factors.

Adam Smith ignored the state and the nation and talked in terms of humanity, of a world-wide economic system that would function to mutual benefit and advantage. List argued that 'history teaches us that the individual draws the largest part of his productive strength from social institutions and conditions.' He attacked Smith's 'boundless cosmopolitanism' by insisting that between the individual and the whole of humanity stood the nation. 'Just as the individual attains intellectual development, productive strength, security and prosperity by means of the nation, so is the civilisation of the human race only conceivable and possible by means of the civilisation and development of the nations.' For the nations to develop and to become fully civilised they would have to become industrial states in which there was a 'balance of productive forces', so that the full potential of the state could be realised. Adam Smith's views on the international division of labour would simply condemn certain states to dependency and backwardness, and were further evidence that classical political economy was an ideological justification for British economic domination.

Whereas Adam Smith and his followers argued that if all were left well alone, international peace and understanding would necessarily follow, List insisted that if things were left alone as they were at the present level of development, British hegemony would be guaranteed. For List it was only when a nation had reached a sufficient level of industrial development, which was only possible with protective tariffs, that international harmony and free trade were possible. There was nothing in List of the mean chauvinism of the late nineteenth century. His patriotism was liberal and humane, directed against the petty tyrannies of the small German states, and inspired by the desire to secure for every citizen a decent standard of living. The classical political economists argued that Germany should be content to remain a country producing agricultural goods for export, eau de Cologne, and toys for the world's children. List insisted that Germany had the raw materials, the climate, the hard-working and intelligent people to become a prosperous industrial state.

Opponents of the protective tariff argued that it would lead to rising prices. List replied that it would unleash the productive forces that slumbered within the nation and lead to wealth and prosperity. It is for this reason that he preferred to call the protective tariff the 'educational tariff', an essential part of a programme of constitutional and legal reform, of education and of national renewal. Once the harmonious balance of the *Agrikulturmanufakturhandelsstaat* (the state which combined agriculture, commerce and industry) had been reached, then the 'educational tariff' had done its work and the state could face the competition of free trade.

This romantic vision of a world of equal partners, although tempered by List's awareness of the poverty and suffering that accompanied the process of industrialisation, had a serious flaw. Protectionism, far from leading to understanding and co-operation, increased the tensions and hostilities between states and made the realisation of List's cosmopolitan aims all the more difficult. His talk of forcing Holland and Belgium into the *Zollverein* and of forming a Continental alliance against England was hardly a sound basis for international understanding.

List's masterpiece, *The National System of Political Economy*, published in 1840, was a powerful and highly readable battle-cry for the industrial bourgeoisie of Germany, but in the short term it had little effect. The bourgeoisie was too feeble to force its ideas on a politically divided Germany in which aristocratic and bureaucratic inertia combined with a distrust of these liberal notions. A man of enormous energy and dynamic presence, List finally admitted defeat and committed suicide in 1846. This was a tragic end to a remarkable life.

Railways

Although his schemes for protective tariffs were frustrated, List had far greater success as a propagandist for railways. Just as he was enormously important in raising the consciousness of the manufacturing and commercial interests to the needs for a united German economic area, so too was he a pathfinder in the field of railway construction. The opening of the Stockton to Darlington line in 1825 excited considerable interest among far-sighted Germans. Peter Beuth from the Prussian Finance Ministry and the architect Schinkel were sent on an official visit to England to study the railway. The industrialist Friedrich Harkort pointed out the need for a railway system in Germany, and the Finance Minister Motz quickly realised that the railway could be a useful weapon in the struggle to extend the Prussian customs area.

This enthusiasm for the railways was shared by very few, hence the importance of the propaganda of men like List, Hansemann and Camphausen. More cautious souls argued that Germany's economic development was as yet so modest that railways could not be justified. Joint-stock companies were still a rarity in Germany, and it was difficult to see how capital could be raised for railways, which were high-risk ventures in all but few places where traffic was very dense. Frederick William III of Prussia failed to see any point in arriving in Potsdam an hour or two earlier. Ernst August of Hanover was appalled at the idea that 'any cobbler or tailor could travel as fast as I'. The aristocracy thought that the railway was an alarmingly democratic institution. Finance Ministers worried about the loss of revenue from toll roads. Innkeepers and ostlers felt that they would be ruined. Goethe told Eckermann that the railway would unite Germany, a prospect which was most alarming to less progressive spirits.

For men like List these arguments were further reasons why Germany needed railways. Railway-building would be the means whereby Germany would be able to industrialise and modernise and eventually to equal the economic power of England. Backwardness was an argument for the railways, not against them. List insisted that Germany had a greater need for railways than had England, for coastal shipping was only of limited use in Germany and there was no comparable canal system. The railway would be complementary to the *Zollverein*, an essential means towards the unification and strengthening of the German economy and the German nation.

Given the misgivings and the suspicions of governments, it is hardly surprising that private initiative provided the initial spur to railway-building. Industrialists in the Wuppertal area were determined to reduce the freight rates on coal, which over a distance as short as 20 miles could be as high as twice the initial cost of the coal. A committee was struck to discuss the building of a railway to transport the coal, but failed initially owing to the opposition of the coal-carriers, of the mine-owners whose holdings were not on the proposed route, and because of lack of capital. Eventually a horse-drawn railway was built in 1830 by a joint-stock company led by Harkort. These five miles of railway mark the beginning of the German railway system.

Almost immediately upon his return to Germany, List published his work *On a Saxon Railway System as the Foundation of a General German Railway System with Particular Reference to the Laying of a Line from Leipzig to Dresden*, a rather dreary title for a book that was to have such a tremendous impact. List realised that it was not enough to build isolated stretches of railway, they had to be planned as part of a national railway system. In a lesser-known work the young Cologne corn merchant, Ludolf Camphausen, published a pamphlet on the need for a railway from Cologne to Antwerp which should be integrated into a larger system.

As long as governments were suspicious of railways and particularism remained strong, there was little hope for such far-sighted schemes as these. The first railways were built on the initiative of railway committees formed in the great urban centres. In 1832 a committee was formed in Nürnberg under the leadership of the mayor to discuss the building of a passenger line from Nürnberg to Fürth. Similar projects were soon planned for railways between Bonn and Cologne, Leipzig and Dresden, Elberfeld and Düsseldorf, Munich and Augsburg, and in spite of the King's objections, between Berlin and Potsdam.

These early railways were designed primarily as passenger lines. Given the high cost of loading and unloading freight, and the lack of any really long stretches of rail, lines were only built where passenger traffic was already heavy. The demand for railway service could be calculated with a reasonable degree of accuracy when it was a matter of moving passengers over relatively short distances, and this was a vital consideration when planning such costly and risky ventures. Freight service would have to wait for a later stage. In the Rhineland men like Camphausen, David Hansemann, the founder of an insurance company, and the industrialist Friedrich Harkort had more ambitious plans. They wanted lines to the Ruhr and the Weser to provide inexpensive transportation of coal, and they also wanted to extend the railway system as an alternative to the Rhine so as to avoid the crippling tolls imposed by the Dutch on the Rhine estuary. As transport costs on the Dutch Rhine were thirteen times those of the Prussian Rhine, a railway from the Rhineland to the Belgian border and a second line to Bremen were attractive prospects. Antwerp and Bremen could then become viable alternatives to Rotterdam and Amsterdam. Local representatives of the Prussian civil service, men like Koppe and Krüger, enthusiastically supported these schemes.

In spite of this interest and the far-reaching and imaginative plans, there was little railway-building in the early 1830s. In 1835 the short stretch from Nürnberg to Fürth was completed. It was easy to build and, given the density of traffic, was an almost certain success. The first stretch of the Leipzig to Dresden line was finished in 1837 and the project was completed in 1839. The success of the Nürnberg–Fürth line and the propaganda efforts of List and his supporters for the

Dresden–Leipzig line encouraged investors to put their money into railway shares. As early as 1835 the Dresden–Leipzig line had a share capital of 2 million thalers. This triggered off a frantic wave of speculation in railway shares which reached its peak in 1836. A year later the bubble burst, partly due to the unexpected expense of the railways and the fact that there was no immediate return on the investment, and partly because of the cyclical crisis in the British economy which had severe repercussions in Germany.

Although many had taken a beating in 1837–8, the German bourgeoisie now realised the vital importance of railways if the German economy was to expand and prosper. If anything, the experience of the depression strengthened their resolve to tackle the problem of British competition, and they knew that without railways this would not be possible. Investors also got used to the idea of investing in railway shares and the unfortunate experience of the depression did not mean the end of private investment in railways. Governments and the aristocracy were beginning to lose their strong feelings of opposition to the railways. As one satirist pointed out, if the railway was the work of the devil, at least he was a clever devil. By the end of the 1830s governments had come to the realisation that railways were vital to the economic strength, the political influence and the military might of a state and they could no longer be opposed or ignored. The main problem remaining was one of finance. If a proper network of railways were to be built, the government would have to invest heavily. Private investors would not put their money into stretches of railway that were unlikely to show much of a profit, and after the experiences of the depression they had lost their initial enthusiasm for railway shares.

The states had many misgivings about the private railway companies. Once they had overcome their objections to railways, they tended to argue that they should no more be controlled by private interests than the roads. They also felt that a system where all the profitable stretches of railway were in private hands and the state was left with the task of building expensive and unprofitable railways was most undesirable. In November 1838 the Prussian government passed a law which enabled the state to take over private railways after thirty years of operation and on payment of adequate compensation. The greater the emphasis on the political and strategic importance of railways, the more reluctant were governments to see railways in private hands. On the whole, the railway enthusiasts like Hansemann, Camphausen and List preferred private capitalism to state intervention, even List hoping that his grandiose scheme for a German railway system centred on

Berlin would be built by private interests. But they were also impatient and wanted to get the railways built as quickly as possible, and this they knew was not possible without state intervention. Furthermore, if the railways were to be built not merely to meet a known need but to stimulate further growth, then the state would have to intervene.

In spite of the success of the Nürnberg–Fürth line, most similar attempts to build private lines in Bavaria failed owing to lack of capital. In 1843 the Bavarian government agreed to build a railway from Nürnberg to Hof and Lindau, and another line from Munich to Augsburg was planned shortly afterwards. The Bavarian Minister-President, von Abel, announced that he would never allow such an important institution as the railway to fall into private hands. Other south German states also began to build railways, Baden in the late 1830s, Württemberg in 1843. With the exception of Baden, these railways were built with capital from the sale of bonds. Baden preferred to finance railway-building from current revenue. Railway bonds were a secure and guranteed investment which would not yield the windfall profits of the early railway shares, but gave a comfortable interest and were thus an attractive investment. A major problem was that bond issues could not be made without the approval of the parliaments. In Prussia the railways became a constitutional question because the King had promised in 1820 that he would not borrow any more money without first seeking the approval of a constitutional assembly. Thus in Prussia railway-building could not begin without a major constitutional change, for the bourgeois representatives in the assembly would not accept a new loan without a guarantee of constitutional reform. Thus in 1847 the bourgeois representatives at the united diet which had been convened to discuss a loan for the construction of the eastern railway (*Ostbahn*) voted against the proposal. It was not simply that they were unwilling to finance a railway that was designed for the land-owning aristocracy in the east, but rather that they were determined to use the crisis to win further constitutional concessions and a share in state power.

As railways were deemed essential, and as loans raised dangerous constitutional issues, the only possible alternative seemed to be for the state to guarantee the dividends of private companies so as to encourage investment. Thus the Prussian government guaranteed a 3.5 per cent return on the 31.5 million thalers invested in Prussian railways, and invested over 6 million thalers directly in private companies. This method proved most effective, and there was a second investment boom in railways in the middle 1840s which lasted until the crisis year of 1847. During this period some of the most important lines were built, including those from Berlin to Hamburg and from Cologne to Minden. Berlin, Cologne, Frankfurt, Munich and Nürnberg became great railway centres and, as they developed, the need for connecting railways became more pressing. These were mostly built in the late 1840s and early 1850s. As early as 1843 the link with Belgium was established via Aachen, the link to Austria was finished in 1848 at Kosel, with France at Saarbrücken in 1852, with Holland in 1856, Switzerland near Basel in 1858 and Russia near Königsberg in 1861.

The result of all this activity, in spite of the fits and starts and the economic and political obstacles that had to be overcome, was that Germany by the 1840s had the second-largest railway system in Europe. By 1850 Britain had 10,653 km of track, Germany 5,874 km and France 2,127 km, and equally important was the fact that the Germans recorded the highest rate of growth.

Railway-building created a vast appetite for machinery, iron and steel, coal and metals. Germany was at first quite incapable of meeting this demand. The *Zollverein* statistics show that in 1837 156,452 Zentner (1 Zentner = 50 kilos) of iron and steel were imported; in 1844 this had risen to 1,517,888 Zentner. In the same period a large amount of machinery and equipment was imported. But even in this early period Germany was far from being a backward country that had to import all its technology and skills from abroad. From the middle 1830s very significant advances were made in all branches of industry, investment in capital goods was high, and new skills and techniques were being applied. Although 1842 saw the first negative trade balance in modern German history, this was due to exceptional demand rather than stagnation at home and is indicative of rising total income.

The demands placed on German industry by the needs of railway-building showed up its relative backwardness. In 1834 more than 95 per cent of the iron produced in the *Zollverein* was from charcoal-fired furnaces. Although coke had been used for iron production a century before at Coalbrookdale, and although the average coke smelter in England produced 86,666 Zentner of iron per year in 1839 whereas the average Prussian charcoal smelter in 1837 only produced 9,410 Zentner, there was little incentive for the German iron-masters to modernise their plant. Using basically late-medieval methods, the Germans were able to meet 80 per cent of their domestic needs for iron as late as 1834. In the 1830s some German firms began to use English methods such as puddling and the use of rolling mills, but these were isolated cases and the labour usually had to be imported from England. By 1840 there were only about 40 furnaces using the puddling process in the whole of the *Zollverein*. Steam engines were hardly ever used in iron production.

The directors of the Nürnberg–Fürth railway naturally imagined that they would have to import the rails they needed from England, and therefore appealed to the Bavarian government to be able to import the rails duty-free. The request was denied and the directors were obliged to put the contract up for tender. The contract was awarded to the Remy works at Neuwied, which was the first firm in Germany to introduce the puddling process and to use calibrated rolling mills. But even though this was the most technically advanced works in the country, it found the task of rail production exceedingly difficult. It was unable to deliver the required number of rails on time, and many of the rails that were produced had to be straightened out, a costly and time-consuming process. The locomotives for the railway had to be imported from Robert Stephenson and Company, although the carriages could be made locally by coach-makers.

The Nürnberg–Fürth was a small affair, but even so, German know-how was not up to the necessary level. The requirements for rails for the longer track from Leipzig to Dresden amounted to 2.5 times the annual iron production of the state of Saxony and to 30 per cent of Prussia's bar iron production for 1837. German industry was quite incapable of producing the amounts needed to meet this enormous increase in demand, and most of the rails had to be imported from England. German industry was able to meet the demand for the smaller bits and pieces of railway-building, such as spikes and chairs, but could not produce rails of sufficient quality in adequate quantities. Almost 90 per cent of the rails had to be imported from England, so that in 1844 the *Zollverein* introduced a new duty on bar iron to try to break this monopoly.

Yet in spite of the overwhelming position of British producers, some enterprising German industrialists and engineers saw that the large and growing demand for iron and steel for the railways offered unusual opportunities. Eberhard Hoesch was the first large German producer of rails at his factory at Lendersdorf near Düren. But even he found it more economical to import coke-fired pig iron from England and Belgium which he processed in his 23 puddling furnaces. In 1838 the *Laurahütte* was formed to meet the demand of the railways and began the production of pig iron in coke smelters. The *Gutehoffnungshütte* built a new factory at Oberhausen in 1836 which used the puddling process and had a modern rolling mill, but it found the technical problems of rail production almost impossible to overcome, and the plant was not able to compete with English rails. Even such railway enthusiasts as J.C. Harkort of Hagen had to be content with the production of spikes and chairs, and could not run the risk of large-scale production.

The engineering works were faced with similar problems. Borsig had started his factory in Berlin in 1837 with 8,503 thalers of his own money and 59,000 thalers of borrowed capital, but he was only able to survive in the first lean years by earning his bread and butter with small pieces of machinery for the railways. Maffei started his Munich works shortly after Borsig. As a wealthy man and chairman of the board of the Munich to Augsburg railway he was in a more favourable position, yet his works still used water power, a striking example of the relative backwardness of even the more modern sectors of German industry. In the following year Klett started his factory in Nürnberg in an abandoned spinning mill. The problems facing Borsig, Maffei and Klett were very great. German engineers and craftsmen lacked the experience and skills needed to produce reliable and economical locomotives. The raw materials were exceedingly expensive. There was a lack of suitable coal for smelters. Capital was lacking for the construction of new smelters, and thus it was more economical to import the iron and process it in German puddling furnaces and rolling mills. German ores were either of poor quality or awkwardly placed, and transport was still slow and expensive. It is thus hardly surprising that by 1844 the *Zollverein* was importing ten times more bar iron than in 1837.

The tariff of 1844 had a dramatic effect on the growth of the domestic iron and steel industry. Whereas before 1844 coke-fired bar iron had entered the *Zollverein* duty-free, it was now subject to duty of up to 68 per cent. At the same time, supplies of charcoal in Germany were running short, driving up the price and making the old charcoal furnaces no longer economical. There was thus enormous incentive to increase the production of iron and steel in Germany. By 1850, although only about 25 per cent of the track that had already been laid was produced in Germany, German firms were now able to meet the demand for new rails and German industry kept pace with the increased demand of the 1850s to achieve an extraordinary rate of growth. Borsig had built his first locomotive in 1841, based on an American model, but, in 1843, 89 per cent of all the locomotives were still foreign. With the help of the tariff and the increased demand of the late 1840s, German producers were able to increase their share of the market and gradually drive out foreign competition. By 1858 Borsig had built 1,000 locomotives.

The development of the locomotive industry is typical of mechanical engineering in general during the 1840s. In the 1830s textile machinery, for example, was imported in considerable quantities from France and Belgium. By the mid-1840s Germany was able to meet much of its own needs. England lifted its ban on the export of machinery in 1842, but this was largely a recognition that the ban had not been effective. A counter-measure by the *Zollverein* was the new tariff in 1844 which increased the duty on machinery acting as a further stimulus to domestic industry. The days of the small workshop had now passed. Engineering works were organised for large-scale production, using machine tools that were usually steam-driven: Prussian government statistics show that by 1846 more than half the engineering works used steam engines. Production was rationalised and machine tools became more specialised in their function during this critical period in which Germany rapidly became one of the leading producers of machinery.

The spurt in the manufacturing industries in this period can best be seen in the increased demand for crude iron in the *Zollverein*. In 1834, 121,093 tonnes were consumed, in 1847 this had risen to 414,094 tonnes. A large part of this increased demand came from railway-building. This demand could not initially be met by domestic production, and imports were high until German producers were gradually able to meet the requirements of the home market. Thus, by the mid-1840s, most of the rails were made in German rolling mills. By this time the puddling process was widespread, without which there could not have been such a dramatic increase in output.

By 1841 more than half the furnaces in the Bonn and Dortmund area used the puddling process. Prussia tried hard to catch up, and by the crisis year of 1847, 70 per cent of iron production was produced by the puddling process. Germany lagged far behind England in the introduction of coke-fired furnaces, and even by the mid-century charcoal was widely used. The Saar, which had the largest number of coke furnaces in Germany, was exceptional in that it had 30 per cent of its furnaces coke-fired in 1847, at a time when in England charcoal was no longer used in the production of steel. In Prussia even as late as 1850 only 18 per cent of the furnaces were coke-fired.

Germany was thus less successful in the production of crude iron than she was in the production of iron goods such as rails and wrought iron. German producers were not able to meet the challenge of British and Belgian crude iron which, until the reforms of 1844, entered the *Zollverein* duty-free. In this situation it was exceptionally difficult to obtain the necessary capital for the heavy investment in new furnaces. The new tariff appears to have had some effect. Between 1840 and 1845 imports to the *Zollverein* of crude iron rose from 36,765 tonnes to 132,927 tonnes. During the same period domestic production hardly increased. Between 1844 and 1848 German crude iron production increased from 171,148 tonnes to 229,161 tonnes. In the period from 1834 to 1848 crude iron production in Germany doubled. This increase in domestic production was not sufficient to meet the rapidly increasing demand, and it was not until the 1850s, with the formation of the joint-stock companies and the massive investment of capital in new furnaces made possible by protective tariffs and the steady demand for rails, that Germany was able gradually to shake off its dependence on imports of inexpensive British and Belgian iron.

The example of the Krupp works gives some indication of the scale of German industry. When Friedrich Krupp died in 1826 the firm employed four workers. By 1835 his son Alfred, the real founder of the firm, had increased the number of workers to 67 and first used a steam engine. By 1846, 122 workers were employed and the firm was an average medium-sized enterprise.

The 1844 tariff, the improved economic climate from late 1848 and the state guarantees of the interest on railway stock all helped the industry. The production of coke-fired iron increased eightfold in the 1850s. Prussia produced more than ten times more steel by the puddling process in 1860 than in 1850 in spite of the severe recession in 1858–9. Cast steel production increased more than 22 times in the same period. Although the number of locomotives in Germany increased 150 per cent between 1851 and 1860, no foreign locomotives were imported after 1854. As early as the late 1840s, all railway carriages were made in Germany. In the 1850s, Germany began to export locomotives and carriages, and by the 1860s this became a major export industry. Heavy investment in the iron and steel industries led to greatly increased productivity, and this investment was made possible in large part because of the almost guaranteed market for iron and steel in the railways.

The railways thus provided the major stimulus to the Industrial Revolution in Germany. They encouraged massive investment in the iron and steel industries and in engineering. They were the direct cause of the enormous increase in the production of iron and steel. They caused major technological changes in these sectors and gave the necessary incentive for the complete modernisation of German industry. The result was the creation of larger, more effective and rationally organised factories which in turn increased the demand for steam power, machine tools and specialised skills and techniques. Even firms like Krupp, which had at first remained somewhat aloof from the railway industry, were swept along by the current of change. By the 1850s Krupp was beginning to make large numbers of specialised items for the railways, including wheels, axles and springs, and it can be argued that demand for such items was decisive in making Krupps into a large firm. Over-all production of the company increased ten times in the 1850s, an impressive growth rate that was not untypical of German industry, and which was due in large part to the effects of the railway boom. Railway-building thus helped to revolutionise German industry, and the formation of a comprehensive railway system was also a tremendous technical advance in a country that had poor roads and an inadequate canal system.

Railway-building and the increased demand for iron and steel had an immediate effect on coal-mining. Between 1835 and 1847 German coal production increased 162 per cent. In the 1840s steam engines were gradually introduced in the mining industry to drive pumping and winding gear. Such equipment made it possible to reach the coal deposits of the Ruhr which lay buried under thick marly soil. In 1841 the first mine near Essen began production, and by 1850 the Ruhr was producing over 1.5 million tons of coal a year. The great coal barons were to become household names: Haniel, Stinnes, Grillo and the Irishman Mulvany. Coal was still extracted without the use of machinery at the coal-face, and this continued to be the case until well into the twentieth century, but this does not mean that the mining industry was not affected by the Industrial Revolution. Huge investments were needed to rationalise and modernise the industry and, although part of the increase was due to the increase in the rate of the exploitation of labour, by specialisation and the careful planning of shift work, the coal industry could not have expanded as fast as it did without steam power, railways, improved roads and canals. The mines ceased to be small operations employing a handful of miners and became huge capitalist enterprises organised along the lines of the most advanced industries. At the coal-face little had changed, but the industry itself underwent revolutionary changes, beginning in the mid-1830s and quickly gathering momentum.

The Textile Industry

The critical period from 1834 to 1847 had a less dramatic impact on the modernisation of the textile industry. By the end of this period only 2,628 cotton looms in Prussia were mechanically operated, whereas 116,832 were traditional handlooms. Very much the same is true of wool and linen weaving. Power-operated machinery was more common in spinning, but both in cotton and wool German industry was unable to compete with British goods. British industry was still so far advanced that even higher *Zollverein* tariffs were of little help to German manufacturers. It seemed impossible to break the British monopoly, and the best that could be achieved was for German industry to hold its own against an overwhelming competitor. Thus the textile industry, and particularly the cotton industry, could not play the leading role in the Industrial Revolution in Germany as it had in England. In Germany it was the railways which performed this critical function. Investment in railways stimulated the growth of heavy industry and engineering which marks the beginning of an Industrial Revolution in Germany.

The tragic figures of the Silesian weavers, decimated by hunger and typhus, exploited by ruthless entrepreneurs and fighting a desperate and hopeless battle against the machinery that was replacing their own labour, have a special place in the history of the German working class and were an inspiration to artists like Heine, Gerhart Hauptmann and Käthe Kollwitz. Their fate was the direct result of the backwardness of the German textile industry, and it was a truly tragic fate because the solution to that problem necessarily involved the end of the handloom weavers.

From the foundation of the *Zollverein* to 1848, German industry was able to meet an increasing share of the domestic demand for yarn. Although the amounts were somewhat modest, it marks a reversal of the trend before 1834 when British yarn threatened totally to swamp the German market. Between 1836 and 1840, 29.4 per cent of the yarn was of German manufacture; in 1846 to 1850, 34.6 per cent. The production of yarn doubled between 1832–3 and 1834–5 and trebled from 1835 to 1848. Cotton weaving also increased during this period, but not at the same rate. The industry was relatively backward and was unable to match the productivity of spinning. German spindles produced an average of 27 pounds of yarn per year in 1849, whereas British spindles averaged 40 pounds. The average British factory had 20,000 spindles, the German only 1,473. With such small-scale production and low productivity it is hardly surprising that German cotton goods were expensive and unable to compete with British goods. For this reason the export of cotton goods from the *Zollverein* declined in the 1840s.

The woollen industry was somewhat more successful. With the formation of the *Zollverein*, German wool manufacturers were gradually able to meet the challenge of British, Belgian and French imports. The factories of Prussia and Saxony made considerable progress and increased their export of woollen goods. Switzerland, Italy, Spain and Turkey began to import German cloth, and even in Belgium specialised cloths from the factories around Aachen were able to compete in a highly protected market.

The Silesian linen weavers were thus something of a special case, working under semi-feudal conditions in an industry that was quite incapable of competing with British and Belgian linens. The linen industry was the one branch of the German textile industry which stagnated and then declined in the second half of the nineteenth century. In Bielefeld improved yarns were spun mechanically for linen, and the bleaching process for linen was also improved, but the Silesian weavers were the poorest members of a declining industry. Linen production in Prussia increased 31 per cent between 1834 and 1849, but this was a poor performance when measured against that of cotton and wool production. After 1850 the industry declined.

Agriculture

An expanding industry increased the demand for agricultural goods. This was met by a steady improvement of farming methods, and to a lesser extent by increasing the amount of agricultural land. German agriculture was able to feed an expanding population, and to increase exports. The three-field system was gradually abandoned, the smaller farms following the example of the great estates. The result was that the amount of fallow land was greatly reduced and much new land brought under cultivation. The major change in the period between 1834 and 1848 was, however, in the application of science to agriculture. The outstanding figure was Justus Liebig, the inventor of artificial manure.

Liebig was born in Darmstadt in 1803, the son of an apothecary. In 1822 he went to Paris and studied under Gay-Lussac. Thanks to the patronage of Alexander von Humboldt, Liebig was appointed professor of chemistry at the University of Giessen at the age of 24. Liebig was the first man to build a teaching laboratory in Germany and insisted on a rigorous experimental approach which had little time or sympathy for natural philosophy and abstract theorising. Along with Wöhler and the Swedish chemist Berzelius, Liebig was the founder of modern organic chemistry.

When Liebig began his work the process whereby plants extracted nourishment from the earth was unknown. Lavoisier had shown that plants took part of their nourishment from the air, but obviously this insight had little practical significance for farmers. The air was free and plentiful, and foodstuffs for plants could hardly be added to it. Obviously manure worked, the problem was to find out how. Liebig discovered that plants extracted nourishment from the earth, and that this nourishment had to be replaced. In this sense plants were 'made' from raw materials, just as were nails or cotton cloth. Agriculture was an industry, and the earth had to be supplied with the necessary materials. Thaer and others had shown that careful husbandry and crop rotation could preserve the land, but in the long run the productivity of the land dropped. Liebig was determined to find out the materials which nourished plants so that the land could be made to produce more. He said, 'when the farmer sells the fruit of his fields he also sells his fields.' Agriculture was a culture of robbery, less harsh than in the past, but robbery none the less. The phosphoric acid, potash and lime which were robbed from the land had to be replaced, and the best way to do this, according to Liebig, was by direct application of the chemicals rather than by the use of natural manures, although he also recommended bone meal, ashes and guano.

Liebig did not live to see the growth of the fertiliser industry which was based on his work. During his lifetime the chemicals had to be imported from England, where his ideas were enthusiastically received. He was a brilliant propagandist and populariser of his ideas, and his boundless optimism was infectious, if a trifle exaggerated. He greatly underestimated the importance of climate, and he undervalued animal manure. He failed to see the use of the rotation of crops, and the need for a proper relationship between crops and livestock. His own model farm in Giessen was a disastrous failure, much to the delight of his many opponents. He refused to accept the criticisms of John Bennett Lawes and Joseph Henry Gilbert that plants do not obtain a sufficiency of nitrogen from the air and that it had to be added to the soil. Berzelius criticised him for lack of experimental rigour and for his excessively vivid and poetic imagination – an attack which Liebig could never forgive, and one which was particularly wounding to a scientist who had done so much for empirical research. Yet Liebig was one of the very greatest of scientists. It is not just his discovery of the three basic organic compounds – fats, carbohydrates and proteins – or the discoveries of chloroform and chloral which sprang from his research, it was his attitude towards agriculture as an applied science which, for all its shortcomings, was to have a profound effect in the course of the century and to transform agriculture in much the same way that other technical change had transformed the manufacturing industries.

Liebig's book, *Organic Chemistry and its Application to Agriculture and Physiology*, was published in 1840, and although artificial manures had been used before in a haphazard and unsystematic manner, it marks a decisive date in the history of agriculture. Historians of science are quick to point out that Liebig's work was not entirely original, that Carl Sprengel (1787–1859) had already reached much the same conclusions, and that his methods were sloppy. Liebig thus rejected the humus theory on the grounds that the first plants would not have been able to survive because there would have been nothing for them to feed on, since humus was made up of decaying vegetable matter. Much the same argument could be used to deny the sexual reproduction of man. These criticisms are beside the point. Liebig had a tremendous impact not only because of his scientific genius but also because of his ability to disseminate his ideas in a popular form. The *Organic Chemistry* is a brilliant book that had an immediate impact. Sprengel's work has none of this sparkle and was ignored and soon forgotten. Davy's book on agricultural chemistry, published in 1813, also failed to have a great impact.

As a result of Liebig's efforts a number of agricultural research centres were built in Germany in which a great deal of detailed and specialist research was conducted, which in turn helped to improve the productivity and profitability of German agriculture. From the 1840s potash was widely used as a fertiliser, Germany having large deposits of potash. Saltpetre was imported from Chile, phosphates from England. From the 1860s ammoniacal water from gasworks was used, even though Liebig had denied its efficacy. The first superphosphate factory in Germany was built in 1855.

The use of chemicals in agriculture made modest progress in the 1840s but it marked the beginning of a revolution in agriculture. But this was not the only example of the application of technology to agriculture. From the 1840s there was a steady improvement in the design and quality of agricultural machinery, which was no longer built by the village smith, but produced in modern factories which used the latest techniques. Iron ploughs replaced wooden ones, they cut deeper and cleaner furrows. Mowing machines, seed-drills and threshing machines enormously increased the productivity of agriculture and saved much back-breaking labour. By mid-century steam engines rather than horses were used on the larger estates to drive this new machinery. Steam-driven tractors were introduced in the 1860s. These new techniques and machines were beyond the means of the small farmers and were often uneconomical in areas where there was an ample supply of cheap labour. Progress was thus slow, but gradually agriculture was transformed to become a modern industry. The increase in productivity was satisfactory but unspectacular, the number of animals growing faster than the increase in crop yields.

Economic Growth in the 1840s

German economic development from the foundation of the *Zollverein* was relatively rapid, very uneven and quite unique. Industrial productivity grew far more rapidly than agricultural productivity, creating something of an imbalance. The 'Prussian way' to modernisation, with the great estates of the land-owning aristocracy still showing remnants of the feudal order, the feudal estates gradually becoming capitalist Junker estates, was part of the reason for this slow development. Within industry it was heavy industry – mining, iron and steel and mechanical engineering – which led the way, and not light industry as in the English Industrial Revolution. The transport industry, particularly the railways, consumed the bulk of investment capital and acted as a major stimulus to economic growth.

The formation of the enlarged estates and centralised and rationalised land holdings was less a result of commercial competition than of the liberation of the serfs and the compensation extracted for that freedom. Another important factor was the comprehensive adjustment of land holdings carried out by government officials, which created out of numerous dispersed holdings efficient and workable units. The increases in agricultural production were more the result of a rationalisation and intensification of existing methods than of the investment of capital and the large-scale introduction of modern machinery and methods.

Capitalist production was most advanced in mechanical engineering where modern industrial methods of machine-building were rapidly replacing the old handicraft skills. Workshops gave way to engineering works, capital investment was relatively high, and productivity increased greatly. In textiles the handloom weavers were able to survive a little longer, but their standard of living declined steadily. From the late 1830s their position became hopeless and their decline rapid, partly as the consequence of the crisis in the British textile industry, and partly from the competition at home of modern industrial production. Yet even as late as the 1860s many textiles were still woven on handlooms, even though spinning and finishing were now entirely mechanised. Even in the more traditional handicrafts, factory production was becoming more common. The leather industry is the most striking example. With the growth of the towns, the building trade, once the province of the small entrepreneur and craftsman, was becoming the modern capitalist industry of the late nineteenth century. The need for large investments in order to remain competitive, particularly in mining, metallurgy and engineering, hastened the tendency towards the formation of large firms, the concentration of capital and the destruction of the small productive units. Although by 1848 this process had only just begun, it was already in evidence.

The population of the German confederation, excluding the German-speaking parts of the Austrian Empire, was about 46 million. The population of Prussia had reached 15.5 million. Industrialisation was thus taking place at a time of rapid population growth which added to the problems of the movement of population to the urban areas. It is a measure of the extent of industrial growth of Prussia that between 1816 and 1847 the increase in the number of factory workers, apprentices and servants was greater than the increase in the population. The largest increase was in the number of factory workers, which in Berlin was more than 170 per cent. The towns were growing rapidly. In 1835 the population of Berlin was 265,122 and by 1846 had increased to 108,502.

There can be little doubt that the industrialisation of Germany was well under way before the 'great spurt' of the early 1850s, but what is much more controversial is the role of the state in encouraging industrial development. The absolutist state was highly suspicious of joint-stock companies, which it saw as dubious associations of a potentially troublesome bourgeoisie. For this reason the Prussian state made the licensing of joint-stock companies exceedingly tiresome and difficult. Between 1826 and 1850 the average of new joint-stock companies in Germany was between 4 and 5 per year. Given the fact that there appears to have been sufficient capital available for investment, and interest rates were on the whole fairly low, it would seem that the attitude of the state was an important contributory factor to the slow growth of the joint-stock company as a form of industrial organisation. Industrial entrepreneurs in the 1840s found it exceedingly difficult to obtain sufficient capital, and this at a time when the economy was progressing smoothly, and the initial stages of industrialisation when risks were very high had already been largely overcome.

The manner in which the liberation of the serfs was carried out was also an inhibiting factor for economic growth. Semi-feudal remnants in the agricultural sector were a direct cause of rural poverty, which in turn restricted the domestic market. Without a sizeable middle-income group with a relatively high elasticity of demand, light industry had little chance of rapid expansion, and hence the importance of heavy industry in the German Industrial Revolution. Industrialisation was a serious challenge and threat to the social and economic position of the aristocracy, and it is thus hardly surprising that the state, in which the aristocracy played such an important role, was often less than enthusiastic about industrialisation.

It would be a serious mistake to see the role of the state solely in such negative terms. From the eighteenth century the absolutist state, whether in Germany, France or Russia, had realised the importance of industry for the economic, political and military strength of the state. The bureaucracy encouraged the growth of industry and was to forge the links that were to bind the middle class to the absolutist state. Thus in Germany industrial modernisation did not entail political modernisation. The civil servants of the nineteenth century continued the work of the enlightened absolutist state by gradual reform, honest administration, and by encouraging economic growth. But this delicate balancing act between a liberal economic policy and restorative aristocratic domestic politics was exceptionally difficult. Industrialisation caused a redistribution of wealth and property, it created new classes and changed the face of society and yet the old élites preserved their monopoly of state power. Increasingly pressing was the question of whether the resulting tensions between rich and poor, bourgeoisie and proletariat, industry and agriculture, aristocracy and middle class could be restrained and assuaged by a continual process of reform that would preserve the unity of state and society, or whether they would explode in a social and political revolution.

Those civil servants who carried on the traditions of the great reformers of the Napoleonic era were convinced that the unity of state and society could be preserved by the emergent third estate. Men like Peter Beuth, who was Director of the Department of Industry and Trade in the Prussian Ministry of the Interior from 1818, the Prussian Councillor of State Kunth, or the south German Nebenius hoped to open the way for the bourgeoisie to develop its own initiative and talents, industrial society enabling the completion of the reform work of Stein and Scharnhorst. Although Beuth encouraged individual enterprises by granting subsidies, by importing foreign machinery, and by persuading foreigners to build model factories in Prussia, the real key to replacing the outworn and restricting state lay in the education of the people to meet the challenge of the new society. They enthusiastically welcomed the new industrial age, and argued that if Germany were to remain an agricultural state, it would never be able to secure the welfare and happiness of a rising population. They answered the reactionary sentimentalists who longed to preserve and strengthen the old rural way of life by pointing out that foreign competition would destroy the handloom weaver and the village artisan even more effectively than domestic industry which, for all the immediate disruptions which it caused, was the only hope for survival. As Beuth pointed out, an army commander, however much he disliked gunpowder, was unlikely to be very successful with bows and arrows. Not only did men like Beuth see industrialisation as an essential means for national survival, they also saw machinery as the way in which men would complete their mastery over nature so that mankind could become truly emancipated. Thus industrialisation was not only an economic and political imperative, it was also moral educator.

Education

An essential part of their efforts to modernise and industrialise Germany was their programme of educational reform. If the people were to use modern techniques effectively, they would have to be educated. Without educational opportunities the competitive desire for self-betterment would be dulled. An ignorant people could never use technology as a means to self-realisation and self-liberation. This was to prove a tremendous undertaking, for the majority of the German population was illiterate. In 1825 Kunth discovered that only one-third of the master craftsmen in Grünberg in Silesia could write their name with any confidence. Factory owners were of two minds about the desirability of educating their illiterate workers. Some were unwilling to give them the free time to go to school and feared that education might give them dangerous ideas. Others, like Harkort, argued that education created needs, and that in order to satisfy these needs the worker would become hard-working and thrifty. Frederick William III of Prussia felt that these newly aroused needs would breed social discontent and that education was the first step towards revolution.

Modest reforms were made in the elementary school system (*Volksschulen*). Teachers were very poorly paid and often had to take other jobs to supplement their income. They also tried to teach as many children as possible, as they were paid according to the number of pupils. Most teachers were inadequately trained, and the curriculum failed to meet the needs of the time by largely ignoring the sciences and history. Statistics of school attendance are rather spotty. In 1835 it appears that 75 per cent of school-age children actually attended school in the province of Prussia, whereas in Posen it was only 61 per cent. Thus although the Prussian government had introduced the first steps towards compulsory education as early as 1717, it lacked the means to carry out this enlightened measure. New schools were built to provide education for the growing population, but universal education was still a distant ideal.

Just as the reformers had rather romantic notions of the moral value of modern technology, ideas that were to be brilliantly attacked in the early 1840s by the young Karl Marx in his writings on alienation and reification, so their vision of an education self-improving population was far from realised. As 'realists', they attached the humanistic *Gymnasium* as bastions of intellectual snobbery dedicated to the study of useless subjects, such as the dead languages of classical antiquity. In their place they wished to support the *Realschulen*, in which the natural sciences would replace the classics as the basis of the curriculum, although the classics were still compulsory. Even Goethe, the archetypal 'universal genius' of the eighteenth century, came to the conclusion that the age of the specialist had come, and that the wise man should concentrate on becoming a master of one area of human knowledge and endeavour. *Realschulen* were founded in the eighteenth century to provide the rudiments of a practical education for businessmen and farmers, but in the early nineteenth century they were seen as a means to overcome the relative backwardness of the Germany economy by turning, as Friedrich Naumann was to say, dreamers into workers.

The technical universities (*Technische Hochschulen*) played an important role in providing a supply of highly trained specialists. Tulla had founded the engineering school in Karlsruhe on the model of the *Ecole Polytechnique* where he had studied. He refused to make the new school a department of Heidelberg University and insisted that it should be fully independent. In the 1820s similar institutions were founded in the leading German states. In 1825 the Karlsruhe engineering school amalgamated with the school of architecture, and Nebenius became the director of the new university. Although these technical universities did not match the great French schools, they played an important role in educating the engineers and professionals who were so badly needed, and in the course of the century they became important centres of research and learning.

In Prussia Peter Beuth was the great champion of technical education. Beuth was appalled at the lack of mathematical and scientific knowledge of even the most brilliant graduates of the Berlin *Gymnasium* and was determined to correct what he felt to be the essential weakness of Humboldt's educational reforms which placed too great an emphasis on the classics. In 1821, after considerable opposition, he opened the first trade school (*Gewerbeschule*) in Berlin. The trade school was but a part of Beuth's comprehensive plan for the encouragement of industry in Prussia. English machinery was imported illegally and carefully studied at the school. Industrialists were encouraged in their efforts to manufacture machinery in Germany. Thus a young Westphalian named Egells was sent by Beuth on a study trip to England, and on his return was able, with Beuth's support, to open his own workshop in the north of Berlin. In 1825 he built his first steam engine; his first foreman was none other than August Borsig. Beuth also founded the 'Society for the Encouragement of Industrial Diligence in Prussia' on the model of the English 'Society of Arts' as a means of propagating his ideas among businessmen and industrialists, scholars and civil servants. He played a major part in securing an effective law protecting the holders of patents.

Beuth's trade school also trained teachers for the provincial trade schools which were built after 1820. By 1838 there were twenty such provincial schools in Prussia. With the growth of the provincial schools, Beuth was determined to improve the standards of the Berlin school. In 1827 the Berlin Trade School was renamed the Berlin Trade Institute, when reform of the curriculum had made the school into a true polytechnic.

The upper classes still regarded industry and the technical professions with snobbish disdain, and the technical schools were looked upon as grossly inferior to the old universities. The protagonists of the technical schools saw their struggle against the old universities as part of the struggle of the new against the old, of the steam engine against the handloom, of the locomotive against the coach. The 'humanists', although often liberals, tended to look back to the simpler times when it was possible to be an 'all-round man', and had serious misgivings about specialisation and the rejection of the old educational values. The 'realists' had the zeal of genuine missionaries and, although their ideas were often exaggerated and extreme, there can be no doubt that they had a tremendous effect on the industrial development of Germany. Particularly in the second Industrial Revolution, in which more sophisticated technology was applied to industry in metallurgy, textiles and the optical industry, but above all to chemicals and the electrical industry, this investment paid handsome dividends. With an adequate supply of highly trained engineers, chemists and mathematicians graduating from the technical colleges, Germany was to lead the world in many of the most advanced sectors of industry and technology. Beuth had hoped that education would enable Germany to match the economic power of England, and it is partly due to his efforts, and those of like-minded men, that Germany was to overtake Britain as an industrial nation sooner than even the most sanguine of the reformers could have hoped.

3 THE SOCIAL IMPACT OF ECONOMIC DEVELOPMENT 1815–1850

The economic changes that had taken place between 1834 and 1848 had a dramatic effect on the social and political climate in Germany. The 'social question' now became a pressing problem as demanding of the attention of the liberal bourgeoisie as constitutional reform or the unification of Germany. Although the industrial bourgeoisie were rapidly becoming masters of the economic life of the country, they were almost entirely excluded from the political process. Yet while the middle class was growing in confidence and beginning to demand a voice in decisions which affected its vital interests, it was increasingly becoming aware of the threat from below by radical democrats and socialists who wished to extend the liberal notions of democracy and reform far beyond the point that the bourgeoisie found acceptable. Radical republicanism was the political expression of the frustrations, uncertainty and deprivation suffered by the artisans whose livelihood was relentlessly being destroyed by industrialisation, but above all by the new industrial proletariat whose radical socialism was beginning to demand the overthrow of bourgeois society. Thus in Germany even before a liberal-democratic bourgeois order had been established, there were demands for its overthrow.

Agricultural Labourers

The liberation of the German peasantry coupled with a continuing rise in population placed an intolerable strain on the rural economy. Peasant holders were not sufficient to provide a living for the increased population. Village handicraft industries, although they had been able to expand owing to the abolition of the guild system and the restrictions on artisanal labour, and although there was an increased demand for some products that could be produced on a limited scale, were unable to provide a sufficient number of jobs, and many industries, such as textiles, were being destroyed by factory-produced goods. With the overwhelming competition of British and local mass-produced goods, even if the landless peasant could find a job in the textile industry, his position was wretched indeed. In 1845 the average weekly wage of a linen weaver was 42 per cent less than the average of the lowest-paid agricultural labourers. Although the weavers were better paid than the unfortunate spinners, their wages fell well below what the authorities deemed to be an acceptable minimum income.

Part of this unemployed population managed to find work as day-labourers on the larger estates. The improvements in agriculture, the reduction of fallow, the winning of new land and the intensification of production increased the demand for labour. Labour-saving machinery was only rarely used in the first half of the century, so agriculture was able to provide employment for part of the increasing population. In western Germany it was quite common for the agricultural labourer to work part-time for a large farmer, and to spend the rest of the time cultivating his own plot of land. These *Häusler* scarcely existed east of the Elbe by 1850, for their holdings had been largely absorbed into the Junker estates during the period after the liberation of the peasantry. In the east the common form of part-time labour was that of the *Insten*, who did not own their small holdings, but received them in lieu of wages under contracts that lasted for a limited period, usually one year. On the Junker estates payment in kind or in leases of land were quite common, as were labour contracts. This clearly shows that a semi-feudal mode of production was still in force in which a modified form of serfdom survived. The *Insten* were no longer tied to their landlords by hereditary bondage, but they were obliged to relinquish their freedom for the time that they were under contract. The Junkers preferred this form of labour because during the agricultural crisis they found it difficult to find the cash to pay wages and thus payment in kind provided an attractive alternative. Furthermore, contracted labour, paid partly in kind, provided a less abrupt transition from feudal to capitalist production. The relationship between landlord and peasant had changed, but it was not a startling novelty. For these reasons the landless labourers who looked for work were seldom welcomed on the Junker estates, except perhaps at harvest-time.

As the Junkers gradually grew accustomed to the new methods of agriculture and as the economy pulled out of the slump into a period of steady growth, they began to see the positive advantages of wage labour. Long-term contracts might tie the worker to the land and ensure a submissive labour force, but they also entailed obligations by the employer. The Junkers came to realise that it was more profitable to hire labour when it was needed than to maintain a full complement of workers throughout the year. The *Insten* were thus gradually replaced by day-labourers. They were forced out by gradually reducing the size of the land granted to them and by reducing payments in kind, and at the same time refusing to increase the cash payments proportionately to the loss of alternative modes of payment. As the value of its output rose, it seemed foolish to waste land on the peasantry. The *Insten* were now faced with the cruel choice of continuing to work under contract under steadily worsening conditions on the grounds that they were at least guaranteed a minimal income during the winter months when work was scarce, or of becoming day-labourers and trying their luck on an overburdened labour market.

The Mobility of Labour

As a result of these changes, there was a steady growth of unemployment on the land, starting in the 1820s and beginning to tail off by mid-century, when rapid industrial growth absorbed the larger population to an increasing extent. There began to be a movement away from the land to the urban centres by artisans and labourers looking for work. Peasants could hope for little better than a position as an unskilled worker in a factory, in the building industry, or as a railway navvy. The artisans hoped to find opportunities in the cities to continue their trades, but they found this increasingly difficult. In the early stages of industrialisation many of the factory workers were peasants who still kept their domicile on the land and who only worked part of the time in the factories. The railways were largely built by itinerant labour of this sort; day-labourers from the countryside, unemployed from the towns, handloom weavers and apprentices. This striking mobility of labour was further increased by the completion of the first phase of railway-building, by which time it had become a matter of some concern to the authorities who did not wish to see their states overrun by the unemployed in search of work. As a result, restrictions were placed on the free movement of labour in parts of south and eastern Germany. The industrialists of the Rhineland and Ruhr managed to resist this movement and were able to secure an adequate supply of labour from outside.

A rising population, a shortage of work and a politically stifling atmosphere caused many Germans to emigrate, mainly to the United States where opportunities for gaining a decent living in conditions of greater freedom seemed so promising. The wave of German emigration to the United States began in the 1830s and steadily grew. After the failure of the revolutions of 1848, the motives of the emigrants were largely political and there was a mass exodus of liberals and radicals who had seen their hopes dashed and who were to play an important role in the political life of the United States in the late nineteenth century. Between 1830 and 1870 some 2.5 million Germans emigrated to the United States. Emigration was thus an important safety valve, in that part of the unemployed population left the country, but far more important was the fact that governments were glad to see the last of so many political malcontents and critics of the existing order.

With the difficulties and expense of travel and the many barriers placed in the way of the free movement of peoples within Germany, most of those who left their villages merely travelled to the next town in search of work. Thus close ties remained between the new town-dwellers and the rural population and, as we have seen, many town workers maintained their residence in the country. Berlin was the one major exception to this rule. As a great capital city it attracted people from all over the country, yet even in Berlin the bulk of the recent immigrants to the city came from the immediately surrounding areas. It was not until the period of rapid industrialisation in the 1870s that those who left the land began to travel long distances to find employment in the urban areas, in the course of which process Germany ceased to be a predominantly rural country, the bulk of the population now living in towns.

The influx of labour from the rural areas served further to depress the living standards of the urban workers. The handicraft industries in the towns rapidly reached saturation and from 1842 the proportion of artisans to the total working population did not rise. During the 1850s many of the artisans who were unable to make a living at their trade found employment in industry, but before these boom years, and particularly in the 1840s, the life of many urban artisans was exceptionally hard and precarious. This process of the proletarianisation of the artisans was of particular advantage to the German industrialists, who were able to draw on an adequate supply of well-trained and highly skilled workers who were quickly able to adapt to the new techniques of factory production. The unskilled peasants and land labourers tended to become unskilled factory workers, working under the direction of the erstwhile artisans. The skills of this important sector of the German working class were to have a tremendous impact on the course of German economic development. In engineering, fine mechanics and the optical industry, industries in which the Germans were soon to excel, the skilled artisans were quick to learn their trade from the entrepreneurs, and in turn trained new cadres of skilled workers. Thus from the very beginning of German industrialisation there was a distinct hierarchy within the industrial working class and a distinguishable 'aristocracy of labour', whereas in England this process did not occur until a much later stage of industrialisation.

The Formation of the Working Class

Generalisations about the origins of the German working class are extremely difficult to make as there are so many regional disparities and differences between branches of industry. A historian of the period of early industrialisation, Wolfram Fischer, has suggested three basic divisions. First, there was the textile industry where there was a high percentage of women and children working and where there was a gradual transformation of cottage industry into factory production and a close connection between factory workers and the rural working class. In this group of industries are also to be found the sugar, tobacco and food industries. Second, there were the mines, steelworks and chemical industry where the labour force was largely male and usually from the rural areas. Few of the workers had any previous experience of home industry, coming usually from purely agricultural areas. Workers in these industries were cut off from their previous life on the land and had to adapt themselves to a completely different style of life. The third group included engineering and the manufacture of precision tools and instruments. In this group of industries the percentage of artisans was very high, forming the élite of the proletariat.

The diverse origins of the German proletariat and its divisions between skilled and unskilled, guild member and free worker, native and immigrant, townsman and peasant delayed the formation of a clearly articulated class consciousness and helped to create a complex stratification within the working class. Workers in the all-male engineering industry regarded themselves as superior to workers in the textile industry which was less skilled and where the majority of the work-force was composed of women and children. Within the skilled industries there was a hierarchy of skills which by no means always coincided with the hierarchy of master craftsman, foreman, worker and apprentice. The exceptional skills needed in a process of industrialisation in which engineering played such a tremendously important role should not be overlooked. The brutalised and mindless labour of the unskilled factory worker was certainly a striking and unpleasant feature of industrialisation, but it was by no means the entire picture. From the very beginning of industrialisation in Germany there was a clear division of labour and a wide range of skills among the industrial working class. These differences were further underlined by clear legal distinctions between various groups of workers which often dated back to pre-industrial social distinctions of gradations within the estates. A good example of these differentiations and distinctions is the Georg Bodmer engineering works in St Blasien, one of the earliest manufacturers of machinery in Germany. In October of 1809, although there were only 74 workers employed, they were divided into 20 different categories, of which 14 were handicrafts.

Wide differences of status and function are also reflected in wage scales. Again it is difficult to generalise, because the more skilled and specialised the industry, the greater was the tendency for there to be wide differentials between the highest-paid and the lowest-paid workers. Generally speaking, the relationship of the highest-paid to the lowest-paid was 1:5 or 1:6. In the Krupp works the relationship was 1:5 in 1845. Wage differentials between industries, and between branches of the same industry, were also very great. Differentials within branches of the textile industry for workers in Halle in 1783 were almost 1:7. On the basis of very limited evidence it would seem that wage differentials of industrial workers tended to diminish during the period of industrialisation, but that rises in nominal wages from the 1830s tended to be offset by rising prices.

The pressure of population and the movement to the towns tended to have the effect of depressing the wages of the ordinary factory workers, and only those who were masters of the *arcana* of industrial production could maintain their relatively high wages. With the industrial growth of the 1830s, the demand for labour grew and wages tended to move upward. In this decade wages rose by about 5.5 per cent, in the 1840s by about 10.5 per cent, and in the 1850s by about 16.5 per cent. Kuczynski's estimates, which are open to serious doubts although they are still the best we have, argue that these gains in nominal wages failed to meet the rise in the cost of living which rose 16.3 per cent in the 1830s, 16 per cent in the 1840s and 20.7 per cent in the 1850s. Only the very highest-paid workers earned sufficient to support a family. Women and children were thus forced to work. Most working-class families were seriously undernourished and badly housed. Although the question of the standard of living cannot be confidently answered, it is clear that unemployment was a permanent threat, and in times of economic crisis could take on catastrophic proportions. With no special services for the unemployed, this frequently led to starvation and bread riots. Working conditions in the factories were dreadful, and the discipline harsh. Working hours tended to increase throughout the early period of industrialisation. It is thus hardly surprising that the wretched handloom weavers resisted to the last becoming factory workers, and it would be absurdly cruel to condemn as hopelessly reactionary those who experienced progress as a disruption of their family life and as a loss of their remaining freedom and dignity.

Pauperismus – the Germans used the English phrase to describe a growing and alarming phenomenon – was less the direct result of industrialisation, of deliberately depressed wages and the cyclical crises of over-population which were such a chronic feature of the English experience, than of the inability of the German economy to absorb a population that was growing as a result of a combination of a higher birth rate, a lower death rate, earlier marriages and larger families. These paupers appeared to contemporaries as a new class, quite unlike the poor of old, a menacing anti-social growth within a society that was in an uneasy transitional stage from an ordered authoritarian society based on the estates to a modern industrial society. Many felt that drastic measures were needed to stop the growth of this class or society would be unable to meet the problem without revolutionary upheaval.

Restrictions were placed on the marriage of the poor in some states, civil servants issued grave warnings that something had to be done, but there were few helpful suggestions. Dr Weinhold suggested the compulsory infibulation of the poor, a grim measure that found little support in the medical profession. Some braced themselves for a social revolution, others hoped that restorative politics could prevent this disaster, or that the teachings of the church could save the godless drunken mob from its sinister purpose to overthrow existing society.

Although revolutionary activities by this class were the hope of socialist intellectuals and the dread of the liberal and conservative circles, both were distortions of reality. The *classes dangereuses* were demoralised and divided and lacked a clearly defined political ideology, for which spontaneous outbursts of frustration and rage or wild Utopian dreams for a better future were no substitute. Even the industrial workers were divided among themselves, uncertain of the world around them, and restrained by repressive legislation. In 1845 the Prussian government prohibited any associations of the working class that were designed to secure higher wages. Yet in spite of this measure strikes occurred in the 1840s, although they were usually small-scale, poorly organised, and soon crushed by the authorities. It was not until the revolutionary year of 1848 that strikes became large-scale, highly organised and determined. A number of important concessions were won, particularly a shortening of the working day, but most of these gains were to be lost in the reactionary period of the 1850s.

The beginnings of a trade union movement in the workers' clubs, the early strikes, and the demands for far-reaching changes in society that were far more fundamental than modest increases in wages or some shortening of the working day are all clear indications of the gradual formation of a distinct working-class consciousness. Although this working class was divided within itself and can be divided into factory workers, semi-proletarian artisan-outworkers, and a traditional artisanate, and within each of these groups there were clear hierarchical divisions, yet it was increasingly bound together by common resentments and frustrations. Workers felt estranged from and menaced by the society around them. Their response to this situation varied from the carefully articulated programmes of constitutional and social reform of the labour aristocrats of 1848 to the spontaneous violence of the inarticulate mob. It gradually became clear that the causes of the present miseries were not to be found in supernatural forces that were beyond man's control, or in modern industrial technology as such, but rather in the social relations of an emergent capitalist society.

The Bourgeoisie

If the working class was divided and uncertain, the rising bourgeoisie was equally unsure of its place within this new society, and the attitude it should take to the pressing problems of the day. Middle-class demands for a political voice in a society in whose economic life they were playing a vital role threatened to be overtaken by the radical democratic spokesmen of the working classes. The bourgeoisie was determined to secure what it felt to be its rights and to create a liberal social and political order that would correspond to the modern capitalist economy, but they also feared that if they did so they would open up the floodgates of revolution, which would challenge their own hard-won position. Although there was some agreement over the extension of the power of parliamentary bodies and a restriction of the power of the bureaucracy, bourgeois liberals could never accept the radical republicanism of the left, to say nothing of the revolutionary socialism that was beginning to win some adherents in the working class. Overriding all these problems was the distinct possibility of what Jacob Burckhardt in 1846 was to call the 'day of social judgement'.

The attitude of the bourgeoisie towards the state was also highly ambiguous. As liberals they distrusted the authoritarian state with its schoolmasterly attitude. In place of regulation by the state they wished to have self-government in economic affairs. The economy should be left to the free play of market forces, and economic society should be separated from the state. The nightwatchman state of the Manchester liberals was an ideal that might be attained by constitutional reform, yet it was an ideal that appeared increasingly unrealistic and even undesirable.

The industrial and commercial middle classes could never become wholehearted in their demands for the dismantling of the 'civil service state'. They were well aware of the importance of agrarian reform, the *Zollverein*, educational policies, direct investment and encouragement of new techniques, the abolition of the restrictions of the guilds and the modernising efforts of the liberally inclined bureaucrats. In part, they owed their newly found wealth and importance to the efforts of a bureaucracy which, according to the teachings of the classical political economists, they should despise and reject. The absolutist state had, under the exceptional circumstances of a catastrophic defeat and the need for national renewal, begun the process of reform and had laid the foundations of economic freedom. The bureaucracy could not be seen simply as the executive organ of the semi-feudal authoritarian state, nor was a bureaucracy as such seen as wholly evil. The liberal Rhineland industrialists, for example, were affectionately attached to the Napoleonic bureaucracy of western Germany.

List had argued that the ideology of Manchesterism was a means to secure the domination of British industry in the world market. Others were equally sceptical about the effects of the free play of market forces which were clearly something of a mixed blessing. Social tensions, the disruption of traditional ways of life, grinding poverty, urban squalor and the ever-present threat of violent disruption were as much the product of capitalism as were economic growth and the prosperity of the fortunate few. Indeed, there was a growing awareness that perhaps the absolutist state might be needed to protect what gains had been made from the destructive rage of the dispossessed and exploited. The bourgeoisie was eager to dismantle the system of aristocratic privilege, but they had no desire to include the lower orders in civil society. For all the talk of equality before the law and the extension of democratic rights that was common to liberal thinking, the bourgeois as factory-owner was as much concerned to be absolute master of his workers as was the Junker on his estates. Increasingly the bourgeoisie looked to the state to protect its interests against the demands of the working classes, and this identification of interests was to blunt the demands for reform. Agrarian conservatives regarded the social problem as the inevitable consequence of industrialisation, and Engels' indictment of the condition of the working class in England was greeted in the conservative press as a timely warning of the necessary evils of the new age. Liberals were at something of a loss to know what to do, for a system which had promised happiness and prosperity seemed to bring the opposite to an alarming and perplexing degree. The old Freiherr vom Stein could only think of emigration by the excess population. Others hoped that co-operative efforts by the workers, on the English model, would save them from total deprivation. Some argued that only in old-fashioned charity was there hope, whereas others remained true to the political economists and were convinced that the free workings of the economy would eventually solve the social problem. To arch-conservatives the restoration of the guild system and a determined opposition to capitalism was the only hope of salvation.

Under the influence of British and French reformers, and particularly the Benthamites in England, an important group of liberals called for state intervention to protect the interests of the working class, for adequate factory inspection and the encouragement of co-operative efforts by workers. Their spokesman was Robert von Mohl, who was supported by such well-known figures as Mevissen and Harkort. These ideas were to find their way into the state-socialist notions of German social democracy via Rodbertus and Lassalle.

The most interesting and influential of these pre-March liberal thinkers was Lorenz von Stein whose studies of the French socialists had convinced him of the reality of the class struggle, which was the key to any adequate understanding of the social process. Stein drew the Hegelian distinction between state and society, in which society was rent asunder by the conflict of the classes, which in turn tried to seize control of the state to pursue their own sectional interests. The state's purpose was to remain aloof from the sordid struggles of class interests and to promote the common good. The state had therefore to intervene to stop the class struggle getting out of hand, by raising the economic and intellectual level of the lower orders and restraining the rapacity of the wealthy. Six years before the publication of the *Communist Manifesto*, Stein had said that the spirit of Communism was stalking Europe, 'a dark and sinister spirit, in which no one wishes to believe, but whose existence everyone recognises and fears'. Judicious reform by the state was for Stein the only alternative to revolution and the only way to exorcise the ghost of Communism. These notions of a state that was independent of the class struggle and which incorporated the true interests and values of the people were a far cry from the traditional liberal view of the state, and are a direct response to the failure of liberalism to cope with the social question, which in Germany was rapidly becoming as important a question as the creation of a modern liberal constitutional state, and which threatened to deflect liberal thought into conservative channels. From Stein came the idea of a social monarchy which was to be so appealing to William II at the outset of his reign, and the belief that social problems could be administered away. The social question and the constitutional question could thus be reduced to administrative questions. Stein is a key figure in the development of the Bismarckian compromise between a modern industrial society and an agrarian conservative hierarchical state. He clearly saw the tensions that were to arise between modernisation and restoration and although his prescriptions were but panaceas, it proved possible to maintain an awkward balance between these two forces for a remarkably long time.

The Revolution of 1848

Seen in terms of the development of both the bourgeoisie and the working class, the revolution of 1848 came at an unfortunate time. Middle-class liberals wanted constitutional and social reforms that would change the face of society, but they were also uncomfortably aware of the radicals breathing down their necks. They felt themselves isolated and powerless, caught between the reactionaries and the radicals, unwilling to make a step in either direction for fear of reaction from the other side. In the end they preferred to stay with the old and the familiar than run the risks of the new. The working class found itself in the centre of the political stage at a time when it had no clearly defined understanding of its position or of its goals and when its hostility towards 'respectable society' was barely sufficient to overcome the divisions and contradictions within its own ranks. It was not so much that the liberals 'betrayed' the revolution as some of the sterner readings of the events of 1848 would have it, but rather that the demands of the radicals were not the demands of the liberals, and that given the choice between social revolution and compromise, they opted for the latter. It was unfortunate for the course of German history that the liberal bourgeoisie was forced to make this choice in 1848 and that they made the decision that they were almost bound to make, but their course of action was determined by the particular social, economic and constitutional development of Germany, not by their perfidy or bad faith.

The problems which the politicians in the Paul's Church in Frankfurt were called upon to solve were immense. There was general agreement that national unity was a desirable goal. In the age of the railways, the division of Germany into small sovereign states seemed more than ever absurd to progressive thinkers. The confusion caused by different codes of commercial law, by different currencies, and by different weights and measures was increasingly irritating, the more so as the experience of the *Zollverein* had shown that co-operative efforts were possible in these fields. Indeed it would be fair to say that national unity was the prime concern of the liberals, but they were unable to settle the tricky problem of deciding the frontiers of Germany. The national aspirations of Germans came into conflict with the national aspirations of Poles, Czechs, Danes and Slovaks. The liberals were anxious to preserve the German royal houses for, as Dahlmann argued in his speech on the constitutional question, they were a guarantee that tradition and obedience would be preserved. But even so cautious an approach to the national question implied the destruction of the Vienna settlement of 1815 which had already been badly shaken in 1830, and it raised the all-important question of the relative strength of Prussia and Austria.

In Prussia many liberals, particularly the progressive industrialists and financiers of the Rhineland, wished to break the political monopoly of the aristocracy, the bureaucracy and the military, which seemed so badly out of step with the development of a modern economic system. They detested radicalism, wished to avoid a revolution, and had no sympathy whatever for popular demands for the sovereignty of the people, but they were acutely aware of the backwardness of the Prussian constitution and looked enviously to England and France for models of constitutional and administrative excellence. Liberal demands for constitutional reform were often couched in terms of dire warning that unless changes were made, Germany would experience the horrors of a social revolution. By supporting industrialisation and the modernisation of the German economy, the bureaucracy had created something of a sorcerer's apprentice. The resulting social tensions could not be contained or mastered without major changes in the political and social structure of the country or violent confrontation. The bureaucracy was unable in the reactionary climate of the Pre-March to continue the tradition of the great reformers of a 'revolution from above', and lacked the confidence to break their ties with the traditional elites and enthusiastically embrace the cause of reform. In the face of mass poverty, bitter resentment and the steadily growing demand for reform, all within the context of economic uncertainty and depression, the bureaucracy suffered from a curious paralysis of the will.

Part of the cause of this inability to act was the widespread feeling that life had improved and was improving. Ranke, in a much quoted phrase, referred to the Pre-March as those 'halcyon days' and expressed a widespread feeling that went beyond a mere sentimental hankering after the 'good old days'. For the bourgeoisie things had improved greatly. The terrible waste and frivolity of the eighteenth-century court was a thing of the past. The brutality and fickleness of court justice and the crime and violence of the cities had been reformed and improved. Life was more restrained, civilised, rational and 'bourgeois'. For the middle classes, including the better-placed artisans, life was appreciably better in 1848 than it had been in 1800. But for the vast mass of people who lived on the margin of existence, and in some parts of Germany this was as high as 40 per cent, any further depression of their living standard spelt disaster. The crop failure of 1846 led to a sharp rise in food prices, and for the poor this meant desperate hunger and even famine. As the production of such key staples as rye and potatoes fell to almost half the normal amount, it is hardly surprising that food prices began to rise steadily from the winter of 1846 and did not begin to fall until the summer of 1848 as a result of a satisfactory harvest. The agricultural crisis caused widespread unemployment, thus worsening an already critical situation.

There can be no doubt whatever that the disastrous effects of the rise in food prices from 1846 were a major causal factor in the revolution of 1848. Certainly contemporaries feared that the starvation of the masses was the beginning of a social revolution. Frederick William IV of Prussia saw in the 80,000 victims of typhus in Silesia, which was directly caused by starvation, the 'seeds of the overthrow of existing conditions'. But as Rudolf Stadelmann has shown, it is a mistake to see the revolution of 1848 purely in terms of economic hardship, either in the long or the short term. It was the result of a widespread feeling that the day of reckoning had come, that the old order had failed and had lost its legitimacy. Life had become too complex and too hectic, menacing changes loomed on the horizon, the old certainties were lost. The world of the railways, the factory, the steam engine and applied science could not be mastered by the autocratic state, however enlightened its servants, and in its underworld were menacing forces that threatened to break loose and disrupt the ordered certainties of the familiar social world.

These dire prophecies of doom were symptoms of the fact that the political and constitutional structure of society was contradictory to the social and economic reality and needs of a rapidly modernising society. There could be no easy answer to this problem, for there were as many solutions as there were special interests. In the ranks of the revolutionaries there were two main groups, those who enthusiastically supported industrialisation and modernisation, and those who saw in industrialisation the cause of their present misery. After the first heady days of March 1848 these contradictions became increasingly acute. The successful and enterprising bourgeois found the constraints and restrictions of the semi-feudal aristocratic state unjustifiable and demeaning. The journeymen, the most radical and outspoken group in the revolution, were not anti-capitalist but rather demanded that within a capitalist mode of production they should be given their just deserts. They no longer enjoyed the protection of the guilds and were forbidden from forming associations to protect and further their interests. In the crisis year of 1847 work was hard to find, and high prices were not matched by any increase in wages. But between the journeymen and the bourgeoisie was a deep ideological split which was soon to become open antagonism. The ruined master craftsmen demanded the end of factory production, a return to the days of the handloom and the guilds. The revolutionary conservatism of the master weavers of Krefeld, for example, was a far cry from revolutionary socialism, from the democratic demands of the Chartists, or the co-operative schemes of the French left, and is a measure of the relative economic and political backwardness of Germany in 1848.

Friedrich Engels, whose writings on 1848 are the basis of most later studies of the revolution, argued that since the employers were divided among themselves between bourgeois and petty bourgeois, the working class was equally divided between factory workers and the employees of the artisans. The first group saw their future within the factory system, the others in a restoration of the handicraft trades. Divided between land-labourer, day-labourer, journeyman and factory worker, scattered over a thinly populated country and with few key central points, it was too early to speak of a working class. Without true class interests, each pursued his own separate interests. With a weak and divided working class, an aristocracy whose day had passed, and a petty bourgeoisie that had neither strength nor a viable programme, the bourgeoisie was the class that could have taken the leadership in 1848.

The bourgeoisie of 1848 was not equal to the task of taking on this role. They had already made their historic compromise with the old order. It was impossible for a class that had benefited to a great extent from the efforts of the absolutist state to demand its total destruction. The bankers, industrialists and businessmen were no more willing to mount the barricades than were the liberal professors and writers to emerge from their studies. Those bourgeois who had bought estates and were busy aping the ways of the aristocracy were lost to the progressive cause. The liberal bourgeoisie was thus in a hopelessly isolated position, caught between the radicals and the reactionaries. Without mass support and with no armed force behind them they could do little but wait on events until the decisions of the day were made by blood and iron.

The Prussian Ministry of 29 March 1848 that followed the fighting on the barricades in Berlin is a perfect example of the dilemma and weakness of the German bourgeoisie. It was headed by Camphausen and Hansemann, two moderate liberals, leading figures in the economic world, men of outstanding ability, foresight and decency. Within their Cabinet were aristocrats like von Auerswald, who sympathised to a degree with the aims of the liberal reformers. They worked with the old bureaucracy, and made no changes in the administration nor did they attempt to control the army. In short it was a government without power. The King moved to Potsdam in April, where he was surrounded by his army and came totally under the influence of the reactionary *camarilla* of von Manteuffel, Leopold von Gerlach, von Rauch, von Neumann and Count Dohna. Power was in Potsdam and not in Berlin, and it was only a matter of time before it would be used against the liberals.

The Camphausen-Hansemann government was determined to eradicate the unacceptable face of the revolution, to maintain law and order, and to restore confidence in the economy. The revolution would be carried out in an orderly and decent manner by means of the united diet, the economy restored by massive credits offered through state banks (the *Diskonto- und Beleihungskassen*). But these steps were too cautious to appease the radicals and republicans, and the romantics and hotheads who called for revolution, not reform. The growing impatience of the masses and the warning of the class battle of the

June Days in Paris made the liberal bourgeoisie more anxious than ever to compromise with the existing order. In Frankfurt the same split occurred, the moderates seeking the protection of Austrian, Prussian, Hessian and Württemberg troops against the radicals who were outraged at the armistice of Malmö, which they saw as a betrayal of the revolution and of the national cause in Schleswig and Holstein.

The failure of the liberal bourgeoisie in 1848 makes it all too easy to ignore the significant changes that occurred as a direct result of the revolution. In April 1849 the King of Prussia dissolved the second chamber of the *Landtag* which had been elected by equal suffrage according to the constitution granted in 1848. The new house of representatives was elected according to a three-class franchise designed to secure a majority for the conservative aristocracy. In fact the liberal bourgeoisie was soon to win a majority in the house and to precipitate the constitutional crisis of the 'new era' in the early 1860s. The liberals were also able to secure the creation of a Prussian Ministry for Trade, Industry and Public Works, whose Minister was von der Heydt, who came from a Rhenish banking family, who had sympathised with the liberals in the Pre-March, and who had served in the Camphausen-Hansemann government. After 1848 von der Heydt became increasingly less sympathetic to the liberal cause, but he remained an important figure linking the big bourgeoisie of the Rhineland with the aristocratic reactionaries in Berlin.

In many of the German states remaining feudal rights were abolished in 1848. Thus the patrimonial courts (*Gerichtsherrschaft*) were abolished in Saxony, Bavaria, Hesse, Hanover and in Prussia. The freedom of movement of the peasantry was greatly increased as a result of these measures. Thus the process which had begun in 1806 was virtually complete in 1848. It had been painfully slow, and was both cause and effect of the gradual and intermittent development of the German economy. Also as a result of the revolution, the question of compensation for the loss of feudal rights was finally settled in most of the states.

The Camphausen-Hansemann ministry was responsible for the creation of the first joint-stock bank in Germany, which in the economic history of Germany was one of the most significant events of 1848. The failure of the Schaffhausen Bank, seriously overextended by investing in some 170 concerns in the Rhineland and unable to survive the depression following the crop failure of 1848, was the cause of considerable concern. With its extensive investments it was imperative for the Rhineland industrialists that the bank should be saved. Thanks to the efforts of the Finance Minister, Hansemann, supported by Mevissen and other prominent figures in the economic life of the Rhineland, the bank was reconstituted as the *Schaffhausensche Bankverein* with a capital of 4,187,000 thalers, of which about 3 million were immediately issued. The new bank had to move cautiously at first to restore the ruins of Abraham Schaffhausen's old bank. The bank only accepted term deposits for which between three months and a year's notice of withdrawal was required. A very modest rate of interest was a deliberate policy to keep deposits low, and most of the bank's business consisted of trying, in the bank's words,

> to induce the capitalists of the country, by recommendations based on exhaustive investigations, to turn idle capital toward such enterprises, which, when properly launched, in response to existing requirements, and offering the guarantee of expert management, bid fair to yield reasonable profits.

With the security of guaranteed government support the bank was soon actively involved in promoting new business ventures, particularly in transport, insurance and mining.

Efforts by the liberals to stimulate the economy by direct government investment and guaranteed loans were a direct response to the economic crisis. The failure of the crops in 1846 was followed by the international economic crisis of 1847; this had an immediate effect on the German economy which had expanded markedly in the 1840s. Thus a depression in the world market coincided with a domestic depression caused by rapidly rising food prices and a corresponding reduction of the spending power of the majority of the population. Critical sectors of industry, such as the machine-building industry in Berlin, which was forced to reduce production by 42 per cent, were seriously affected. The poor performance of the German economy in 1848 was less the result of the disruption caused by the revolution than the effects of a cyclical crisis. Indeed the revolution, as the example of the Prussian March ministry shows, enabled the state to play a far more active role in stimulating the economy than had hitherto been possible. Furthermore, the modest gains made by the journeymen and workers in securing higher wages did something to pull Germany out of the depression faster than would otherwise have been possible by encouraging domestic demand. It was the slackening of investment and the contraction of the market in 1847 that was the main cause of the reduction of output in almost all sectors of industry in early 1848, and not the sudden panic-stricken reaction to the barricades in March.

By making concessions to liberal economic demands, the old authoritarian monarchical state had made the necessary adjustments to enable it to survive in the industrial age. The leading representatives of commerce, industry and banking were easily satisfied, being content to make the best of what had been gained rather than run the risk of allowing the radical republicans to push the revolution further to the left. Faced with this threat, the liberals were only too eager to embrace the conservatives. The attractive prospect of economic growth as Germany pulled out of the slump was for most an adequate compensation for the failure of the middle class to gain the share of the political power which they felt was their due. Once again disillusioned liberals turned their backs on politics and returned to their insurance companies, their banks and their factories. For many even the modest degree of co-operation between the bourgeoisie and the old ēlites in parliamentary bodies, their franchise carefully designed to ensure the domination of the aristocracy, was enough. In their modesty they had asked for little more.

The old order had feared the revolution, had weathered the storm, and emerged with a new confidence. Madcap schemes for the revival of the old economic order could be abandoned as the economy entered a new period of prosperity which also helped the Junker estates where the benefits of past reforms and new techniques were clearly evident. Thus even though Germany was plunged into a period of grim political reaction the process of reform was not wholly halted, and the state continued to make concessions to the world of private capitalism. Modest advances were made in social policy, in law reform and in the easing of restrictions on the formation of joint-stock companies and co-operatives.

The bureaucracy lost much of its liberal impetus after 1848. It began partially to undo some of the achievements of the past by introducing new restrictions on the free exercise of a trade and by partially restoring some of the privileges and controlling rights of the guilds. But there was no question of restoring the old economic order, as some outspoken conservatives demanded. Modest reforms continued, some of them of considerable importance, such as the abolition in 1851 of the 'direction principle' in the Prussian coal-mines, by which private mine owners were obliged to follow guidelines laid down by the state mines. The state continued to withdraw from direct control of the economy, and the work of the *Zollverein* in creating a united and free German economic area continued. Free trade united the agrarians, the businessmen and the commercial bourgeoisie and this policy helped further to stimulate the growth of the German economy, even though it was bitterly opposed by the industrialists who were still demanding protection against competition from abroad, and by the protectionist south Germans and Austrians. A policy of free trade coupled with modest social reforms and a concern for the fate of the handicraft trades made up the economic policy of the period of reaction, which coincided with a boom in the world economy. This boom stimulated the growth of the capitalist economy at a time when it was still possible to hinder the development of a modern society. That the boom coincided with the reaction is a significant result of 1848, for it further hindered the development of a modern society in Germany and further heightened the contradiction between the economic and the political life of the country.

4 THE 1850s: GROWTH AND CRISIS

Banking and Investments

In the boom years from 1850 to 1857 Germany made a significant step forward towards becoming an industrial state, in spite of the political tendency of the reaction to slow down and to modify this process. The German landscape was changed with the building of new factories, rapid expansion of the railway network, the widespread introduction of steam-driven machinery and the concentration of production in the new factories that were built to meet the increasing demand for industrial goods. The building of new factories, the purchase of new machinery, the need to sink deeper mine shafts and to build larger blast furnaces all required considerable sums of capital. The traditional methods, such as the direct investment of merchant capital, were no longer adequate. Companies like Krupp, which were able to survive in this rapidly expanding and increasingly competitive economy by ploughing back their profits in order to modernise their plant, were exceptional cases. The only way in which capital could be accumulated quickly and effectively was by the joint-stock company. Particularly in mining and smelting, the joint-stock company played an increasingly important role in industry in the 1850s.

Prior to the 1850s, investors in Germany had been extremely cautious. Railway stock with its guaranteed dividends was the only attractive investment to those who were looking for security. Industrial enterprises with inadequate capital reserves, struggling to survive in a harshly competitive climate, were far too risky. Even the banks were regarded with suspicion, and the banks did not encourage small private deposits. In the uncertainties and anxieties of the revolutionary year money was hidden under floorboards and buried in the garden; it was not invested in industry or in banks. It was not until 1851, when confidence was restored and something of a speculative boom began, that money began to be invested. What had been a trickle soon became a flood. Between January and August 1851, private deposits in the Prussian Bank rose from 4.75 million thalers to 9.33 million thalers. The bank now had so much money deposited that it did not know what to do with it and took the extraordinary step of asking depositors who had not used their accounts for some time to withdraw their money.

The failure of the Schaffhausen Bank in March 1848, widespread unemployment, uncertainty and disruption necessitated a drastic reappraisal of economic policy. To the liberals like Camphausen, Mevissen, Mansemann, or von der Heydt, the answer lay in making cheap credit available to stimulate industrial production, secure full employment and guarantee a decent living wage to the working people. Private profit would go hand in hand with the growing prosperity of the masses. A healthy economy was thus deemed to be the best antidote to radical political demands and inchoate social unrest. The conservatives were at first unwilling to dismantle the restrictive measures they had introduced in the 1840s to restrain speculation, to forbid joint-stock banks or the purchase of options, and continued to feel that in the last resort the best guarantee against revolution was the army.

Those conservative bureaucrats who felt that something had to be done to help the economy through the crisis hoped that this could be effected by means of the Prussian Bank, and feared that the unrestricted growth of private banking and of joint-stock companies would mean the end of state control of the economy. It was not simply that the state was regarded as being a moral regulator of the economic life of the country, being far above the sordid jealousies of the market-place, but also that the economy would soon be dominated by the new money of the industrial sector which would then be given power to determine the fortunes of a land-owning aristocracy which desperately needed credit. Thus the schemes of the liberals were regarded by many more traditionally minded bureaucrats as a sinister threat to the social and political order. Economic domination of the aristocracy by the bourgeoisie would alter the power structure of the state, destroy the checks and balances of Pre-March society, and mark a major step forward towards the creation of a modern industrial state.

The key figure in this conservative policy was Christian von Rother. Rother had done much in the 1830s and 1840s to stimulate industry by means of the Prussian Bank, of which he was director, which was known by the rather misleading title of the Overseas Trading Corporation (*Seehandlung*). Rother carried on the old mercantilist traditions of state-controlled industry into the age of the Industrial Revolution. Factories run under the auspices of the Seehandlung produced woollen cloth, gunpowder, armaments, mined ore and spun cotton. It was actively engaged in most of the key industries of the time. Rother hoped by these means to overcome the worst problems of the social question by providing adequate employment, particularly in regions of low employment, decent working conditions, and an up-to-date and efficient industry. But by 1848 it was clear that these measures had failed. State enterprises, criticised in many quarters, were wasteful, expensive and provided unfair competition, and were simply not sufficient to meet the pressing needs of an economy in turmoil and a population without work. It was no longer sufficient to inject a few thousand thalers here and there to help out some needy industrialists; the economy needed the transfusion of millions. The liberals could argue that without drastic measures a true revolution would break out, and that economic liberalism was preferable to the horrors of 'Communism' – that sinister word which was applied indiscriminately to all radicals.

Demands from businessmen, the collapse or near failure of several banks, the bankruptcy of a number of industrial enterprises and a menacing growth in unemployment convinced Rother that his liberal critics were correct. But as the Seehandlung had insufficient funds to meet these demands, Rother resigned, leaving the direction of the economy to liberals like Camphausen and Hansemann. They immediately set about trying to find the credit with which to prop up respectable society against the assaults of the dispossessed and frustrated radicals.

Their strategy was to offer large low-interest loans to help industry, and to encourage businessmen to form associations which would support and guide the efforts of the government in Berlin in a form of economic self-determination. Even these efforts were not enough, and by April Mevissen was asking Hansemann to provide 5 million thalers to establish new issuing banks, 2.5 million thalers to buy shares in order to drive share prices up, and 5 million for the issue of new bank notes.

Hansemann only went part of the way to meet these demands. The salvage operation of the Schaffhausen Bank was the first step. Somewhat to the distress of local business interests, the bank was placed firmly under government control at least for the initial stages, before it was considered safe to let this new joint-stock bank stand on its own feet. This was not because Hansemann wanted to continue the policy of men like Rother, but rather that he distrusted traditional bankers, who had done so little to further industry and who were one of the causes of the crisis. His ideal was for joint-stock banks that would truly serve the interests of industry and commerce as well as the small entrepreneur. The new banks would not serve the interests of the traditional state apparatus, but of the commercial and industrial bourgeoisie. They would bring about the revolution in the economic world that had failed to materialise in the political field. Whether new banks would be prepared to do this of their own accord, or whether because of their conservatism they would have to be directed by state control was a question that divided the liberals: the question of whether they were likely to remain in power was never discussed in this context. In fact Hansemann, caught in the cross-fire of conservatives and radicals, ceased to be Finance Minister only two weeks after the new Schaffhausen Bank was formed..

Before leaving office Hansemann had been able to secure royal consent to a measure allowing the formation of joint-stock issuing banks that were to be controlled in part by the government, and which were not able to issue more than a total of 8 million thalers in notes of which 4.5 million were for the eastern provinces and 3.5 million for the western part of Prussia. The implementation of these measures was left to the new Finance Minister, von Rabe, and the Trade Minister, von der Heydt. They would only consent to the formation of banks that paid particular attention to the needs of Prussia east of the Elbe, so that the original liberal intention of altering the balance of power within Prussia by means of a bank policy was drastically changed. The joint-stock bank was not necessarily a means to modernisation and social change, but was directed by government policy to strengthen the conservative elements within the state.

The *Bank des Berliner Kassenvereins* is an example of the kind of bank that flourished under this new régime. Hansemann, who remained very much in the centre of affairs as the director of the Prussian Bank, was highly critical of this new formation. For him it served the private interests of a group of prominent Berlin bankers who had obtained state guarantees for their banking exploits and who would look to their own gains rather than the welfare of the economy as a whole. Hansemann wanted a bank for the small businessmen whom he saw as the backbone of the liberal movement, not state aid for the rich and powerful.

By 1850 Hansemann could do little more than use the Prussian Bank as a means to pursue his financial-political goals. Business and industry were supported as far as possible, much to the fury of the agrarians. Von der Heydt counter-attacked by attempting to strengthen the new issuing banks to break the monopoly of the state bank. This situation rapidly became intolerable, with the Finance Minister, supported by the land-owning aristocracy, attacking the state bank, which in turn was determined to frustrate the efforts of the Minister and could count on the support of the Seehandlung. But Hansemann's hands were tied. The Prussian Bank was not allowed to support joint-stock companies, so this vital part of his banking policy was left entirely in the hands of the private banks, whose capital holdings were as yet too modest to have any great impact on industrial development. Von der Heydt's final *coup* against Hansemann was the mine reform, which reduced taxes by 50 per cent and eased many restrictions on mining. This appeased many liberals, leaving Hansemann with little support. In 1851 he retired from the Prussian Bank to return to private business. He immediately set about the creation of a completely new bank, the *Direktion der Diskontogesellschaft*, which was so cunningly constituted that it slipped through all the rules and regulations governing the formation of new banks, so that in spite of the objections of the government and of the banking world it could not be stopped.

The bank was a very small affair, dealing only with the business of its 236 members, and in the first years of operation was unable to play a particularly important role in the economic life of the country. In 1856 the bank was reformed to become the *Diskontogesellschaft*, one of the great German banks. By this time Hansemann had lost much of his concern for the little man and his bank aimed to have a commandite capital of 20 million thalers and his eye was on much larger undertakings.

The rise of the *Diskontogesellschaft* was only possible within the context of the boom years from 1850 to 1857. These years saw the formation of many other banks which in turn played an important role in fuelling the boom. With the rather disappointing growth rate and rapid fluctuation of the economy before 1850, and the sensitivity of the economy to the performance of the agricultural sector to a degree that would be unthinkable in a developed economy, the system was badly in need of adequate credit facilities. Capital was readily available for investment. The gold discoveries in California and Australia and an increasing demand for European goods caused a steady flow of the metal to Europe. In a healthy economic climate investors began to increase, until by 1852 there was talk of a boom on the Berlin stock market. Whereas in the past German investors had placed their money abroad, often in government securities, now foreign speculators began to look to the German market for quick profits in a young, vigorous and rapidly expanding industrial economy.

The hectic activity of the 1850s, with the formation of many major new enterprises in heavy industry and mining, placed an intolerable strain on existing credit facilities. The private banks simply did not have the means to meet the enormously increased demands for capital. Credit restrictions and state interference hampered the activities of even a new formation like the Schaffhausensche Bankverein, and one joint-stock bank was hardly enough to meet the needs of a boom which was altering the whole structure of German economic life.

The Prussian government still refused to allow any more joint-stock banks, and remained convinced that an extension of the state banking system was both adequate and desirable. Even requests by the Schaffhausen Bank to open branch offices were refused. In this situation the only hope that the industrialists and businessmen of the Rhineland saw was to form a bank outside Prussia in a state where economic policy was not dictated in large part by the needs of eastern agrarian interests. Their model was the *Credit Mobilier* of the Pereire Brothers, a credit bank designed to promote new companies whose capital should come in large part from small private investors. The spectacular success of the Credit Mobilier, in spite of the grave warnings of the conservative bankers, was a tremendous encouragement, particularly to men like the Cologne banker Abraham Oppenheim, who had been one of the original investors in the Credit Mobilier, and was a business associate of the Foulds family, who were the Pereires' main backers.

It was on the initiative of Mevissen and Oppenheim that the first German credit bank was founded. Their first attempts in Frankfurt came unstuck owing to the opposition of the private bankers, headed by Rothschild, who realised the challenge presented by the new bank and who distrusted its 'liberal' overtones. The Bank of Commerce and Industry (*Bank für Handel und Industrie*) was formed in 1853 in Darmstadt in spite of shrieks of protest from the Frankfurt bankers. The Archduke of Hesse allowed the Karlsruhe banker von Haber to form the bank, although Mevissen and Oppenheim were the guiding forces behind it. The new bank had many similarities with the Schaffhausensche Bankverein. Its by-laws were based on those of the Schaffhausen Bank, but it was allowed a much wider field of action in underwriting large loans, circulating bonds and arranging mergers and forming new companies. Unlike the Credit Mobilier, the new bank participated in the 'great creations and financial transactions of governments'. State, provincial and municipal loans played an important part in the business of the bank, so that the emphasis was not wholly on the promotion of industry. The *Darmstädter Bank*, as it was soon to be known, was the bank of the future, the bank of the industrial age, encouraging the growth of new concerns, active in the stock exchanges and promoting a certain democratisation of the appetite for speculative profit.

The victory of the Darmstädter Bank over Rothschild and the private bankers was of considerable political significance as Bismarck, who at that time was Prussian envoy to the confederation in Frankfurt, was quick to realise. The Rothschilds were financial supporters of Austria and the south German states, and stood for the *status quo* in the German confederation and for Austrian domination of Central Europe. Bismarck urged his government to support the new bank in order to undermine the Rothschilds and thus to weaken the position of Austria in the confederation, but Berlin would not support these dangerously liberal ideas which would involve supporting industrial against agrarian interests. Frederick William IV of Prussia saw the bank as a disgusting example of French speculative fever and corruption and demanded that steps should be taken against it. The Schaffhausen Bank was warned to steer clear of this undesirable institution. With such determined opposition from the German governments and from the private banks the Darmstädter Bank relied heavily on foreign investment, particularly from France, and on the support of the government of Hesse. Some private bankers, like Bethmann and Oppenheim, invested in the bank to their considerable advantage. The healthy economic climate coupled with the bank's determination to overcome all the difficulties placed in its way helped its considerable success in the early years. A silent partnership was opened in New York as early as 1853, and branches were opened in Frankfurt and Mainz, and connections established in Berlin, Heilbronn, Mannheim, Breslau and Leipzig. The success of the bank, its flexibility and its determination to play an active role in the industrial development and growth of the country made the Darmstädter Bank the model on which many of the later great German banks were based.

According to Prussian law all joint-stock companies had to be approved by the government. Company by-laws and any amendments to them had to be sanctioned by the government. Infringements of these by-laws could be punished by the dissolution of the company. A company's capital was carefully scrutinised to see that it did not drop below a minimum of 50 per cent of the original stock. A company could not be dissolved without government permission. Companies had to be deemed to serve the public interest and it had to be shown that a joint-stock company was the only way in which the necessary capital could be raised. A further law in June 1852 gave the state even more supervisory powers over joint-stock companies. Books could be examined at any time by government officials who were also empowered to attend any meetings of the board.

Obviously the application of these provisions depended very much on local conditions and on the zeal of individual civil servants, but the threat of such interference was tiresome and inhibiting. In general it is safe to say that the Prussian state was less averse to joint-stock companies after 1848 than it had been in the Pre-March. On the one hand there was a deep-rooted distrust of modern industrial society, which found its most effective ideological expression in a condemnation of speculation and materialism, and which saw the joint-stock company in industry as a dangerous innovation, but on the other hand there was a growing realisation that Prussia needed industry to maintain her position in Germany and in Europe and that the state could not simply turn its back on the modern age. Controlled industrial expansion, if needs be by means of the joint-stock company, but with careful state control and supervision, seemed to many civil servants to be the ideal solution. It became increasingly obvious that industrial expansion could be most effectively secured by means of joint-stock companies, and that if one wanted the one, it was necessary to accept the other. Thus economic policy of the years of reaction after 1848 was contradictory and fitful. The attitude of the government was highly ambiguous, and this ambiguity was of itself a hindrance to the full development of Prussia's industrial potential.

Although the number of joint-stock companies formed during the boom was rather small, it marks a significant increase over the previous years. In Prussia between 1850 and 1857 there were 85 new joint-stock companies formed, and 12 companies were given the right to increase their capital holdings. In Saxony 61 new companies were formed during this period. In the first half of the nineteenth century only 37 industrial companies had been formed on a joint-stock basis in Prussia. Of the new companies the majority were in mining and smelting, particularly in mining, where the lowering of taxation and the abolition of certain restrictions by the Prussian government had made investment more attractive. Rapid industrial growth had greatly increased the demand for coal, and the state authorities agreed that only by means of the joint-stock company could sufficient capital be raised. This argument was turned against the sugar industry, where joint-stock companies were refused on the grounds that other adequate sources of capital were available. No doubt the fact that the state feared loss of revenue from duty on imported sugar was an important consideration, as was the fear of some Junkers that their small sugar refineries would not be able to compete with large joint-stock companies. Some already existing companies converted themselves into joint-stock companies in order to obtain the capital needed for expansion. In this process many companies were completely reformed and reorganised. This course of action was typical in the iron and steel industry of the Rhine and Ruhr. Many of the new coke-fired blast furnaces were built by newly formed joint-stock companies. The joint-stock company thus played a vital role in modernising important sectors of industry at a time when capital accumulation was still a problem as a result of the relative backwardness of the German economy. In spite of the many restrictions and difficulties, Germany would not have made the significant gains in the 1850s which marked the arrival of the country among the great industrial nations without the increase in the number of joint-stock companies.

Even with the new joint-stock companies and marked increase in the activity on the German stock exchanges, capital was still difficult to obtain. Agrarians had little inclination to invest in industry. The bourgeoisie was not wealthy enough to provide sufficient funds for investment. Profits of industry were not high enough to finance major improvements. It was thus necessary to attract capital from other parts of Germany and from abroad if the needs of industry were to be met. Nearly 40 per cent of the capital invested in the Prussian mining industry came from outside Prussia. Much of this capital came from France and Belgium, a small amount from Holland, whereas English capital was hardly represented. The Prussian government was concerned that industry should not fall into foreign hands, and for this reason insisted that the majority of the board of directors and the president of a company had to be native citizens. Foreign capital thus played an important role in stimulating industrial growth without any loss of control to outside interests. From the records of these early joint-stock companies it is a striking fact that a sizeable proportion of the investors were civil servants, which provides clear indication that the state apparatus was by no means unanimous in its suspicious attitude towards joint-stock companies. It would seem that it was mostly the middle and lower civil servants who invested their savings in shares, and only seldom their superiors. Modest sums were also invested by the land-owning aristocracy, sometimes the profits from the sale of land, or even a speculative flutter of the kind they liked to decry in their public utterances. They preferred to invest in the mining industry of Upper Silesia, where the aristocracy played an important role in industry. It was hardly a loss of caste or a dangerous act of liberalism to invest in the concerns of von Pless, Count Ballestrem, von Schaffgotsch or Henckel Donnersmarck.

From home investors the largest percentage of funds came from commercial interests followed by industrialists. The banks made a more modest contribution, for reasons that have already been outlined, although the banks played a vital role as intermediaries between investors and industry, and particularly in helping to interest foreign investors. Some figures are clearly prominent among the thousands of nameless investors, and they represent a new type of capitalist. Gustav von Mevissen was on the board of six mining companies, the president of two industrial concerns, the president of the Darmstädter Bank and the Luxembourg International Bank, as well as being chairman of the board of three further banks, including the Schaffhausensche Bankverein, and on the board of two other banks. Other figures who appear on more than one board of directors in the new companies were later to become widely known: Thyssen, Stumm, Böcking, Hoesch, Siemens.

These were certainly not the days of the small investor, in spite of Hansemann's hopes in 1848 for a form of 'people's capitalism'. Shares were usually in 100-thaler denominations (1 thaler = £6.50 sterling) which was far too expensive for the little man. Usually investors bought large blocks of shares. In the hectic years of the 1850s the demand for new capital was incessant, as companies grew as fast as possible to cash in on the expanding market. Share issues were cumbersome and rarely sufficient, and the companies relied heavily on bank loans. With reasonable profit rates and with a booming economy this system worked well enough in the initial stages of the boom, but soon the economy grew dangerously overheated and highly susceptible to any recession. When the crisis came in 1857, many companies were grossly over-extended and bankruptcies were common. As many of the Westphalian companies were still in the process of formation, there were few gains for the shareholders.

Banks thus played an important role in these critical years. Although the amount of share capital they controlled was by no means overwhelming, it was important, and without short-term bank loans few of the great German firms could have expanded so fast or have survived the depression. The regulations governing the formation of joint-stock companies did not allow them to be controlled by a narrow clique, and board members were only given a maximum number of votes, regardless of the amount they had invested. Partly for this reason, bankers were on many important boards and the beginnings of the close association of bank capital and industrial capital, which is so characteristic of Germany by the late nineteenth century, can clearly be delineated.

In the 1850s investment in the railways continued to play a critical role in stimulating industrial output. Railways offered a safe investment, but some also promised high speculative gains. The need for an extension of the railways network was apparent not only to industrial and commercial interests, but also to the military. Railway-building could thus satisfy both the aristocracy and the bourgeoisie, for after the initial resistance to railways, they were now regarded as not only desirable but essential. Investment in railway stocks had a positive effect in livening the stock markets and the capital market. Railway-building further helped heavy industry, providing the critical marginal demand which for undercapitalised companies with low profit margins was out of all proportion to the actual demand. Heavy industry was thus not wholly dependent on the railways for its well-being, for it had its own specific sectoral problems of investment and output, but given the narrow room for manoeuvre left to heavy industry, any changes in investment in railways was bound to have a tremendous impact. The periods of heavy investment in railways, in 1844, 1846, 1854–7, 1863 and 1864, coincide with periods of high demand for iron and machinery, for coal and steel. Periods of depression from 1848 to 1852 and from 1858 to 1861 coincide with marked falling-off of railway investment.

The 1850s saw the completion of a proper railway network in Germany. With the formation of adequate railway links across the length and breadth of the country, the transportation of goods rather than people became increasingly important, and thus the impact of railway-building on the economy as a whole was much greater. The first railways were built largely for passenger transport. In the 1850s the transportation of goods increased sevenfold, and the number of passengers doubled. Although there was a remarkable increase in the volume of traffic, the actual length of railway that was built in the 1850s was not as great as in the 1840s. The improvements thus came in large part from an increase in the efficiency and density of railway traffic. Profits jumped for, the initial large investments having been made, the marginal revenues were considerable.

Industrial Growth in the 1850s

Just as the Prussian government was determined to keep a close watch on the joint-stock companies, so were they anxious to keep a close eye on the railway system by building on the state railways rather than allowing private railway companies to challenge their hegemony. The responsible Minister, von der Heydt, wanted a railway that would serve the interests of the state, not the sectional interests of the bourgeoisie, and he wanted a railway system run by submissive civil servants rather than aggressive businessmen and troublesome workers. He was concerned that the railways were manned by democrats, and he issued an order in 1852 that all 'democrats' should be dismissed forthwith from the railways. Here von der Heydt came up against his erstwhile colleague Mevissen, chairman of the Rhineland Railway Company, which was regarded as dangerously democratic in Berlin.

The Prussian railway system was gradually extended and financed by state-guaranteed loans. The *Ostbahn*, which had been such a burning issue in 1847, was built. A number of small private railways were bought and amalgamated with the state system. Three private railway companies were allowed to be formed in Prussia in the 1850s, and other companies were allowed to increase their share capital, but these companies played a very minor role. Outside Prussia, the private railway companies were of much greater significance and there was a brisk trading of railway shares. Saxony and Bavaria tended to follow the Prussian example of building up the state railway system and discouraging private companies.

The expansion of the railways in the early 1860s was a result of a defeat of von der Heydt's railway policy by the liberals in the house of representatives (*Abgeordnetenhaus*). The liberal bourgeoisie no longer needed state guarantees of railways, for the railways were proving highly profitable. They now wanted to get their hands on the distributed profits of the railways by the dividends paid on shares, which were now a far more attractive prospect than the fixed interest on government bonds. In the 1850s only 611 km of private railway had been built, while the state railway laid 2,249 km of new track. In the 1860s private companies built 2,856 km and the state railway 2,375 km. Included in the figures for the state railway in the 1860s is the entire Hanover railway system, which was taken over by the Prussians in 1866.

By the 1860s Germany had the largest railway network in Europe, and although the total length of track was less than that in England, the gap was narrowing. In the production of machinery Germany still lagged behind, but here too important advances were made. The 1850s saw the final triumph of the steam engine, so that on average every factory had two steam engines. Machine tools became increasingly specialised, so that the all-purpose hand operated drills and lathes were a thing of the past. Machine parts were standardised and interchangeable, which made a dramatic increase in production possible, and resulted in a corresponding increase in the productivity of labour. Although mass production techniques had yet to be introduced, the first steps had been taken towards the complete mechanisation of production. The machines themselves were now built by machines using precision tools which were faster and more accurate than the hand-operated tools of the past. German manufacturers were determined to catch up with the English in this vital branch of modern industry. They may have lacked the experience, but they eagerly applied new techniques and the discoveries of the engineers. At the world exhibition of 1862 German machine tools could hold their own with the best of British machinery.

These improvements resulted in a steady decrease in the amount of machinery imported into Germany. An export of German machines began, particularly to Russia and to Austria. By 1863 the *Zollverein* was exporting more machines than it was importing and machinery was to form an important part of Germany's steadily growing export industry.

For this reason the machine-builders were champions of free trade, unlike the heavy industrialists of the Rhine and Ruhr, of the Saar and Silesia. They saw the possibilities of an expanding export trade and lost their fear of English competition. Machine-builders were found throughout Germany: Borsig and Schwartzkopff in Berlin, Maffei in Munich, Henschel in Kassel, and Schichau in Elbing. They were less regionally conscious and less traditionally minded than the heavy industrialists and thus tended to be more liberal in their politics as well as their economic ideas.

The 1850s also marked the end of the old charcoal furnaces for the production of iron and steel. By 1860 only 9 per cent of wrought iron production in Prussia was by the old method. Although the revolutionary process of Bessemer converters and the Siemens-Martin process were not introduced until the next decade, iron and steel production was increased by refining existing techniques, by abandoning the old methods, and by the widespread introduction of massive steam-driven machinery. The large amounts of capital needed to build coke-fired furnaces were now more readily available with the easier access to share capital. Thus in 1851 only 25 per cent of Prussian blast furnaces were coke-fired, and by 1860 it was 70 per cent, a dramatic example of the high level of investment during the boom years. The productivity of the individual worker in the iron industry rose from 421 Zentner in 1852 to 585 Zentner in 1858.

These massive investments and the striking increase in productivity had a direct effect on costs. German iron and steel could not compete effectively with English and Belgian imports. Imports to the *Zollverein* began to fall, although it was not until the end of the 1860s that more crude iron was exported than imported.

The production of crude iron increased 2.5 times in the 1850s. This was well above the average increase for metals, although steel production doubled in the same time period. A major reason for this increased production was the widespread use of coke, and those areas closest to the coalfields grew fastest. The supremacy of the Ruhr was established, and areas such as the Eifel, which had been well suited for charcoal-fired furnaces, but which were too far from suitable sources of coal, rapidly declined.

In the age of the steam engine and the coke-fired furnace, coal production was one of the main keys to growth. In the industrial area of the Rhineland-Westphalia where coal mines and the iron and steel industry worked side by side, the new centre of German wealth was formed.

Coal production more than doubled in the 1850s, and the production of lignite increased 2.5 times. Iron ore production increased about 40 per cent during the same period. Although machinery was not used at the coal-face until the end of the century, and even then only in a few isolated instances, steam engines for pumps and winding gear were now used on a large scale, enabling deeper shafts to be sunk to reach the rich deposits that lay deep under the surface of the Ruhr. The work-force was greatly increased and the productivity of individual miners improved. Steam power was used to haul coal to the surface, work at the coal-face was rationalised, and the miners were driven harder. In 1850 Germany was producing 5.25 million tons of coal, more than was produced in France, but lagging far behind the 49.5 million tons produced in Britain.

Wages in the 1850s tended to be low and lagged behind increases in output and productivity. Prices therefore tended to remain low, and aggregate supply rose slightly faster than aggregate demand. Mining made considerable profits between 1853 and 1855, which stimulated a further round of investments, so that by the late 1850s falling prices were combined with a falling rate of profit and an increasing difficulty in selling the steadily increasing quantities of coal. This could lead to reductions of production at moments of crisis when the mining industry went through one of its self-generated cycles that was independent from either the agricultural sector or fluctuations of mass purchasing power. This was one of the consequences of a maturing economy which no longer reacted immediately and directly to changes in the agricultural sector.

Germany was still unable to meet the demands of its domestic market and imports to the *Zollverein* remained very high. The industry of the Rhineland was offered new opportunities by the treaty with Hanover in 1851 and the customs agreement with Belgium two years later. But these treaties also enabled British goods to enter Germany more easily. As the *Zollverein* refused to increase tariffs, the only salvation for German industry was to produce large quantities of cheap and nasty goods which would undercut British prices. The other alternative was to specialise in high-quality goods produced on a large scale: Krupp's cast steel axles were famous throughout Europe. In either case large productive units were necessary, either by building up enormous firms or by agreements with other firms. The role of the cartels and trusts, which was to be so important in late nineteenth-century Germany, was in part the result of the problem of a growing economy faced with the almost overwhelming competition of British industry and the need to improve and innovate without fearing domestic competition. German heavy industrialists and the hard-pressed textile manufacturers continued to call for protective tariffs, but as long as the agrarians dominated the political life of the country, particularly in Prussia, and as long as they were convinced that free trade was the best antidote to the final triumph of industrial capitalism, and the best support of an ordered and autocratic society, there was little hope for change.

The Politics of the Zollverein

In the 1850s the *Zollverein* and customs policy were at the centre of the struggle between Austria and Prussia for hegemony in central Europe. Under the forceful and able leadership of Schwarzenberg, Austria began a policy of centralising the Habsburg monarchy under the government in Vienna. At the same time he was determined to frustrate any liberal plans for a 'greater Germany' and to bring the German confederation firmly under Austrian control. It was not enough to destroy the Prussian-dominated Erfurt Assembly and thus to frustrate

Prussian ambitions for a 'small Germany' controlled by Berlin. The convention of Olmütz in November 1850 had secured these aims, much to the shame and resentment of the Prussians. It would also be necessary to break Prussia's economic strength by challenging her authority over the *Zollverein* by means of a carefully conducted scheme for a customs union which would ensure Austria both the political and the economic domination of central Europe. This scheme appealed to the Austrian Trade Minister Bruck, who hoped that by means of an association with the prosperous and expanding *Zollverein*, the stagnant Austrian economy could be given a new lease of life.

Such ideas had little appeal to the Prussians. The Austrians still were in favour of protective tariffs which were unacceptable to the free-trading agrarian interests, and the Prussian government knew full well that the Austrian proposals were designed to promote Austria's power-political interests. In a central Europe dominated by German Austria, Prussia would be reduced to the rank of a second-class state. The Prussian government was thus to use the weapon of free trade to beat off the attempts by Austria to win its way into the *Zollverein*. The political and the economic interests of the land-owning aristocracy coincided perfectly, and the political argument could be used against those who were asking for protection, so that protectionism could almost be made to seem like treachery. This feeling grew stronger as Bruck pointed out the advantages of protection to the manufacturers and industrialists in Germany, men who hardly needed to be converted. But the protectionists had little political influence in the years immediately after the failure of the revolution of 1848. Having welcomed the help of the reactionaries against the radicals in the revolution, they had little desire to press the political question and were thankful for the peace and quiet that the conservatives had restored to Germany. Free trade was a heavy price to pay, but it was certainly preferable to threats of revolution and overthrow.

Plans for a customs union with Prussia were first suggested in an anonymous article which Bruck placed in the *Wiener Zeitung* in October 1849. The Prussian Ambassador, Bernstorff, interpreted this as a sinister plot by the Austrians to crush Prussia, a view that was thought a little excessive by the Foreign Minister, Schleinitz. The Prussians did not reject the idea out of hand for fear of appearing too negative and thus alienating the protectionists within the *Zollverein*, but they hoped to postpone and water down the proposed customs conference as much as possible. Delbrück, the Prussian specialist on customs duties, pointed out to his government that the Austrians would not be able to accept a low *Zollverein* tariff without serious disruption to their economy, and also that the members of the *Zollverein* were tied to Prussia by self-interest and by the economic strength of Prussia. Prussia could therefore face the prospect of negotiations with Austria with a certain confidence.

Bruck, with his extraordinary vision of an Austrian-dominated *Mitteleuropa* controlling the trade routes to India via Trieste and Egypt, realised that time was running out. The *Zollverein* treaty would be due for renewal in 1852, and it was thus vital to move before 'all the German states have to bow to the will of Prussia for the next twelve years'. Prussia was in a weak position as Radowitz's schemes for a 'small Germany' were hardly viable. The German states were attracted by the Austrian proposals, some for economic reasons, others, like electoral Hesse, because they disliked Prussia's German policy. The Prussians decided to postpone the issue further, along lines suggested by Delbrück, by proposing a trade agreement with Austria and to postpone the customs union until the tariff question was settled. As tariff negotiations were likely to be exceedingly long and complicated, this seemed to be an excellent way to put off the entire affair. It soon became clear that the German states were unable to agree in what ways the tariff should be reformed, and Prussia had, at least for the time being, frustrated Bruck's schemes that had seemed so promising only a few weeks before. Olmütz was a resounding victory for Austria; now Schwarzenberg hoped for an economic Olmütz.

As both Prussia and Austria looked around for allies in the forthcoming debate in the Bundestag on the tariff issue, Prussia scored a major success with the trade agreement with Hanover in September 1851, which was supported not only by the agrarians as an important step in the direction of free trade and opening up the export trade to England, but also by industrialists who welcomed an expansion of the domestic market at a time when output was rising. The German states began to realise that they could profit from the struggle between Austria and Prussia to pursue their own economic aims, and this made Austria's attempts to alter the whole nature of the *Zollverein* by making it Austrian and protectionist all the more difficult. Prussia used threats to renegotiate the *Zollverein* treaties and boycotted a meeting of the *Zollverein* states in Vienna. Delbrück's calculations were correct. However much the German states distrusted or even disliked Prussia, they realised that their economic well-being rested in large part on their membership in the *Zollverein*. Even the most anti-

Prussian of the states, Bavaria, Baden and Württemberg, feared the isolation of southern Germany, and knew the vital importance of access to the North Sea ports; hence the significance of the agreement with Hanover in 1851 which opened up the routes to the north. Prussia could afford to take a firm line. If the worst came to the worst she would rather have a small north German *Zollverein* than be part of an economic organisation in which Austria would have the right to veto. These negotiations vividly show the trade-creation effects of the *Zollverein* at a time of rapid industrial growth. Within fifteen years of its formation, the small states could hardly survive without Prussia.

Austria, having failed to win the German states away from Prussia, agreed to direct negotiations for a trade agreement with Prussia without talking about an immediate customs union. Prussia agreed because it again postponed the issue, and Austria was in favour because she felt that this was the first necessary step towards an eventual customs union. The resulting trade agreement of February 1853, the *Mitteleuropa* Agreement, satisfied both parties in these respects. Prussia made a vague promise of a customs union and agreed to consider the *Zollverein* and Austria as one customs area – a meaningless formula as there was still a customs barrier between the two. Austria was obliged to lower her tariffs, so that German industry had new opportunities to compete on a more competitive basis.

The *Zollverein* treaties were renewed six weeks after the *Mitteleuropa* Agreement so Prussia had gained twelve further years in which to negotiate with Austria from a position of strength. In Austria industrialists were anxious that the tariff should not be lowered, and viewed their government's schemes for an arrangement with the *Zollverein* with the deepest suspicion. With such powerful support against the customs union within Austria, Prussia could well afford to postpone any decisions. Austria's position was further weakened by her inept handling of the Crimean crisis. In an atmosphere of economic uncertainty and with the disruption of her markets in the Balkans, Austria was no longer such a valuable trading partner. Austrian schemes for tariff reform lost their immediacy, and some gloomy souls predicted that if Austria were to join the *Zollverein*, even on favourable terms, it would lead to her economic ruin. The diplomatic and economic weakness of Austria encouraged Bismarck to demand an all-out assault on Austria's position in central Europe with the aid of foreign powers. This was too excessive and dangerous a proposition for the conservative Prussian government under Manteuffel, who preferred to use Prussia's relative strength after the Crimean War in order to negotiate with Austria to secure favourable terms without stirring up the hornets' nest of nationalism and liberalism.

The Depression 1858–1861

By 1856 signs were already beginning to appear of the impending depression which was to prove to be the most severe economic crisis that had yet affected the industrialised world. First signs were seen on the Paris market where bonds were sluggish. Interest rates were raised in London and New York. In Germany share prices began to fall badly. With the end of the Crimean War production had been stepped up even though the prices of raw materials remained high. As there was no corresponding increase in purchasing power manufacturers were obliged to stockpile and look for further loans to tide them over until the market picked up. The American harvest of 1857 was particularly successful, but this had the effect of depressing prices and the business cycle began its downward trend.

In August 1857 the Ohio Life and Trust Company went into receivership. This was but the first stage of a large number of bankruptcies of insurance companies, industrial companies and banks. Interest rates reached 24 per cent by the end of August and on discounts in New York even reached 100 per cent. Britain, recovering from the badly administered and costly Crimean War, and now engaged in China and India, was also seriously affected by the slump. Over-speculation and lack of liquidity resulted in many bankruptcies, including the failure of the Western Bank of Scotland, and the bank rate was raised to 10 per cent. Although the crisis was not as serious in England as it was in America, the effects of the commercial crisis were transmitted rapidly to England's trading partners on the Continent.

The newly formed German banks were able to weather the storm by careful housekeeping and by subsidies from the state. In mining the industrialists formed associations to protect their interests, and the main burden fell on investors rather than the mining companies, which had largely completed their first round of major investments and thus did not have any great call for capital on a market that was contracting rapidly. The failure of the stock market and the relative immunity of most large firms from the worst aspects of the crisis caused a widespread disenchantment with the joint-stock company. Small investors had been badly hurt, and the conservatives had their worst fears confirmed that the joint-stock company did little but encourage thoughtless and improvident speculation which was seen as the direct cause of the present difficulties. Stock prices fell to 50 per cent of their face value. Wholesale prices fell 30 per cent. Even the banks, which had played such an important role in financing the industrial expansion of Germany, began to lose their enthusiasm for stock promotion and investment in industry. Industry thus lost one of its main sources of supply of capital and increasingly had to rely on the issue of fixed-interest securities.

The main effect of the crisis in Prussia was that it affected the traditional sectors of the economy such as agriculture, the wholesale trade and the capital market more than the newly expanded and improved industries. With the catastrophic fall in prices these sectors were more anxious than ever to pursue a free-trade policy to unload excess commodities. In Austria the situation was quite different in that it was industry that was hardest hit, and therefore the calls for protection were louder than ever. Thus in terms of the Prussian and Austrian rivalry Prussia emerged from the crisis in a strengthened position, the more so as the effects of the disruption of world trade had been more severely felt in Austria.

This is not to imply that industry in Germany was not seriously hurt by the crisis. Rapidly falling prices caused a cut-back in production. This was clearly visible in the textile industries in the last quarter of 1857 and early 1858. In heavy industry the effect was somewhat delayed. Engineering and machine works were the first to be hit, followed by a fall in the amount of coal produced in 1859. In large part, however, the crisis in heavy industry was one of falling prices rather than reduced production, of a reduced rate of growth rather than complete stagnation or even decline. As Germany relied heavily on imports, part of the reduction simply involved buying a smaller percentage of goods and raw materials from abroad.

The causes of the depression in Germany from 1858 to 1861 were not only exogenous, they lay also in the development of the German economy during the 1850s and in some cases they were largely specific to certain sectors, though exacerbated by external factors. Many industries were undercapitalised and thus very susceptible to any changes in the economic climate. Some had tried to grow too fast and had tied up all their investments in long-term projects which were not to become profitable until the 1860s. Part of the reason for the falling prices was the fierce competition among rapidly modernising firms where production was increasing steadily. Profits were being squeezed by price-cutting precisely at the time when money was getting harder to find and interest rates were rising and when nominal wages showed an upward tendency. Reduction in the amount of railway-building in the late 1850s closed off heavy industry's most valuable market for marginal production. The measures taken by industry which included cut-backs in production, reduction of the work-force, wage cuts and further rationalisation of production did, however, place German industry in a favourable position for further expansion once the immediate crisis had been overcome.

In agriculture the shock had at first been considerable. Agricultural output reached a peak in 1856, and prices dropped to their lowest level in 1858. The fall in prices thus came after the downward trend in the business cycle. This timing is important because it shows that the fall in agricultural prices did not trigger off the crisis, and it strengthened the conviction of the agrarians that the crisis itself was the result of faulty economic policy that was too protective of the economy. This conviction became all the stronger when grain exports picked up again due to increased exports to England. The crisis thus not only strengthened Prussia and the *Zollverein* against Austria, it also strengthened the alliance of the land-owning aristocracy and the commercial bourgeoisie behind a free-trade policy whose leading spokesman was the English-born John Prince-Smith, who represented Stettin in the Prussian House of Representatives. The 'Manchesterism' of the Manteuffel era was a curious hybrid, for although Manteuffel enthusiastically endorsed Prince-Smith's views on free trade, which he knew to be in the vital interests of the export-oriented Junker-dominated agricultural sector, and, although he was prepared to liberalise the mining industry by removing old and tiresome restrictions, he tried to contain and restrict industrial growth by showing a marked reluctance to allow new joint-stock companies to form, to grant subsidies, or to allow the destruction of the last remaining vestiges of the guild system. Manteuffel also knew that free trade was a powerful weapon to use against Austria, particularly as the depression only served to accentuate the economic dominance of Prussia.

That arch-reactionaries like Manteuffel could support free trade placed in a cruel dilemma those who saw free trade as a step towards the creation of a modern capitalist state, which would push aside the petty princelings and their authoritarian governments and create a liberal democratic national state. Would they have to support an autocratic and politically reactionary Prussia on the grounds that it was the driving force behind free trade in Germany, or would they by opposing Prussia also be undermining the liberalisation of the German economy? Such problems as these underline the peculiarity of the German experience of industrialisation and modernisation and were to become key issues in the 'New Era' and the ensuing constitutional crisis.

The organisational link between the free traders and the liberals of the 'New Era' when, in 1858, Prince William of Prussia was appointed Regent, was the Congress of German Businessmen (*Kongress Deutscher Volkswirthe*) formed in the same year. This new association worked closely with other reforming institutions and clubs throughout Germany. At the first Congress, held in Gotha in 1858, many of the great names of the liberal movement were in attendance: Schulze-Delitzsch, the leading spokesman for the co-operative movement, and Prince-Smith being the best known. The Congress called for a lowering of tariffs and the reduction of state interference in the economy. Thus the liberals supported in part the Prussian attitude towards Austria, and became the spokesmen of Junker interests, even though their long-term goals were so widely different. In the same year the Prussian Trade Association (*Preussische Handelstag*) was formed and the inaugural meeting was attended by none other than von der Heydt. Three years later a German Trade Association was also formed. North and south German liberals united in the National Association (*Nationalverein*), which was a movement of right-wing liberals who placed national unity higher than any liberal democratic principles, and, although many Congress members were also members of the *Nationalverein*, the association had little real understanding of the importance of the economic question. For this reason it was easy for Bismarck to destroy the *Nationalverein* by granting economic but not political concessions to the German liberals. With the success of Bismarck's policies they were all too willing to abandon their liberal baggage and become a respectable association of the prosperous middle class.

The proliferation of clubs and associations devoted to debating economic issues and pressing for the claims of specific sectors of the economy was a direct result of the economic crisis. Free trade was now on everyone's lips, apart from those in heavy industry who were calling for protection and who also organised themselves in associations such as the *Verein für die bergbaulichen Interessen im Oberbergamtsbezirk Dortmund* (Dortmund Mines Association). Economics became a matter of general public concern as society experienced the shock of the first world-wide economic crisis. Germany had suffered less of a crisis of over-speculation than either France or England, partly due to the tight state control over joint-stock companies, but it became obvious that Germany was part of a world-wide economic system and that it had to set its own house in order to be better able to face any future crisis. The resulting debate led to a hardening of the divisions between protectionist Austrians and free-trading Prussians and strengthened the ties between German liberals and Prussian conservatives.

5 ECONOMICS AND UNIFICATION

Germany and the Cobden Treaty of 1860

Although for Austria the disaster of the economic crisis had been followed by the defeats of Magenta and Solferino, Prussia was isolated and unable to exploit the situation to her own advantage. The German states would not have tolerated an outright attack on Austria, and Prussia was becoming increasingly concerned about the attitude of Britain and France. The trade treaty with France negotiated by Cobden in 1860, although it was thought by Palmerston to be far too favourable to the French, and by many Frenchmen to be an attack on the very foundations of the social order which were based on protectionism, was felt by the Prussians to mark an end to the hostilities between France and England and to pose a threat to the conservative order of central Europe. The Prussian Foreign Minister, Schleinitz, was even prepared to agree with the Prussian Ambassador in London, Bernstorff, that 'revolutionary' France allied to England was such a danger that Prussia would have to settle her differences with Austria.

Schleinitz was soon to find himself in an awkward dilemma. Almost simultaneously he was approached by the French with a proposal for a trade treaty and be the Austrians for a defence agreement. Schleinitz would have preferred to begin negotiations with Austria, but other members of the Council of Ministers, including von der Heydt, argued that both options should be left open. They argued that in a dire crisis Austria was bound to stand by Prussia, and that Napoleon III's free-trade policies could be used to benefit Prussia's position against Austria. In June Prince William of Prussia met Napoleon III at Baden-Baden and negotiations with France began. The next month William met Francis Joseph at Teplitz, where a somewhat empty formula of mutual co-operation in Germany was evolved and there was some vague talk of future discussions of the proposals for a customs union between the two countries.

The negotiations after Teplitz ran into familiar difficulties. Austrian protectionists lobbied their government, urging it not to ignore the vital interests of Austrian industry. Prussian free-traders, all the more outspoken after the experiences of the economic crisis, called for a lowering of the tariff and warned of the dangers of making any concessions to the Austrians. The negotiations between Prussia and France went relatively smoothly, whereas discussions with Austria, particularly over a possible military convention that had been suggested at Teplitz, soon reached an impasse, largely because Austria was unwilling to make any concession to the Prussian position. Prussia was encouraged to pursue the negotiations with France not only because of the pressure from free-traders at home, but also because the German states welcomed the move, hoping that it would help to stimulate trade and industry and pull the *Zollverein* out of the slump. Austria persuaded the south German states that the terms of the proposed Franco-Prussian treaty, which envisaged customs dues based on value, rather than the *Zollverein* duty on the weight of specific items, would be disadvantageous to them, whereupon Bavaria and Württemberg refused to accept the draft of the treaty and urged that more attention be paid to the needs of Austria. Austria was also successful in mobilising opinion in Germany to her side. In May 1861 the *Deutsche Handelstag*, representing local groups of businessmen throughout Germany who favoured a 'Greater German' policy, who were not dedicated free-traders and who were concerned about the power of French and British capital in Germany, called upon Prussia to take steps towards a customs union with Austria. The Prussian government ignored this plea. Relations between Austria and Prussia grew steadily worse. Austria signed treaties with the south German states to stop any revision of the federal constitution which might weaken her position. Prussia saw this as deliberate provocation and hastily concluded the trade treaty with France, opening up the French market to German industrial goods and thus offering a large and attractive market to industry, which was beginning to climb slowly out of the recession.

Exploiting the political crisis in Prussia over the reform of the army, which had reached a peak in the spring of 1862 when elections returned a liberal majority in spite of frantic efforts by the government to secure a conservative victory, the Austrians tried to form a customs union with those states which disliked the proposed Franco-Prussian trade agreement. The Austrian Foreign Minister, Rechberg, greatly overestimated the opposition in south Germany to the treaty and overlooked the fact that Austria with her backward and decrepit economy was not a particularly attractive partner. Anti-Prussian resentment and a certain anxiety about the consequences of the trade agreement were certainly present in south Germany, but they were hardly enough to risk breaking up the *Zollverein* and attempting to build an alternative south German and Austrian customs union. Nor did Rechberg realise that the opposition of the liberals to the army reform did not mean that they rejected the government's economic policy. Indeed the newly elected Prussian Parliament (*Landtag*) enthusiastically endorsed the Franco-Prussian trade agreement. The government was able to satisfy the economic demands of the liberals, and thus the way was open for the compromise between the liberals and the autocratic state that Bismarck was so skilfully to accomplish. The 'betrayal' of the liberals in the 1860s was once again determined by economic factors as much as by a desire to come to terms with existing political conditions.

The Austrians knew that once Prussia had ratified the trade agreement with France the customs agreement of 1853 would be in ruins, and that there would be little hope of reviving schemes for a Greater German customs union. Confident of the support of the south German states, Rechberg now planned an all-out offensive against Prussia in the hope of torpedoing the trade agreement with France and destroying Prussia's domination over the *Zollverein*. Prussia would not bow to this pressure. In the general staff, discussions of a possible war with Austria were conducted. Bismarck, from Paris, urged an immediate signing of the trade agreement. The Prussian *Landtag* voted 264 to 12 in favour of the agreement, while the upper house (*Herrenhaus*) was unanimous in support. With such unanimity between liberals and conservatives in Prussia, and with Austria snapping at her heels, the agreement was signed in August 1862. The shape of future alliances was already clear. Junkers and liberals in alliance with France united behind a free-trade policy faced Austria and the protectionists of south Germany.

In spite of the protest notes from Bavaria, Württemberg, Hanover and Saxony (though not from Baden) the south German states were not prepared to go all the way with Austria, but preferred to use Austria as a weapon against Prussian excesses. Aware of the uncertainty in the south German position, the Prussians announced that a continuation of the *Zollverein* would be dependent on the acceptance of the trade agreement with France. Such was the situation when Bismarck was appointed Minister President of Prussia in a last desperate bid to settle the crisis over army reform. Bismarck determined to push the crisis to breaking point in order that the lines would be drawn up clearly on either side. The liberals were horrified at his immoderate language and the dissolution of the *Landtag*, conservatives were equally appalled at his excesses, and alarmed at some of his dangerously liberal-sounding utterances. His programme was outlined in the famous 'blood and iron' speech. He argued that the social and political standing of the traditional élites could best be preserved by binding the liberal bourgeoisie to the existing order by modest concessions and an active and violent foreign policy. Bismarck thus hoped to cement the compromise between the bourgeoisie and the aristocracy by means of foreign policy, of which he was soon to prove such a master, and an important component of that policy was bound to be the question of tariffs.

Bismarck had a great deal of experience of economic policy, but he always saw questions of tariffs and trade agreements in terms of power politics and as a means to cement and strengthen the conservative order in a time of rapid industrialisation. He also knew that he could gain widespread support for a trade policy based on free trade and the exclusion of Austria that would encompass both liberals and conservatives, and that Austria was badly divided in that the industrialists bitterly opposed Rechberg's schemes for a customs union.

The Austrians received a bitter blow in October 1862 when the second congress of the *Handelstag* reversed its position almost completely by adopting a resolution by a narrow majority which called for support for the Franco-Prussian trade agreement and made disparaging remarks about Austria's economic backwardness and the ill-effects of the economic rivalry within Germany. This was a remarkable change in the attitude of the *Handelstag* and obliged the president, Hansemann, who had grown increasingly critical of Prussian policy and was thus more inclined towards Austria and protectionism, to resign in protest.

The Rivalry of Austria and Prussia

The trade agreement with France and the increasing antagonism between Prussia and Austria all happened within the context of a recovering and expanding economy. Prussia was now making a bid to become a great economic power that would stand beside England and France. But would it be able to do this? To Georg von Siemens, later to become director of the *Deutsche Bank*, Prussia would only be able to stand beside the industrial giants if the *Zollverein* and Prussia were to become one, and if Prussia were to annex Schleswig and Holstein. Otherwise Prussia would sink to the level of a colony, 'like Portugal, Turkey or Jamaica'. The consciousness that Prussia had reached a turning-point in its economic development is part of the reason for the extraordinary virulence and aggressiveness of Bismarck's policy.

Prussia thus decided to continue with its trade policy regardless of the objections of the south German states. Complaints and resolutions by Bavaria and Württemberg about the Franco-Prussian trade agreement were simply answered by concluding a similar agreement with Belgium, signed in March 1862, without consultation with the *Zollverein*. On the other hand, the diplomatic experiences of 1863 were cautioning. The pro-Russian and anti-Polish policy of the Alvensleben convention had left Prussia dangerously isolated after a strong reaction from France which led to talks between Paris and Vienna. Bismarck thus determined to continue along the traditional lines of Prussian trade policy of excluding Austria from the *Zollverein*, but at the same time offering to co-operate politically with Austria against the dangers of revolution in Poland, upheaval in Schleswig and even against the challenges to the social order at home. Differences in economic policy could be combined with co-operation against the 'revolution', in whatever guise it might appear. Trade rivalry might be replaced by an agreement to differ.

The Schleswig-Holstein question, which was raised once more when the Danish Parliament called for the incorporation of Schleswig into the Danish state in November 1863, offered Bismarck an ideal opportunity to implement this policy. Co-operation with Austria over the question of the duchies and assurances that the aim of Prussian policy was to be accommodating over the tariff question were combined with an insistence that the *Zollverein* should accept the French and Belgian trade agreements and adopt the Prussian tariff as the basis of any further discussions in the *Zollverein*. Talk of the customs union with Austria, which Bismarck never for a moment believed would ever come about, was the most effective way of keeping the German states in check. With widespread opposition to the idea of a customs union in Austria, and with only Bavaria firmly committed to the union, it was reasonable to assume that time was on the side of Prussia and that eventually the *Zollverein* states would accept Prussia's terms.

Yet even during the war against Denmark it seemed that the *Zollverein* might fall apart and in its place would be two customs unions, a southern union led by Bavaria and including Württemberg, Hesse, Nassau, Hanover and possibly Electoral Hesse, and a northern union under Prussia with Saxony, Thuringia, Brunswick, Oldenburg, Frankfurt, Baden and, with a bit of luck, Electoral Hesse. Negotiations began in Munich for the formation of the southern union, but from the outset it was plain that the object of the new union was to win better terms from Prussia and it was never designed to establish a completely separate customs system. Moreover Austria was the key to the success of the southern union, and she was in a precarious financial situation, faced with mounting opposition at home to any policy that smacked of free trade, and with the Schleswig-Holstein affair she was politically bound to Prussia.

Bismarck's policy was now to get those states which were most favourable to the Prussian position to accept the Franco-Prussian trade agreement. The first such agreement was reached with Saxony in May 1864. Saxony accepted the agreement with France and agreed to renew the *Zollverein* treaties for a further twelve years. Within a few weeks this was followed by similar treaties with Thuringia, Brunswick, Frankfurt, Baden and, after issuing a rather brusque ultimatum, with Electoral Hesse. In October the southern states accepted the conditions of the 'North German *Zollverein*', realising that they had no real choice in the matter. Austria could not offer a viable alliance, and economic interests demanded an arrangement with Prussia and the north. Prussia had thus reformed the tariff, secured the trade agreement with France, placated the economic liberals, excluded Austria and satisfied part of the liberal nationalist demands by the annexation with Austria of Schleswig and Holstein. For Bismarck it was now important to complete the process and to exclude Austria from the German Confederation and break off the remaining links between Austria and the *Zollverein*. In April 1865 Prussia signed a separate treaty with Austria which saw a considerable reduction of the tariffs on most manufactured goods, particularly on metal goods, while corn continued to be free from duty. Tariffs were raised on some commodities such as glass, porcelain and cheese. In the following month the *Zollverein* treaty was extended for a further twelve years.

The *de facto* annexation of Schleswig and Holstein offered an attractive field for investment and expansion, and served to bring a number of industrialists and bankers over to Bismarck's side. Mevissen of the Schaffhausensche Bankverein was the leading figure among those who wished to exploit the possibilities of the provinces, and along with von der Heydt in his capacity as a private banker and Hansemann's son Adolf who had taken over the Diskontogesellschaft, he formed a committee to urge the construction of a canal from the North Sea to the Baltic and the development of Kiel as a naval base.

The Economic Crisis of 1866

Although these developments amounted to an endorsement of Bismarck's policies by a powerful sector of finance and industry, a war with Austria was felt to be a dangerously risky undertaking by most businessmen. There was panic selling on the stock exchanges and a frantic rush to withdraw deposits from the banks. The conviction was widespread that Bismarck was leading Prussia to defeat and economic ruin. Some cool-headed bankers like Bleichröder, Bismarck's personal banker since his days in Frankfurt, and Hansemann made windfall profits out of this situation of panic. The rapid end to the war and the overwhelming Prussian victory did something to restore confidence, although heavy industry was badly hurt by the crisis.

It would be a mistake, however, to assume that the economic crisis of 1866 was purely the result of uncertainty caused by the war between Prussia and Austria. The crisis was by no means confined to Germany but had world-wide ramifications. The American Civil War had ended in 1865 bringing to a close the cotton famine that had only partly been overcome by imports from Egypt and India. The tremendous sense of relief in the business world at the ending of the Civil War soon turned into an excessive speculative enthusiasm, over-production and the bankruptcy of several firms, including a major London bank.

The prosperity of the 1860s in commerce and trade and in banking and industry was interrupted by the war between Prussia and Austria in 1866, but the economy had been showing signs of over-heating as early as the autumn of 1865. There had been a marked move of investment capital away from the traditional and secure government bonds to more lucrative industrial shares. The Berlin banks were increasingly successful in getting foreign capital for investment in Germany and thus making up for their own shortage of capital. The poor performance of the Austrian and Hungarian economies prompted the Diskontogesellschaft to enter the Austrian capital market in search of bargains and to make up for the shortcomings of banks like the Rothschilds in Frankfurt and Vienna who were no longer able to meet the demands of the Austrian government for fresh bond issues. In this process the Diskontogesellschaft gradually absorbed the Rothschilds in Frankfurt. The result of all this activity was that Germany was entering another period of critical over-production less than a decade after the first major world crisis, and only five years after the country had pulled out of that slump. Prices began to fall, the demand for coal dropped, and the stock exchanges became somewhat sluggish even though the prices of many key shares remained high. Political uncertainties after the treaty of Gastein were coupled with growing domestic political tensions. When war looked inevitable stock prices began to fall. Those who hoped that the war would stimulate the economy as the war against Denmark seemed to have done were soon disappointed. Industrialists seriously misjudged the increase in consumption, and orders did not match production. Hoping that the market would pick up, they were faced with a recession. News of the collapse of the English bankers Overend Guerney and Company caused grave concern. The bank rate rose by 50 per cent from 6 per cent to 9 per cent so that the brakes were applied firmly to the economy. But the recession proved to be short-lived. Soon the economy was recovering to enter another period of steady growth. The war had been quickly finished without the serious disruptions that many had feared, and it strengthened and invigorated the Prussian economy and the Berlin stock exchange was more active than ever. But it was not until the victory over France that Germany entered a period of hectic boom that was to last for three exhilarating years.

The crisis in London reached a peak in May, and the war with Austria began in June 1866. Thus the war was fought within the context of a world-wide crisis, and problems of credit and general uncertainty over the outcome of the war were exacerbated by the international crisis. Rising unemployment, sinking wages and the stagnation of the market were made all the more harsh by the failure of the harvest in 1867, the effects of which were made far worse by the determination of the Junkers to maintain their exports. The financial crisis was over more quickly in Prussia than in southern Germany, share prices climbing up again with the euphoria of victory. The tightening of the credit market was exceedingly hard for the heavily indebted farmers, so that the small farmers of southern Germany were particularly hard hit. But governments were also affected. Rothschild in Frankfurt was getting into serious difficulties and was unable to handle the 4.5 per cent Württemberg war loan, floated to pay off the indemnity to Prussia. Württemberg therefore had to increase the rate to 6 per cent to make it more attractive, and was obliged to use the services of other banks in Stuttgart. Württemberg had to throw its loan on the market at 91, whereas Bavaria had to make do with $89^3/_8$. Capital reserves in the south were hopelessly depleted. Thus the south had to look to Berlin, where the capital market was rapidly improving. The days of Frankfurt and the Rothschilds were clearly numbered.

A further blow to the Rothschilds was the termination of their exclusive right to handle Prussian bonds in southern Germany. The

Prussian government now relied more heavily than ever on the Diskonto-gesellschaft, which was to be one of the great victors of 1866.

The Economic Effects of the Defeat of Austria

The reorganisation of northern Germany after the defeat of Austria enabled Prussia to have continuous territory from the Memel to the Rhine. The annexations of Hanover, Electoral Hesse, Nassau and Frankfurt as well as the duchies of Schleswig and Holstein were combined with the creation of a federal state, the North German Confederation, which gave Prussia control of all of Germany north of the river Main. Southern Germany was to be bound to Prussia by military alliances and by economic policy, its liberal elements attracted by the universal manhood suffrage to the North German Parliament which Bismarck managed to push through against the opposition of his appalled conservative critics. Its federal nature was made to appear flexible enough so as not to deter the southern Germans from joining the new confederation. This policy showed almost immediate success. One by one the southern German states, out of a mixture of economic, military and political motives, began negotiations with Prussia.

In order to institutionalise these treaties the Prussian government decided to seize the opportunity of the revision of the *Zollverein* treaty in order to create a 'customs Parliament' (*Zollparlament*) which would be responsible for all questions of tariffs and trade agreements, and would be elected by universal suffrage. A Prussian president and the right of veto would ensure that the new *Zollparlament* would be compliant to Prussia's wishes, and would hopefully be a stage towards the creation of an all-German Parliament, also under Prussian domination, that would complete the task of the unification of Germany, excluding Austria. But the problem was already arising as to whether Austria might change her attitude towards tariffs and also favour free trade, in which case her exclusion from the *Zollverein* might pose problems. The creation of the Dual Monarchy after the *Ausgleich* of 1867 meant that the Austrian government had to pay more attention to the free-trading wishes of Hungarian agricultural interests. The Austrians were prepared to make far more concessions to the southern German states than ever before, and France, angered at Prussia's refusal to come to terms on the question of compensation for the benevolent neutrality she had shown in 1866, was becoming increasingly close to Austria. Bismarck was thus faced with the possibility of a successful diplomatic and economic *coup* by the new Austrian Minister President Beust by creating a common front of Austria-Hungary, the south German states and France against Prussia, thus destroying his plans for a Prussian-dominated small Germany. The thrust of Beust's policy was particularly aggravating because Prussia was still in the midst of organising the North German Confederation, and thus in a weak position to take decisive steps towards securing the complete compliance of the south German states to Bismarck's schemes.

A further problem was the attitude of France. The success of the military agreements with the south German states made the French all the more anxious that Bismarck's schemes for a *Zollparlament* should not succeed. France did not want to see a united 'small' Germany, and knew full well that tariff policy was a means that Bismarck was using to achieve this aim. After the settlement of the Luxemburg question, which was a set-back for French policy, Bismarck decided to move ahead. In June 1867 a conference was held in Berlin between the Ministers of the south German states and the North German Confederation, with Bismarck in the chair. The topic for discussion was the reorganisation of the *Zollverein* along the lines suggested by Prussia. The south German states, pushed by their economic self-interest and seeing no viable alternative, agreed to the proposal for a *Zollparlament* elected by universal suffrage, for an upper chamber (*Zollbundesrat*), and to give the presidency to Prussia.

The *Zollparlament* was designed by Bismarck to satisfy the economic demands of the liberals to placate their nationalist feelings and to divert them from political liberalism. The experiment was designed painstakingly by Rudolf Delbrück who was moved from the Ministry of Trade to become Bismarck's right-hand man and 'chief of the general staff' of the free-trading liberals as head of Bismarck's office as Chancellor. To Bismarck and Delbrück it was a resounding success. Prominent liberals like Miquel (who worked under Hansemann in the Diskontogesellschaft) or Bennigsen (who was particularly involved in railways and was on the board of a number of companies), who led the national-liberal party which included a number of other businessmen and financiers whose main concern was for an economically united Germany, were thus prepared to accept Bismarck's policies. As Bismarck had been so successful with this policy in the North German Reichstag there was every reason to hope that it would work within the all-German context of a *Zollparlament*. The clear identification of Bismarck with the forces of capitalism and nationalism and the support afforded to him by the

National Liberal party was regarded as highly undesirable by the conservatives. The Junkers, even though they were free-traders and supporters of the *Zollverein*, were alarmed at his constitutional experiments, his enthusiasm for universal suffrage and the political company he kept. Those conservatives who came from banking and industrial circles as well as from the upper echelons of the civil service, the 'grandees' of industrial Germany, remained haughtily aloof from the national liberals, but their party, the 'free conservatives', pursued almost identical policies. The free conservatives supported Bismarck's German policy because they realised the opportunities which it offered. Railway-building, armaments, banking and heavy industry all stood to gain from a united German market. The great magnates of Silesia and the bankers of Berlin were all too willing to compromise their pristine conservatism for the sake of the economic advantages which Bismarck's policies promised.

It soon became clear that Bismarck had made a serious miscalculation. The elections to the *Zollparlament* in southern Germany showed how strong was the opposition to his schemes in spite of the massive economic strength of Prussia. Anti-Prussianism in the south was political rather than economic. Catholic clericals, particularists, pro-Austrian 'Greater Germans' and democrats who called for a boycott of the elections proved to have far greater popular support than the businessmen and industrialists who supported any move towards the creation of an economically united Germany. For socialists like Bebel and Liebknecht the elections posed an awkward dilemma. They could neither support the narrow particularists nor the pro-Prussians and they refused to accept the arguments in favour of a boycott. They called for a democratic Germany that would include Austria, for the step-by-step introduction of free trade which would allow time for German industry to be strengthened, and for a reduction of taxation to reduce the heavy burden placed on those least able to pay and to weaken the massive Prussian military establishment. The elections returned a solid anti-Prussian majority and the south Germans immediately set about frustrating plans to use the *Zollparlament* as an instrument of Prussian power. Whether by accident or design, the sermon at the opening service for the session of the *Zollparlament* was preached on the text: 'I have sheep, but they are not from my fold.' Bismarck would have appreciated the point. Caught between the Prussian conservatives and the south German particularists, Bismarck could do little more than bide his time, convinced that the 'national idea' would in the long run triumph over the prejudices of the past and that economic self-interest would help the medicine go down. For the moment it was clear that the elections of 1868 were a firm rejection of the idea of extending the competence of the *Zollparlament* so that it might serve to unite Germany by 'resolutions and majority votes'. Bismarck seemed to have made the same miscalculation that the men of 1848 had made, the men whom he had mocked in his 'blood and iron' speech. The economic strength of Prussia and the attractions of the *Zollverein* did not lead automatically to German unity, even though these factors were of considerable importance in helping Bismarck to achieve the foundation of the Reich.

In spite of the opposition of the Greater Germans and the protectionists, the trade treaty with Austria was accepted by the *Zollparlament* in May 1868. The trade agreement with France was also ratified. Trade treaties were signed with a number of overseas countries, and proposals were put forward for the acquisition of overseas colonies, and among these suggestions were ideas for German colonies in Formosa, New Zealand, Java and La Plata. Delbrück, Michaelis and the free-traders pursued a policy of steady tariff reduction, in spite of the bitter complaints of the protectionist industrialists and south Germans. The tariff on iron was halved in 1870, and the tariffs on many other commodities were either reduced or abolished altogether. Yet in spite of these achievements in the economic field the political unity of Germany seemed as far away as ever. Economic interests and political passions seemed to be pulling in opposite directions, and Bismarck's hope that the political would follow meekly behind the economic proved to be illusory. Indeed the anti-Prussians turned the economic weapons of the *Zollparlament* against Prussia.

Rapid economic expansion in Prussia after 1866, which included ambitious railway projects, resulted in a great shortage of capital, made all the more acute by the expense of the war against Austria. Foreign capital proved hard to get. France preferred to invest in Austria, and the British demanded terms which the Prussians regarded as excessively stringent. The south Germans used Prussia's financial embarrassment to block moves to increase taxes and to continue the lowering of the tariffs. Thus an increase in the tobacco tax, designed to bring in 2 million thalers, was reduced only to allow an extra 200,000 thalers. The left ran an effective campaign against the tobacco tax, arguing that the revenue would be used to increase the army and to turn all of Germany into one vast Prussian barracks. Bismarck was again forced to wait on events, still confident that time was on his side.

Events moved rapidly and were manipulated by Bismarck with ruthless brilliance. The story is familiar how the crisis over the Hohenzollern candidature for the Spanish crown and the heavy-handed French diplomacy was used by Bismarck to provoke France into declaring war and to make Prussia seem the innocent victim. Blood and iron was at last to achieve what resolutions and majority votes on tariffs and trade governments could never do. On 18 January 1871 King William of Prussia was proclaimed German emperor. The success of the German army against France gave it a prestige, influence and popularity such as it had not enjoyed since the days of the wars against Napoleon. The economic interests that had played such an important part in preparing the ground for the unification of Germany now seemed to be eclipsed by the military and the conservatives. Almost half the members of the new German Reichstag were aristocrats. The bankers, industrialists and liberals seemed to have been pushed aside to make way for the heroes of the hour. But this shift in power was not to last very long, for Germany entered a period of rapid growth and frantic speculation, fuelled by the French indemnity and patriotic enthusiasm. In the 'Foundation Years' (*Gründerjahre*) it seemed that nothing could stop the growth of wealth, power and prosperity of the new state. It was hoped that the banks and the factories would complete the task which the military had begun.

Industrial Growth in the 1860s

The economic history of Germany from 1860 to 1870 is not simply a matter of an endless series of tariff negotiations and trade agreements. Less dramatic but profoundly important in their results were the changes taking place within the structure of the economy. Fresh capital was pumped into the Rhineland and Westphalia by the Berlin banks. The Diskontogesellschaft bought up mines and smelting companies that had suffered badly from the depression and Bleichröder followed suit, both in the hopes of gaining a substantial stake in the economic recovery of Germany as the country pulled gradually out of the slump. In place of foreign capital from France, England, Belgium and Holland the joint-stock companies of the Ruhr came to rely on the domestic market. This process served further to underline the growing disparity between the industrial west and the agrarian east. Capital looking for speculative returns moved to the west, so that eastern agrarians began to fear that they would not be able to find the funds to improve their estates and build an adequate transportation network to ensure the competitive sale of their agricultural produce, a situation that was particularly galling as the bank deposits of the agrarians were being used to capitalise industry.

By 1861 there were clear signs that Prussia was pulling out of the slump and beginning a period of growth. Austria, however, showed little indication of recovery, for the disastrous defeat of 1859 placed a heavy burden on a backward economy and destroyed confidence in Austrian bonds. Southern Germany, and particularly the banking centre Frankfurt, felt the effect of this disruption very strongly, so the defeat of Austria in Italy helped to place Prussia in a commanding position for the economic battle in Germany. The Berlin stock exchange experienced increasing activity, and the banks thrived not only because of the increasing involvement in industrial investment, but also because Berlin was becoming a more important capital market as Frankfurt was hampered by the failures of Austria both politically and economically.

The 1860s were also years of important industrial innovations in which the banks and stock exchange were to play a vital role, unlike the earlier period of German industrial development. The foundations were laid in these years of the German dye industry which was to become one of Germany's major industrial achievements. The Höchst works, as they were later to become, were founded in 1863 under the name Meister Lucius and Company, but did not become a public company until 1880. The firm specialised in dyestuffs and drugs. In the same year the Bayer works were founded, but Friedrich Bayer and Company was from the beginning a public company. In 1861 Friedrich Engelhorn started a factory producing aniline colours. By 1865 the company was reorganised, thanks to the efforts of two of Liebig's students from Giessen and a massive injection of capital by the banker Seligman, to become the *Badische Anilin- und Sodafabrik* (BASF) in Ludwigshafen with 1.5 million guilders capital and within a year 130 workers. The company produced a wide range of chemicals, and by 1870 it employed almost 500 workers.

In other branches of industry exciting new possibilities were opened up. The electrical firm Siemens and Halske had been founded in 1847 and specialised in the production of telegraph wire covered in gutta-percha so that it would not be affected by moisture. The firm thrived thanks to government contracts to build telegraph lines, the first of which went from Berlin to Frankfurt so that the deliberations of the Parliament of 1848 could be relayed back to the Prussian capital. In the 1850s Siemens and Halske specialised in underwater cables, the first such cable having been laid by the English between Dover and Calais in 1851. These endeavours proved to be unprofitable, and when their cable from Spain to Oran broke shortly after it was laid the firm faced serious financial difficulties. Halske left the firm in 1867. One Siemens brother went to England, another went copper-mining in the Caucasus. But when it seemed that the firm was falling apart Werner Siemens, the original founder of the firm, discovered the principle of the electric dynamo. He delivered a paper on the device to the Berlin Academy of Sciences in 1866, and from the very outset it is clear that he had discovered something the potential of which was revolutionary, indeed almost as significant as the discovery of the steam engine. By 1872 Siemens employed 543 men and his firm was flourishing, but it was yet to become an industrial giant.

The 1860s also saw a revolutionary change within the steel industry and the beginning of the 'age of steel'. The Bessemer convertor had been invented in England in 1856, and Alfred Krupp was the first European steel producer to introduce the new method in 1860. The Bessemer process was simpler, cheaper and more efficient than any previous method of producing cast steel. It produced in 20 minutes the same quantity as the puddling process in 24 hours. In place of resmelting in crucibles, the method Krupp had used, hot air was blown through molten pig iron through the bottom of the tilting convertor. The carbon in the iron acted as a fuel, raising the heat and enabling some of the carbon to combine with the iron to produce steel. The molten steel could then be tipped into a massive ladle which in turn poured the steel into the moulds. It is a clear indication of the enormous progress that had been made in German industry that the Bessemer process was introduced within three years of its discovery, whereas it had been almost fifty years before the puddling process had any widespread application.

Also in 1856 Friedrich August Siemens, a younger brother of Werner Siemens, began working on the open-hearth furnace which was also used in France by the brothers Emile and Pierre Martin. The principle of the open-hearth process was to use hot exhaust gases from the furnace to heat the draught. The advantage of what was to become known as the 'Siemens-Martin process' was that large charges of iron, either pig, scrap or ore, could be melted at one time. The steel was also a better quality than Bessemer steel and far cheaper than crucible steel. Krupp introduced the Siemens-Martin process in his works in 1865, although the process was not widely used until much later.

The main drawback with both the Bessemer and the Siemens-Martin processes was that only high-grade ores could be used, which for the Germans meant Swedish ore. It was not until 1879 when Gilchrist Thomas discovered a method for extracting phosphorus from the ore that lower-grade ores could be used to produce good steel. But the Bessemer and Siemens-Martin processes were enough to make the 1860s the decade in which the German metal industries made the greatest increase in output in the nineteenth century. The production of cast iron and steel doubled during this period, and cast steel production in the *Zollverein* increased from 34,259 tonnes in 1861 to 161,829 tonnes in 1869. With the construction of large rolling mills, Krupp building his in 1864, the production of items like railway track could be speeded up. Krupp was soon exporting railway track throughout the world. The efficient and relatively cheap production of iron and steel meant that steel was increasingly used as a construction material in place of wood, and iron for boats, railways and weaponry. The age of steel was thus a prelude and a precondition of the age of imperialism, for without it the fleets, the armies and the railways could never have been built.

These increases in the iron and steel industry were only made possible by similar increases in the output of coal and ores and in larger imports of ore. Similarly the achievements of the metal industries stimulated the further growth of coal and ore extraction. Coal production more than doubled in the 1860s, lignite by 75 per cent. Iron-ore production increased more than two and a half times and copper increased at about the same rate. Lead production, by contrast, dropped 30 per cent, but zinc ores increased by the same 30 per cent. These increases were made possible by rationalisation, by the employment of a larger work-force, by stepping up the intensity of labour, and by the introduction of more machinery driven by steam engines. There was no revolutionary change in techniques as there was in the steel industry.

The 1860s saw the foundation of a number of firms that were to become enormously important in years to come. Eberhard Junghans started his clock factory in 1861 and it was soon to become Germany's largest clock and watch factory. In the following year Adam Opel started a small sewing machine factory at Rüsselsheim. Opel had learnt this trade in a French sewing-machine factory, but he was to become world-famous as a manufacturer of automobiles. Ernst Leitz started to work for a small optical company in Wetzlar in 1864. Five years later he was the head of the firm, and the company that was to produce the Leica camera, which became almost a symbol of the skill and excellence of German industry, was on its way. In 1865 Wilhelm Gustav Dyckerhoff, with a building supplier Lang, started a cement factory in Karlsruhe which was the beginning of Germany's largest cement works. Germany was thus laying the groundwork in the 1860s for the next stage in industrialisation in which it was to become so exceptionally successful. This decade saw the establishment of the chemical, electrical and mechanical firms which were to make Germany a world leader in the new technology.

The Bourgeoisie

As the deliberations in the *Zollparlament* and the many interest groups in the 1860s show, the German bourgeoisie was growing in power and influence, even though it was excluded from its rightful share in the decision-making process. In a country dominated by the land-owning aristocracy, it proved difficult for the bourgeoisie to find an appropriate self-image. Some felt an acute sense of inferiority in the presence of the aristocracy, and tried to emulate the habits and prejudices of their social superiors. Others felt a deep resentment of the privileges of the aristocracy and emphasised their independence and achievements in a manner which the aristocracy regarded as vulgar, ostentatious and immoderate. The aristocracy of today are often the parvenus of yesterday, and the German *nouveaux riches* were all too often anxious to follow in the footsteps of those whom they admired and found a new dynasty whose sordid origins in industry and trade would soon be forgotten.

The German aristocracy, with its dread of losing an entry in the Almanach de Gotha, was unwilling to marry off its children to wealthy members of the middle class, so that with very few exceptions, which included at a later period Krupp and Stumm, this avenue of social advancement was closed to industrialists. In place of aristocratic titles the prosperous middle class were awarded their own titles. Those who shared their zealous devotion to God, King and Fatherland and had kept their noses clean in the constitutional crisis might be given the coveted title of *Kommerzienrat* (Commercial Councellor). Holders of the title formed an elite of the new bourgeoisie, and they were bound to the existing order by their desire to be distinguished and rewarded for their devotion to the monarchical and aristocratic system. Service in the army, particularly as a reserve officer, or the purchase of a large estate were favoured ways to improve one's social standing. As army officer and landowner one seemed two-thirds of the way to becoming a true aristocrat.

Yet there were still many bourgeois who were appalled at this aping of the manners of the aristocracy, whom they regarded as a backward and parasitic caste. Their wasteful spending was also in marked contrast to the traditional bourgeois virtues of thrift and hard work, the virtues which Gustav Freytag praised in his second-rate but best-selling novel, *Soll und Haben*, and they had little liking for the army and the behaviour of the officers' mess. These men carried on the traditional disciplined, simple and patriarchal life of the early industrialists, whose life had been a constant struggle to keep going. They valued their independence above everything else, and often refused titles and honours on the grounds that they involved obligations and commitments that they were not prepared to make. Alfred Krupp refused all titles and decorations, was free from any snobbish admiration for the aristocracy, and became the archetypal *grand seigneur* of the new industrial bourgeoisie. Yet he also built a vast and tasteless palace, gave magnificent receptions, went on his travels like some potentate, and ruled his industrial empire as an absolute monarch. His example was followed by all those who had comparable success: Thyssen, Kirdorf, Röchling, Hoesch. Yet for all their consciousness of being a separate caste from the aristocracy, the big industrialists' attitude towards their firms and their works was very similar to that of the aristocratic landowners to their estates. There was the same insistence on the absolute authority of the head of the firm, family or estate and the identical feeling that the firm was a world of its own held together by a community of interests which bound owner and apprentice together in a cause that was far greater than either of them. There was the same rigid discipline and strict supervision coupled with a certain concern for the welfare of the workers, a concern which helped to bind the workers closer to the firm and strengthen the feeling of *Gemeinschaft*, of an organic community. The welfare system provided for the *Kruppianer* was regarded as exemplary, and dates from mid-century. At the same time Krupp would warn his workers to leave politics alone, to accept the existing order, and to spend their free time with their families in breeding and raising the new generation of *Kruppianer*. Such autocratic and patriarchal attitudes show how deeply the leading industrialists were influenced by the ideas and the ideals of the semi-feudal aristocracy. The 1860s thus saw the clear emergence of the 'industrial feudalism' which was to be a distinguishing mark of German life in the late nineteenth century. The industrial magnates were powerful factors in arresting the social and political development of Germany. By and large they were content with the economic policies of the Prussian government and of the *Zollverein*, and began to fear that political democracy might encourage demands for industrial democracy, so that without the autocratic state there could be no autocratic factory. Even those who had pinned their hopes on the emancipatory movements of 1848 and in the constitutional crisis were increasingly disillusioned and looked for the compensation of being master in one's own house and in the share they were able to get from an expanding economy.

Thus either by the distinct style of a Krupp, or by the pursuit of honours, titles and commissions, the bourgeoisie was assimilated by the autocratic and aristocratically dominated state. Their mode of thinking was formed by the pressure to conform to a style of life that was not their own, and a specifically bourgeois style of life was gradually crushed and deformed. A social order that was no longer adequate to the needs of a modern industrial society was thus not only able to survive but was supported and strengthened, either actively or subconsciously, by those elements which should have been among the most determined to overthrow it. By refusing the democratisation of the social and political life of the country the social tensions within Germany were to become increasingly acute, and could only be overcome by manipulative and demagogic politics which, in the long run, made the situation even worse.

The German bourgeoisie had many great achievements to its credit. It had resolutely championed the cause of economic expansion and the results were impressive. It had been the major force behind the unification of the country which, by finally destroying the barriers and divisions within Germany, made further growth possible. But on the other hand, it bears the heavy responsibility that the form in which unification was achieved was marked by reactionary politics and militarism. Unification, far from liberating men from the shackles of the past, subjected Germany to a form of Caesaristic domination that was to stifle the growth of democratic and emancipatory forces.

The success and growing prosperity of the bourgeoisie accounts in large part for its betrayal of the liberal cause. It had too much to lose in the event of a social upheaval which it feared might get out of hand. It was blinded by the successes of Bismarck's policies. Liberals abandoned their political beliefs and preached 'political realism'. Miquel summed up the feelings of many national liberals when he told the voters of Osnabrück in December 1866: 'The time for ideals is over. German unity has moved from the world of dreams to the prosaic world of reality. Politicians have less right than ever today to ask what is desirable, but rather what is possible.'

The Junkers

Although less spectacular, the growth in the agricultural sector was steady throughout the period. It was also subject to the fluctuations that reflected the state of the economy as well as natural conditions. In both 1856 and 1865 agriculture was hurt by a shortage of capital and falling prices. After 1848 the price of land had risen rapidly, and many of the south German states had introduced legislation to forbid the sale of agricultural land if the residue were not deemed sufficient to maintain a family. This did something to stop excessive speculation, but it did not help the process of the formation of larger and more effective productive units. Prussia continued on a liberal course. High land prices, coupled with a real-estate boom in the urban areas, placed an intolerable strain on the capital supply. Thus interest rates tended to go up at precisely the time when farmers were most in debt. When they were hurt by the further problem of falling prices, often fuelled by increased imports, agriculture faced a real crisis.

Land prices rose steadily from mid-century until, in part as a result of the Great Depression, they began to fall in 1877. On the other hand, agricultural tools and machinery were cheaper in the 1860s than they had been in the 1850s due to improved production techniques, economies of scale, competition and the importation of British and French machinery in the free-trade period of the Cobden Tariff. Although prices fluctuated considerably, they were cheaper at the end of the decade than at the beginning.

The relative success of the modernisation of agriculture enabled the east Elbian Junkers to preserve their privileged position and strengthened the confidence and assurance of the traditional élites. Free trade guaranteed them satisfactory markets for their produce and enabled them to obtain the machinery they so badly needed to modernise their estates and improve the productivity of their land. Unlike the poor peasants, the large aristocratic landowners had easy access to cheap credit and a number of tax exemptions. By putting new land under the plough (between 1816 and 1866 the amount of agricultural land in Prussia doubled) and by systematic and modern farming methods the productivity of the land steadily increased and was able to rise at a greater rate than the rise in the population. At the time of the foundation of the German Reich in 1871, the land-owning aristocracy was at the height of its economic power, even though Germany was now an important industrial nation. Their privileged position had been further assisted by the massive injection of capital in the form of compensation for the abolition of the remaining feudal rights which had been ended in 1848. Although more and more bourgeois bought up aristocratic estates they usually became slightly ridiculous copies of the Junkers themselves, taking pride in their ostentatiously Neanderthal political views and their snobbish obsessions with genealogy. Here again the process of the feudalisation of the bourgeoisie worked its magic. The aristocracy looked down on these absurd figures, and were comforted by the fact that they were often far less successful as farmers.

The Working Class

The aristocracy had been able to maintain its political and economic position, and the middle classes shared in the profits of an expanding economy, but the German working class was also becoming more self-conscious and during the 1860s the first modern working-class parties were formed. In 1863 Ferdinand Lassalle founded the General German Workers' Association (*Allgemeine Deutsche Arbeiterverein*), a party which called for universal suffrage and reform within the existing framework of the state. Lassalle's party was social-democratic rather than revolutionary. The Social-democratic Workers' party was founded at Eisenach in 1869. Led by Wilhelm Liebknecht, the Eisenach party was associated with the First International, influenced by the writings of Marx and Engels and more radical in its demands than the Lassalleans. Although the party was to be sharply criticised by Marx, and although its practice was even more restrained than its programme, the party was a loyal member of the International and, unlike the Lassalleans, a determined opponent of Bismarck's reactionary policies. In 1875 at Gotha the two parties were amalgamated to form the Socialist Workers' party (SAP – later SPD). With the amalgamation the party was soon to become a mass party, even though its work was interrupted by Bismarck's anti-socialist laws. Its ideology was a simplified Marxism, and too many concessions had been made to the Lassalleans at the Gotha conference for it to be a revolutionary socialist party. But it was to enable the German working class to have the best organised and most politically educated party in Europe. Without adequate political organisation it was clear that the German working class would be unable to gain its fair share of the increase in real wealth of the country. The party was remarkably successful, for by 1878 it was the fourth-largest party in the Reichstag. Although it may have lacked revolutionary *élan*, and been a trifle too willing to compromise with the existing system for all its revolutionary rhetoric, there can be no doubt whatever that of all the parties in Germany, it stood most firmly for the extension of democratic freedoms and for the emancipation of society from the burden of the autocratic and militaristic state form of Bismarck's Reich.

If the foundations of the Industrial Revolution in Germany were laid in the late 1830s and strengthened in the 1840s, the upward trend from 1848 to 1873 showed that Germany had finally arrived among the great industrial nations. Even the crisis of 1847 which disrupted this development for some years did not reverse this process. Dating the Industrial Revolution in Germany from 1834 to 1873 may provoke the criticism that such a lengthy process can hardly be given the title of 'revolution', but the process of social and economic transformation is highly complex and exceedingly lengthy. The precise dating of the revolution is very often a matter of definitions. Does the revolution date from the introduction of the first machinery that was to transform industry? Does it begin from the time that the first signs of massive capital investment in industry appear? Does it date from the time that there is a sudden dramatic kink in the curve of industrial growth? Or from the date when there is a sharp increase in the *per capita* output of the workers? Each of these criteria have been used by economic historians, either singly or in various combinations, but there is general agreement that the face of Germany was dramatically changed in the forty years after the formation of the *Zollverein*, and that the process was one of intermittent, jerky yet irreversible growth. In this process the 1860s mark the culmination of the previous trend. Whereas the productivity of the individual worker had increased approximately 8.5 per cent in the 1850s, in the following decade it rose by 42 per cent, a dramatic indication of the massive investments in modern techniques that had taken place, the improvement of production processes, but also of the intensification of labour. *Per capita* incomes increased, although the growth of real *per capita* income was retarded by inflation. By 1871 and the foundation of the German Empire, the industrial and the agricultural revolution was successfully completed, but revolutionary change of the political and social order had been halted in its tracks, and many of the modest gains that had been made as sops to the liberal and democratic elements were to be reversed in the course of the reactionary period of the Great Depression.

6 FROM BOOM TO DEPRESSION

The Impact of the Defeat of France

In the euphoric days after the foundation of the Reich there was no talk of depression. Prussia and Germany soon recovered from the effects of the war with France and a period of hectic activity began, stimulated by further liberalisation of the laws governing joint-stock companies, by the enormous boost of morale that the foundation of the new empire gave to almost all Germans, the creation of a unified currency – the German mark – the annexation of Alsace and Lorraine and the five billion gold francs of reparations paid by France. The upward movement of the economy was not hindered by the economic ties to Austria, for Austria also was enjoying something of a boom, thanks to French investments after 1866 which were encouraged by the French government to strengthen Austria against Prussia. These investments continued even after the defeat of France in the Franco-Prussian war, and in part were made possible by a large loan from London.

In order to finance the reparations France was obliged to make a bond issue. In spite of some pessimistic forecasts it was a brilliant success, proving that, although defeated, Paris was the world's greatest money market after London. The issue was over-subscribed, so that the money could be handed over to the German government earlier than anyone had thought possible. Within three years almost the entire debt had been paid.

More than half of these reparations were used to reorganise and improve the German armies and to modernise the fortifications. The armaments industry and heavy industry were thus given huge sums and production was stepped up at an extraordinary rate. With almost 2.25 billion marks spent on the army in these years, the effect on the economy was very great.

More than one billion marks were used by the governments of the Reich to pay off debts and war loans, so that large amounts of funds were made available for productive investment. Money was also set aside to provide for a fund for the war wounded (561 million marks), the building of a Parliament building in Berlin (24 million) and for fortresses (159 million). Further sums were set aside for the building of a railway network in Alsace and Lorraine and for repairing war damages.

As the bond market had been drastically reduced, capital looked for lucrative investment in industry. The money supply was greatly increased. Prices rose sharply with wages following behind. There were over 600 strikes in the three years of the boom, almost all directed at pushing up wages to keep pace with inflation. This marked a very significant increase in the militancy of the working class, and on the whole the strikes were successful, for in these prosperous years the employers could afford a certain *largesse*.

Just as the period of rapid industrial growth after 1848 was marked by the formation of new banks which played a vital role in stimulating further growth, so the years after 1871 were ones of increased banking activity in which important new banks were started. The tradition of German banks as combinations of commercial banks, investment banks and investment trusts was continued and strengthened. German banks only invested modestly in bonds, Treasury bills, promissory notes and bills of exchange. Unlike British banks, much of their capital was invested in industry and trade and was used to help form new enterprises. Banks would group together to form syndicates that bought up the newly issued shares at fixed prices and then sold them to the public, usually keeping a sizeable proportion of the shares themselves in order to control the fluctuation of prices and to engage in speculation. In order to carry out these highly risky operations the banks needed very considerable capital reserves to be able to withstand any wild fluctuations in the economy or a sustained depression. Big banks and big industry were thus closely allied, and the success or failure of the one was to have a profound effect on the other. Traditionally, small German investors did their daily banking with local savings banks, so that the big banks were unable to gain very much from the growing deposits of the professional men and white-collar workers.

With the new spirit of confidence and national pride, many investors who had been reluctant in the past to speculate lost their inhibitions. As a result the amount of money handled by the banks doubled in the three years of the foundation boom. The banks built new branches in the commercial and industrial centres so that the close ties between banking and industry were further emphasised. The joint-stock banks, like the Diskontogesellschaft, the Schaffhausensche Bankverein, the Darmstädter Bank and the Berliner Handels-Gesellschaft concentrated on investment in industry, whereas the old private banks like Bleichröder and Mendelssohn remained more traditional in their banking methods and specialised in government bonds. From 1870 to 1873 the production of cast iron and steel more than doubled, and this was only possible because of the massive investments in the new techniques in the industry, which in turn made great demands on the capital market. This the joint-stock banks were prepared to meet. In the excitement of the foundation years too many banks were started with inadequate financial backing, hoping that speculative gains would serve to build up capital reserves. In Prussia alone in 1872, 49 new banks were formed. Among the great banks that date from this period are the *Deutsche Bank* (1870) formed by Georg von Siemens, and the *Dresdner Bank* (1872). In 1871, 207 new joint-stock companies were floated for a total of 758 million marks; in 1872, 479 for 1.5 billion marks; and in 1873, 242 for 544 million. Capital investment in new companies on this scale was not to be matched for the rest of the century, and only in 1899 did the amount of capital for new companies equal that of 1873, the year when the speculative boom burst.

These years also marked the triumph of the Berlin banks which before 1870 had been unable to play a very active role in company promotions in the Ruhr due to their lack of capital. The Berlin stock market was flooded with industrial shares and government paper lost its previous predominance. Investors seized upon the shares of the large heavy industrial companies of the west. Among the most attractive shares were those of the *Dortmunder Union*, which Hansemann and Grillo had created from the ruins of von Strousberg's industrial empire, or the *Gelsenkirchner Bergwerks AG* and the *Gutehoffnungshütte*. These companies were to become household names, their share prices eagerly studied by all who were in the swim of these exciting years. The new formations combined coal-mining with ore extraction and smelting and rapidly became the overbearing monopolies of imperial Germany; in this the Dortmunder Union was the leading example of a diversified company firmly linked to a big bank.

Before 1871 industrial shares had played an insignificant part in the activities of the stock exchanges, and most firms were small private affairs which were either unable or unwilling to go public. The boom years changed this completely. Only by the sale of shares could companies get hold of the capital they needed quickly and on the scale they required. Massive investments in heavy industry could not be met by the traditional methods of ploughing back profits or by simple bank loans. The net had to be cast wider. The triumph of the joint-stock company in the 1870s made possible the development of productive forces and strengthened the tendency towards centralisation and concentration of capital. Close ties between industry and banking, and the formation of large firms like the Dortmunder Union, which was able to build railways both at home and abroad entirely from its own resources from the mining of the coal to the manufacture of track and the financing of the entire project, were typical products of this period. Many smaller firms made share issues in these years, for few were able to survive without large injections of fresh capital, and such firms were increasingly threatened with being swallowed up by their mighty competitors.

As industrialists sought to increase share capital they naturally looked to Berlin, which had become the financial capital of the new Reich. Here the industrialists of the Ruhr and Silesia came into close association with the bankers and financiers and then with the politicians and civil servants of the capital. Many politicians played an active part in the economic life of the country, like Miquel of the national liberals and Kardorff of the free conservatives, the leaders of the two main parties supporting Bismarck and his policies. Kardorff had close connections with the Bleichröder Bank and with the industrialists of Upper Silesia. With Bleichröder he was largely responsible for the reorganisation of the *Königs- und Laurahütte*, a conglomerate organised on similar lines to the Dortmunder Union. He was also a prominent figure in railways and banking. Kardorff was active not only in the Reichstag but also in the formation of one of the largest interest groups, the Central Association of German Industrialists (*Zentralverband Deutscher Industrieller*) that was to play such an important role in German politics from its formation in 1876. The careers of such men show how fluid were the divisions between civil servants, politicians and industrialists. Men like Miquel were to reach the top of all three professions. Industry and banking were no longer slightly alarming and vulgar provincial concerns, they were recognised as the pillars on which the strength and authority of the new Reich rested. There was also the irresistible attraction of profit. Army officers and bureaucrats, aristocrats and churchmen, politicians and Ministers lost their inhibitions and their aversion to the squalid materialism of counting-house and factory and speculated wildly. Industrial shares thus also served to bind together the old aristocratic êlites and the big bourgeoisie of banking and industry.

This wave of speculation and new company flotations was made possible by a change in the law governing the formation of joint-stock companies. On 11 June 1870, after a rather perfunctory debate, the Reichstag passed a law which abolished the old state concessionary requirement that applied in most states and replaced it by a set of legal norms which did not go far enough to protect against wild speculation and gave inadequate protection to creditors. Not until 1884 was the law changed, due partly to the efforts of the *Verein für Sozialpolitik* (Social PolicyAssociation) and the organisation of German lawyers.

The boom was by no means confined to Germany, although in Germany it was particularly hectic owing to the psychological climate after the foundation of the Reich and because German industrial development had reached the stage where substantial quantitative and qualitative improvements were possible. Thus it was not only German industrial shares that flooded the stock exchanges, but foreign stock also found eager purchasers. Many of the new companies floated in these years were fraudulent and were solely designed for speculative profit on the stock exchange. Boundless speculation, unsound projects, bankruptcy and fraud were as much characteristics of the age as the spectacular growth of heavy industry. Dr Strousberg, whose railway empire had collapsed to be picked up by the Dortmunder Union, ceased to be a popular hero and was denounced as a swindler. In his autobiography he denounced the giddy times of the foundation years, saying that simple speculation became a mania and degenerated into swindle – a remark which prompted a stern historian to quote the German proverb that young whores become old Pharisees (*Betschwester*).

There was indeed much about these years that was unattractive, and there were all too many men like Strousberg who were prepared to mislead and defraud small investors lured by the prospects of large gains. Yet for the German economy to expand and grow, it was essential that the joint-stock company should become the accepted means of initial capital accumulation. The capital resources of the country had to be mobilised, and companies had to get hold of the capital they needed in order to meet the challenges of the new technology and of mass production.

The great magnates of Upper Silesia also found themselves increasingly dependent on the Berlin money market and were unable to maintain their complete independence. The importance of Berlin thus served to create a truly national economy as the particularism and regionalism finally gave way under the centralising effects not only of the new Reich but also of the dominant position of Berlin in banking and finance. Upper Silesian industry also found that only by stock issues could they meet their needs for fresh capital. This process completed the reorganisation of the economic life of the country in which the joint-stock company dominated industry and banking, and in which the major industrial centres were the Ruhr and Upper Silesia, with

Berlin as the banking centre. Berlin was to draw on the financial reserves of the rest of Germany to fuel the development of these two major growth areas.

These developments in the boom years were of great significance not only in terms of economic reorganisation and growth, but also in the changing relationship between government and the economy. The state no longer kept a close watch on the day-to-day operations of industry and finance, but concerned itself with creating a healthy political and fiscal climate in which industry and finance could thrive. Banking and industry was left to bankers and industrialists, and the close relationship between these activities and government were now due to individual and personal ties rather than a conscious attempt to bind the two together. Successful businessmen entered government service, and civil servants with their contacts within the bureaucracy were welcomed by industrialists and bankers and were all too willing to heed the siren call. To work for the great banks and industrial concerns was far more profitable than 'travailler pour le roi de Prusse'.

If the old ēlites were prepared to relinquish direct control over the economy and if some were prepared to join the bourgeoisie in the dance around the golden calf, as contemporary critics were wont to put it, they certainly did not intend to abandon their political power and influence. Indeed these concessions to *Manchestertum* formed the price that had to be paid so that the old alliance of conservative landed aristocracy and liberal bourgeoisie could be patched up, after it had threatened to fall apart in the 'New Era'. It was a concession that they were willing to make, for the prosperity of the years of the foundation of the Reich lured the aristocracy away from its snobbish aversion to industry. The government could continue with its liberal economic policies because they were so clearly successful, not only in promoting the economic domination of Prussia over Germany, but also in providing a succulent carrot to divert the German bourgeoisie from the task of attacking the pre-industrial social and political values, which were so blatantly antiquated and conducive to provoking still further the growing social tensions within a system that appeared to be hard pressed to find a solution to the problem of containing and deflecting social conflicts. Prosperity and nationalist euphoria worked its magic, and all had an eye on the stock exchange. As a Krupp engineer, Ernst Neu, wrote in 1873 before the crash came:

> Es jobbert der Jude, es jobbert der Christ,
> Es jobbert die Krämer und Schreiber,

Es jobbert der Gastwirt, der Prokurist,
Der Rechtsanwalt und sein Kopist,
Es jobbern die Kinder und Weiber.

('Everyone is speculating now: the Jew and the Christian, the shopkeeper and clerk, the innkeeper and the head clerk, the lawyer and copyist, children and women.') Economics could take the place of politics as long as this prosperity held. Once the bubble burst, the problems of crisis management were to become all the more acute because of the failure to provide the liberal political framework in which it might have been possible to contain social antagonisms more effectively.

Thus the foundation of the German Reich also marks the foundation of the new type of massive industrial concern such as the Dortmunder Union and the Gelsenkirchner Bergwerks AG and the beginning of a new set of relationships between government and industry. Industry had come of age, it could no longer be subjected to the bureaucratic control of an autocratic state. The bourgeoisie had been allotted its place in Bismarck's Reich, to prosper and co-operate. Doing the one, it was prepared to accept the other. Industrialisation failed to bring bourgeois democracy to Germany, just as it failed to do so in Japan or Russia. In its place was Bismarck's subtle, cynical and often brutal Bonapartist dictatorship hidden from the eyes of many historians by the constitutional trappings and universal suffrage that failed to fool his contemporaries. Industry had been effectively modernised, in part because of Bismarck's policies, but the social structure remained essentially unchanged.

Although most contemporaries and later historians saw a direct relationship between the foundation of the Reich and an upward turn in the trade cycle, in fact the upturn had taken place before the Franco-Prussian war. 1869 was the critical year. In that one year alone nearly 1,000 km of new railway track was laid, with a corresponding effect on the production of iron, steel and coal.

This healthy growth was soon forgotten with the outbreak of the war which severely disrupted the economy of the country. The war was neither long enough nor hectic enough to stimulate any significant growth of heavy industry and armaments production to offset the disruption of trade patterns, particularly with France, or the damaging effects of mobilisation on the work-force. Most serious of all seems to have been the shortages of coal which drove up prices and caused cut-backs in production and a disruption of the transportation network. Economic *malaise* and uncertainty about the outcome of the war drove up interest rates to 9 per cent. Many branches of industry were hard hit, production had to be cut back, and industrialists feared that Germany was experiencing a repeat performance of 1866.

In fact the downturn in late 1870 was clearly a result of the disturbance caused by the war, it was not a downward movement of the trade cycle. Once peace was restored, the economy could move onward and upward, as it had in the eighteen months before the outbreak of the war. The effects of victory were thus all the more dramatic because they made such a vivid contrast to the poor performance of the economy during the war months, which in turn seemed particularly gloomy because they followed a period of steady growth and prosperity.

The Beginning of the Great Depression

The boom years were uneven in their effect on different sectors of the economy. The poorest performance was in the textile industry, but even here it is unlikely that the figures were quite so disappointing as some historians have suggested. Nor did the annexation of Alsace-Lorraine have any marked effect on the German textile industry, for the textile industry maintained its close connections with France thanks to certain preferential tariffs. Nevertheless, it is clear that the performance of the textile industry was disappointing when measured by the achievements of heavy industry in this period. A more serious sign of trouble was the increasing shortage of investment capital. Wild speculation and massive investment programmes swallowed up available capital. Increases in the money supply were soon used up in the same manner. Interest rates continued to rise, and investors were willing to pay these rates in the hope of making even greater gains so that the rates were pushed up still further.

As long as the economy continued to expand, as it did in the early months of 1873, these problems could be largely ignored. Industry could afford high interest rates, higher wages, and even reductions in the working week, provided that the economy continued to grow. Even though there were signs in both Britain and the United States that production was stagnating, the German economy continued at an impressive rate of growth. Confidence remained high, even though there were ominous signs from Vienna that all was not well. By the end of the third quarter of 1872 there was an indication of a steady downward trend in prices on the Vienna stock exchange. Early in the following year it was clear that capital reserves had dried up. In spite of continued speculation and increases in the rate of interest, prices continued to fall. Speculators and manufacturers lost heart. In May 1873 the Vienna market collapsed.

For southern Germany the collapse of the Viennese stock market was a disaster. Banks in Munich, Frankfurt and Stuttgart were hard hit, but for the time being Berlin was able to hold its own with sufficient reserves to meet the immediate crisis. However, investors became increasingly cautious, fearing that Berlin prices might follow the path downward. There was a noticeable drop in the demand for luxury goods which had done so well during the boom. The result was an excess of liquid funds and a fall in the interest rate. Purchasers who expected prices to fall postponed their orders, resulting in further stock-piling. Prices began to fall, unemployment to rise.

Although Berlin appeared to be weathering the storm in spite of a widespread feeling of anxiety and uncertainty in September it was badly hurt by the crisis in New York, and particularly by the collapse of the important bank of Jay Cooke and Company. German investors had been particularly attracted by the American market with its higher interest rates and often spectacular profits. But when 83 railway companies in the United States were unable to meet their payments, shares in other railway companies fell disastrously. In October the Berlin Quistorp Bank, which had been dealing extensively with American railway shares, collapsed. This failure set in motion a rapid fall in prices on the Berlin stock exchange. Investment dried up, production was reduced, prices of raw materials which had been driven very high in part by excessive commodity speculation fell, and domestic demand, particularly for more luxurious items, was greatly reduced.

The collapse of the Berlin stock market did not result in a sudden and dramatic cut-back in industrial production. Industrial enterprises were understandably cautious, and some smaller companies were hard hit. Bankruptcies were not infrequent. Production was cut back, but gradually and without undue panic. The collapse did not discredit the new free commercial spirit that had finally triumphed in 1870. The joint-stock banks and industries continued their close co-operation, indeed they were obliged to work closer than ever together to survive through the depression. Amalgamations and fusions were easier to achieve, given the abolition of the tiresome restrictions on joint-stock companies. In this climate the larger companies strengthened their position, smaller concerns were often either forced into an amalgamation with a large competitor, or were unable to continue. This was particularly true in banking. The big banks such as the

Diskontogesellschaft, the Darmstädter Bank, the Deutsche Bank and Dresdner Bank (the 'Four Ds') had sufficient reserves to survive, and took over a number of new small banks that were less fortunate. The immediate effect of the crisis was thus to secure and strengthen the position of the big banks and to strengthen their hold on the economic life of the country. The big banks were strong enough to save any of the firms that they had helped to form, which included huge conglomerates like the Gelsenkirchner Bergwerks AG. But in return for their support they were able to demand and get very considerable influence over the operation of these companies.

This remarkable success by the newly formed big banks is a striking feature of these years. Although the Deutsche Bank had only been started in 1870, it was already in a commanding position. Thanks to outstanding management, which included Georg von Siemens and Hermann Wallich, the bank steered its way safely through the difficulties of the depression. It was able to do so because of the wide range of its activities and its sober and careful assessment of future events. The Deutsche Bank was careful to encourage deposit business which gave it capital reserves for profitable investment. By the end of 1871 the bank already had nearly 5 million marks in deposits, by the end of the Great Depression in 1894 this had risen to almost 75 million and by 1908 it had reached a staggering 779.5 million marks. More than any of the other banks, the Deutsche Bank specialised in the financing and stimulating of industrial exports from Germany. Among its first branch offices were those in Hamburg, Bremen and London, to be followed by further branches in the Far East and America. The immediate effects of the depression were very damaging to the bank's overseas operations and some of the foreign branches had to be closed down, but the bank was able to fall back on its current account business and strengthen this aspect of its activities. With the onset of the age of imperialism, the overseas activities of the Deutsche Bank were again to become vitally important when the bank saw itself as using financial means to fight Germany's political battles.

The Deutsche Bank was able to exploit the difficulties of the smaller banks in order to extend its network throughout Germany and to strengthen its position as a deposit bank. Thus the bank was able to get a firm foothold in Frankfurt by picking up the pieces left after the failure of the *Frankfurter Bankverein.*

Although a somewhat smaller operation, the other new bank, the Dresdner Bank, also specialised in deposit banking. Starting in Saxony, the bank bought a number of smaller banking houses. Avoiding undue speculation, the bank was closely involved in the textiles and brown coal industry of Saxony and in promoting trade between Berlin and the south-east of Germany. By 1881 the head office was moved to Berlin from Dresden, marking the beginning of the bank's activities as a truly national bank. The Dresdner Bank was the only provincial bank that was able to establish itself firmly in Berlin and to take its place beside the other great banks that to an increasing degree influenced the course of the German economy.

The success of the joint-stock banks also marked the decline of the private banks that had played such an important role earlier in the century. Thanks to their close government connections, bankers like Delbrück, Bleichröder and Mendelssohn survived and even prospered, but even they were increasingly dependent on the joint-stock banks. Immensely rich, ennobled and showered with orders and decorations, the private bankers had lost much of the substance of power, a fact that their closeness to the government and the court often served to obscure.

By 1874 the effects of the depression were becoming clearer, as industry continued to cut back production. The consumption of raw iron fell by nearly 30 per cent in the course of the year. Most of this reduction was due to sizeable cut-backs in imports, so that the domestic iron industry was not so badly hit. Engineering companies still had orders to meet, and it was not until the end of the year that orders began to slacken. Railway-building continued as projects that had been started in the period of prosperity were brought to completion. Orders for engines, rolling stock and rails helped to stabilise the economy and prevent a disastrous falling-off from the peak year of 1872. In the iron-producing industry prices were maintained at a high level in spite of the drop in demand, and there is reason to believe that contemporaries were right in thinking that it was due to agreements between the major producers to maintain prices. Coal production dropped off slightly, but by no means catastrophically, and prices were stable.

The textile industry was able to profit from the fall in the price of raw materials to expand production slightly, even though the crisis was causing difficulties to some sectors of the industry. In general it seems that the larger and more modern firms were best able to cope with the situation, and that the hand-weavers, particularly in the linen industry, found it increasingly hard to survive. Industries that were more immediately susceptible to fluctuations in the business cycle were less fortunate. The luxury trades faced an immediate and rapid decline. The building industry had a very lean year in 1874 partly due to the slump, but also because excessive activity in the previous years had led to there being a housing glut, and builders were obliged to borrow money at high rates of interest to finance empty apartments.

The downward trend in industrial production continued in the following year, but again it was by no means a dramatic collapse. For all the depressing reports from local chambers of commerce, the evidence indicates that production levels were only slightly reduced, and in some vital sectors, such as the coal industry, there was even an increase in output. As orders that had been placed before the crisis were gradually filled, there was a distinct drop in the mechanical engineering industry, and even in the production of railway engines and track there were the beginnings of a decline. Industrialists found it increasingly difficult to maintain prices, so that in the coal industry sharply falling prices could not be offset by an equivalent increase in production. Similarly, although the textile industry managed to maintain its level of production, prices continued to fall.

The trend of falling prices, increased unemployment, reduced production, caution and even anxiety continued in 1876. The Borsig locomotive works reduced its work-force by 50 per cent between 1874 and 1876. Many other engineering firms were obliged to make similar reductions. The sharp reduction in output in this sector – Borsig produced 166 locomotives in 1875 but only 80 in the following year – led to a decrease in the demand for iron and steel. But coal production increased, though prices continued to fall. The second half of 1876 appears to have been particularly difficult for German industry as the effects of the depression really began to be felt. By this time even the textile industry, which had managed to survive the crisis better than most, began to feel the full effects of the depression. Speculative purchases of cotton and wool when the price fell tended to make the statistics on textile production appear rather better than would otherwise be the case, for increases in the imports of raw cotton did not necessarily mean that cotton production increased.

The Call for Protection

Initially the depression had hurt investors badly, but industry and finance escaped the worst consequences of the world-wide crisis. As the depression continued, industry also began to suffer. The massive investments they had recently made increased the tendency to over-production which initially had been offset by full order-books from the time when the economy was in full swing. As the market shrank, industry was forced to reduce prices when even their determined efforts to co-operate to maintain price levels could no longer work. Heavy industry found it difficult to make a profit. With falling prices and over-production compounded by the competition of cheap foreign iron and steel, it is hardly surprising that demands for the protection of German industry were voiced once again. Heavy industry argued that protective tariffs alone would save them from ruin, but the agrarians, commercial interests and the majority of politicians still insisted that free trade would bring salvation, and that the interests of the German people could not be sacrificed to the selfish interests of the industrialists of the Ruhr and Upper Silesia. Heavy industry could only weather the storm by fixing prices, but this could not protect them from foreign competition. Excess production was dumped on foreign markets at prices as much as 40 per cent below the domestic price level, but this was an act of desperation along the lines of Andrew Carnegie's 'law' that it is better to keep on producing, even in bad times and at a loss, than to shut down factories. Obviously such a solution would not work in the long run, and as the depression continued and the economy showed no signs of recovery, something radical was needed if heavy industry were to survive in such a hostile climate. On the other hand, these increases in exports during the depression, even under such critical conditions, were vital to heavy industry, and some industrialists feared that protective tariffs would cut off this outlet without offering any compensating advantage at home. Protective tariffs were a gamble to an industry that was firmly established and in a country that could now be measured against the world's leading industrial nations.

Heavy industry did not stand alone in its demands for protective tariffs. The textile industry had traditionally been protectionist, and was now suffering from the double effects of the liberal tariffs with France and England in the 1860s and the depression. Some industrialists, particularly in Württemberg, feared the competition of the technically highly advanced and productive textile industry of Alsace and Lorraine.

The big joint-stock banks, whose fate was now so closely linked with that of heavy industry, also became converted to the protectionist cause. The banks became increasingly alarmed as share prices continued to fall and they became convinced that protection was the essential first step towards the recovery of industry and the salvation of their massive investments.

Initially there were two principal reasons why the protectionists had grounds for hope. A nation that had been formed by war needed a strong industrial base, and none was more conscious of this fact than the Chancellor. Second, social tensions were becoming ever more apparent as the depression wore on, and it was argued in some circles that protection was the price that would have to be paid for social peace. The 'war in sight crisis' and the 'red peril' were thus to be used by the protectionists as proof that their policy was correct and that the national interest was truly at stake, not merely the sectional interests of a handful of overbearing capitalists. But for the time being the agrarians were firm in their opposition, and it would need some dramatic change to get them to alter their thinking on the tariff question which had remained unchanged for half a century.

Heavy industry had supported protective tariffs for many years, but it was not until the depression of 1873 that it began to organise itself effectively for political action. In November 1873 industrialists in the Rhineland and Westphalia organised the Association of German Steel and Iron Industrialists (*Verein deutscher Stahl- und Eisenindustrieller*), with the purpose of forming a national interest group that would lobby the government and the Reichstag to encourage increased government spending, particularly on railways, so that Germany could be pulled out of the slump. The members knew perfectly well that the Reichstag would not accept any increases on the tariffs on iron and steel, so it devoted most of its energies to attempting to make sure that tariffs were not reduced any further, as seemed highly probable. Working closely with the *Verein* was the appropriately named Long-name Association (*Verein zur Wahrung der gemeinsamen wirtschaftlichen Interessen in Rheinland und Westfalen* — Association for the Protection of the Economic Interests of the Rhineland and Westphalia). Both associations were concerned that they should not become too parochial and were determined to co-operate closely with their fellow industrialists in Upper Silesia. A meeting between leading representatives of western and Silesian heavy industry in Berlin in December 1873 ended with general agreement that a common strategy was essential.

The organisational leader of this new alliance was Henry Axel Bueck, who was general secretary of the Long-name Association as well as secretary of the North-West Group of the Association of

German Iron and Steel Industrialists. Bueck had started his career as an agriculturist and free-trader. He had played a prominent role in various agricultural interest groups where he attracted the attention of the industrialists not only for his exceptional organisational ability, but also for the sympathy and understanding he showed for the problems of industry – an attitude which clearly set him apart from most of his fellow agriculturalists. He was hired by the industrialists to run the Long-name Association in 1873 and was to prove the key link man between agricultural and industrial interests. Bueck converted these interest groups into highly effective pressure groups with considerable influence in government circles. As a manipulator of public opinion and as an intermediary between industry and government, Bueck was the first great architect of the profoundly harmful anti-democratic pluralism of the interest groups of imperial Germany. In his footsteps would follow the Navy League, the Army League, the Colonial League and the Pan-Germans, all of which were to play a reactionary role in German society by providing a form of plebiscitory pseudo-democracy in place of the strengthening and extension of parliamentary democracy and of civil liberties and freedom.

The formation of these interest groups, which were complementary in their activities and closely linked, was a further stage in the development of the close links between industry and the hierarchical and autocratic state apparatus of Bismarck's Reich. These industrialists had no sympathy whatever for liberal democracy which they saw as a threat to their own autocratic position within the giant monopolies. The interest groups of the industrialists were thus designed not to challenge the political structure of the Reich, but rather to strengthen it and purge it of democratic elements. In these terms, protective tariffs were not a high price to pay for the enthusiastic support and co-operation of what was rapidly becoming the single most powerful group within German economic life.

At first the Association of German Iron and Steel Industrialists had little success. Delbrück and Camphausen remained true to their free-trade principles. Civil servants and politicians had little sympathy for the captains of heavy industry, and indeed many of them felt that their present difficulties were deemed to be a just reward for their past greed. Faced with such a negative response, the industrialists concentrated on forming a united front of all those who wanted protectionist tariffs. In southern Germany this scheme was particularly successful, and the protectionists scored their first major triumph when the traditionally free-trading *Kongress Deutscher Volkswirthe*

(Congress of German Economists) accepted by a narrow margin a motion favouring protection at their meeting in Munich in September 1875. But any such successes by the protectionists simply provoked the free-trading agrarian and commercial interests to bombard government offices with memoranda on the evil effects of protection that would increase domestic prices and cause still further social unrest. Such pleas met with a far more receptive response than the cries of woe from the Ruhr and Silesia. On the other hand it became increasingly difficult to argue that the salvation of the economy lay in free trade when the system was performing so poorly. As the depression deepened those who argued that something had to be done could not be dismissed out of hand.

The position of the protectionists was also strengthened by Bismarck's political difficulties in the Reichstag over the struggle against the Catholic Church, the *Kulturkampf*, and his attempt to undermine the budgetary rights of the Reichstag by the proposed 'Eternal Law', which would establish the size of the army of the future and remove the army from any sort of parliamentary scrutiny. As the army was coming under increasing attack from the 'enemies of the Reich' – the socialists, Catholic centre party and progressives – Bismarck was all the more determined to defend this 'pillar of the Reich' from attack. The 'Eternal Law' failed, and in its place he had to accept a seven-year Bill which increased the size of the army which now consumed 70 per cent of the Reich budget. The debates over the 'Eternal Law' had been very hectic, and Bismarck had put on his usual performance of threatening to resign, of painting a ghastly picture of an impending socialist revolution and foreign war, and it further narrowed the basis of his political support. Having become politically estranged from the old conservatives to the point that he had tried to restructure the Prussian upper house in an attempt to undermine their political power, and having totally alienated the liberals and the left, he was completely dependent on his narrow coalition of free conservatives and national liberals. But it was precisely in these groups that protectionism found its strongest supporters. Bismarck's schemes for the nationalisation of the railways, which also involved an ingenious scheme for undermining the budgetary rights of the Reichstag, were also supported by protectionist industrialists who hoped for large state orders for new railway building, but opposed by the liberal enthusiasts of free enterprise. This scheme also failed and Bismarck's cunning schemes for budgetary reform and the reorganisation of the Reich were in ruins. His foreign policy had fared little better with the blundering 'war in sight crisis' fresh in everyone's memory. In a hostile world with few free-trading nations and with his domestic policy supported only by the protectionists, it seemed that either Bismarck would fall from power or that he would have to come to terms with those who were clamouring for protective tariffs.

Knowing the strength of opinion against protectionism, Bismarck at first moved cautiously, refusing to make any commitments to the heavy industrialists. He was, however, prepared to throw the arch-enemy of the protectionists, Delbrück, to the lions, there having been numerous differences of opinion between the two men over the railway issue, the relative positions of Prussia and the Reich, and Bismarck's growing disenchantment with the Prussian Ministers.

The protectionists, having failed in their attempts to gain the support of the Reichstag majority, decided to change their tactics and win over the Chancellor to their cause. Preliminary discussions between Bismarck and the industrial leaders were encouraging. In December 1875 Kardorff invited some prominent figures in the industrial world to Berlin to discuss a common strategy. From this meeting emerged what was to become the most powerful interest group in imperial Germany – the Central Association of German Industrialists (*Zentralverband Deutscher Industriellen*). The new association declared total war on the pernicious theory of free trade, which it saw at the root of Germany's present economic distress, and called for a common front of industry, agriculture and handicrafts to revitalise the German economy. The new association was officially founded in February 1876. Attempts to get the Association of German Steel and Iron Industrialists and the Long-name Association to amalgamate with the Central Association failed, for the new organisation was regarded by many as far too radical in its demands for protection and the older associations preferred a more cautious approach. The Central Association was both more outspoken and strident in tone and more representative of industry as a whole than any of the previous interest groups. It soon achieved its aim of being the acknowledged voice of German industry.

While the protectionists were reorganising their forces, changes in the agricultural sector were taking place which were eventually to guarantee the success of the protectionist cause. By the time the Central Association was formed, agrarians were becoming increasingly concerned about the fall in the price of grain. The completion of an efficient European network of railways, the falling price of coal and the general depression of wages had made it considerably easier for foreign producers to sell on the German market. The influx of foreign corn, particularly from Russia, further alarmed the agrarians, who were already affected by the falling price of grain in the German market. By 1875 prices had dropped between 12 and 15 per cent, and lacking the capital completely to restructure agriculture to exploit the possibilities of the international market in the most effective manner, the agrarians were becoming more enthusiastic for the idea of the 'protection of national labour', as the Central Association was proposing. As it became increasingly difficult to meet the challenge of foreign competition from the east or from America, the simple answer seemed to be protection. From the outset the agitation of the Central Association had a virulent nationalistic tone which was to find a resonance east of the Elbe once economic pressures pushed the leaders of 'rye' and 'iron' together. Following the lead of the industrialists the agrarians formed their association – the *Vereinigung der Steuer- und Wirtschaftsreformer* (Association of Tax and Economic Reformers) only a few days after the formation of the Central Association. This agrarian association claimed to stand for the values of 'Christian economics', a thinly disguised appeal for support from anti-Semites who were becoming increasingly vociferous as the depression was blamed by some ideologists on 'Jewish capitalism', and concentrated chiefly, as the name of the association implied, on the reduction of taxes on agricultural property.

At first the Association of Tax and Economic Reformers favoured free trade for agriculture, but from the outset it realised that free trade was not a universal panacea, and that in certain circumstances it had to be abandoned. The 'reformers', with their Prussianism, their militarism and their conservatism shared many of Bismarck's political views. They were less enthusiastic for the Reich and antagonistic towards Bismarck's suggestion for a social policy, which they attacked with slogans about independence and the importance of being able to stand on one's own two feet, but as they became convinced of the importance of protective tariffs, the way was open for Bismarck to change his domestic political alliances and form his new coalition in support of his ultra-conservative and repressive 'welfare state'.

The year 1876, with the formation of the Central Association and the 'Reformers', the gradual abandonment of a doctrinaire free-trade position by the agrarians, and the dismissal of the 'General Staff Chief' of the free-traders, Delbrück, was an important turning-point in the formation of the new alliances that were to dominate the economic and political life of Germany for the years to come. These tendencies were speeded up by the fact that 1877 was a particularly bad year for the German economy. Coal production fell disastrously. The consumption of crude iron dropped. Engineering production was cut back still further, and the machine-tool setter was particularly badly hit. Only in the building trades, when some city councils decided to undertake new building projects, partly to create jobs and partly to take advantage of low prices and low wages, was there some improvement.

The economy continued in this depressed state in the following year. The production of crude iron and of coal increased somewhat, but the consumption of crude iron, which is a more accurate gauge of industrial production, declined somewhat compared to the previous year. Things began to improve in 1879, although the depression was by no means over. The nationalisation of the Prussian railway system which Bismarck had been forced to accept as an alternative policy to the nationalisation of the entire German railway system converted the holders of railway shares into state bond-holders. Capital was thus made available for more speculative ventures, and some entrepreneurs took advantage of this situation to float new companies. Although there was nothing comparable to the boom in new company formations of the Years of the Foundation there was a more lively activity on the Berlin stock exchange, and grounds for a certain cautious optimism. The spectacular recovery of the American economy in 1879 was also of great help to the Germans. Exports to the United States in 1879–80 rose from $31.8 million to $53.5 million, much of which was iron and steel to fuel the American railway boom. The engineering industry was less fortunate, but the textile industry saw some modest improvement as manufacturers speculated that the rising prices of raw materials would continue and that the price of finished products would become firmer. Yet in spite of an over-all improvement in the economy; it was clear that Germany was still in the midst of a depression, and although there was a general expression of relief the business world knew that it was far too soon to speak of a recovery.

Although the effects of the depression were uneven, affecting different sectors of the economy at different times and with varying intensity, there can be no doubt that the crisis from 1873 until the brief upturn in economic activity in 1879 was the longest depression in German history and the most profound in its effects, apart from the Great Depression from 1929 to 1932. By 1876 both the Kaiser and Bismarck were convinced that something would have to be done for the iron and steel industries, but the free-trade faction within the Prussian Ministry of State, led by the Finance Minister Camphausen, argued that the fault lay with the industry itself for expanding far too fast in the prosperous years after 1871, and that protection would simply make the situation worse. For the time being the free-traders, even without the presence of Delbrück, were able to keep the upper hand. Some encouragement was given to the protectionists by the results of the Reichstag elections of 1877. The liberals lost a quarter of their seats and split into two groups of national liberals and progressives. The conservatives, and among them particularly the 'Reformers', did well. The Catholic centre party had also become increasingly protectionist, hoping that it might find allies in its struggle against the *Kulturkampf*. Encouraged by the possibility of finding a conservative and protectionist majority in the Reichstag, the protectionists renewed their propaganda efforts. Meanwhile the 'Reformers' had overcome their initial objection to working with the Central Association and agreed that in this crisis situation a common front was needed in defence of the 'Christian state' against its enemies in the liberal and socialist camps. An all-out political offensive was launched in which a tariff on the value of imports was a key demand.

Bismarck's efforts in 1877 to push a moderate tariff reform through the Reichstag failed, and the Chancellor retired to his estate at Varzin for a long holiday during which he finally decided that the time had come to restructure the Reich with the help of a conservative and right-wing liberal coalition and on the basis of a protective tariff. His successes were at first modest. Against the free-trading arguments of the Prussian Ministry of State he was able to secure the extension of the 1868 trade agreement with Austria which at least avoided the reduction of tariffs, and as the extension was only provisional it enabled Bismarck to raise the whole question of tariff reform, and to use the arguments and the propaganda apparatus of the protectionists against the free-traders, who still had such a powerful position within the Prussian government.

The Reichstag majority naturally enough opposed Bismarck's schemes to undermine the budgetary rights of the Reichstag by means of a tax reform and increased tariffs and to restructure the power base so as to rule through Prussia rather than through the office of the Reich Chancellor. Even though the Catholic centre party was prepared to give limited support to Bismarck's proposals, especially since the death of Pius IX and the end of the *Kulturkampf*, it was clear that a Reichstag majority was only possible if the liberals could be divided once again. With the resignation of the three leading liberals in the Prussian government, the Finance Minister, Otto von Camphausen, the Minister of Trade, von Achenbach, and the Minister of the Interior, Friedrich von Eulenburg, Bismarck was at last free of the 'Manchester men' who had blocked his earlier attempts at change.

An assassination attempt against the Kaiser in May 1878 gave Bismarck the opportunity he was looking for to bring in legislation against the social democrats which he hoped could also be used to split the liberals. The legislation was poorly prepared and rejected by the Reichstag. A second attempt on the Kaiser's life in early June, in which the Kaiser was wounded, caused a public outcry. Bismarck, in spite of the advice of his Ministers to the contrary, was determined to exploit this temporary explosion of public opinion in favour of the monarchy and law and order to call new elections for the Reichstag in the hope of gaining a pliable majority. The elections were fought on a virulent anti-socialist platform which called for a complete reform of domestic politics and the common effort of patriotic elements to rescue the country from revolution, outmoded and doctrinaire economic doctrines, and from the economic crisis. In this election campaign the 'Reformers' and the Central Association played a prominent role. Captains of industry like Krupp and Stumm ran for Parliament, mouthing familiar platitudes about preserving Christian culture and restoring a sense of moral purpose to the public life of the nation. To the protectionists the answer to the threat of revolution and aimlessness was prosperity, and prosperity was only possible with protective tariffs. Thus the struggle against social democracy was intimately linked to the question of tariff reform.

The elections were by no means a complete success for Bismarck. The liberals were still the largest party in the Reichstag, but they were divided on economic questions and the elections had shown a rightward swing in the party's composition. The centre party held the balance of power in the new Reichstag, but although the party was protectionist it was unlikely to support any Draconic measures against social democracy such as Bismarck had proposed. In the new Reichstag 204 members formed a group that demanded protective tariffs, calling themselves the Free Economic Association (*Freie Wirtschaftliche Vereinigung*) and including members of the conservative and centre parties. The association asked the Chancellor for a commission of enquiry into the tariff question.

Yet there were still many obstacles in the way. Industrialists did not favour high agricultural tariffs, which were bound to have an immediate effect on the cost of living and therefore on wage demands. The southern states objected to the increase in indirect taxation which would free the Reich government from the need to ask the state for subsidies (the 'matricular contributions') and thus diminish control over the Reich budget by the *Bundesrat.* Bismarck answered these objections by claiming that without finance reform and an increase in the tariffs the threat of a socialist revolution would grow. Agriculture and industry would thus have to settle their differences in defence of the 'monarchical principle' which alone could save the Reich from growing parliamentarianism and socialism. Thus for Bismarck questions of finance and the tariff were seen in terms of strengthening his conservative and authoritarian state, as an extension of the anti-socialist laws.

The reactionary thrust of Bismarck's scheme was certainly not lost on the social democrats and the progressives. In lively debates in the Reichstag and in a vigorous press campaign they denounced his efforts to halt the reform movement and increase the price of bread. Indeed the price of bread became so central to the issue that the proposed tariff on iron passed the Reichstag with a substantial majority, while some representatives of industrial interests joined with their sworn enemies to the left to defeat the proposals for an increased tariff on corn.

The deadlock over the finance reform was finally settled by the ingenious proposal of the centre party deputy, Franckenstein. Under the 'Franckenstein Clause' the revenue to the Reich from customs and the increased tobacco tax could not exceed 130 million marks. Any excess revenue was then to be divided up among the federal states. As 130 million was not sufficient for the Reich government it would still have to call for the matricular contributions from the states. The states would thus maintain a degree of budgetary control and have the added advantage that the contributions would be financed in part by revenues from the Reich. With this acceptable compromise on the finance question the way was open for approval of the agricultural tariff. On 12 July 1879 the Reichstag accepted the proposals for protective tariffs and for an increased tobacco tax. Both conservative parties, the centre party, and a few national liberals voted for the proposals. The remaining national liberals, the progressives and the social democrats voted against.

The formation of the new coalition of landed aristocracy and industrialists behind the tariffs of 1879 was by no means totally harmonious. Agrarians had not lost their suspicion of industry, which they saw as being at the root of much that was evil in the modern world, and their concern for Germany's place in the new industrial world did not always override their desire to obtain machinery and equipment as cheaply as possible from foreign producers. Similarly the industrialists felt that the high price of bread fuelled social unrest and ran counter to their policy of securing peace at home by general prosperity. As Germany became an industrial country, and as the population continued to grow, it was obvious that the agrarians' belief that the country could be independent from foreign sources of food was an illusion. If that were so, then high tariffs would simply increase the cost of living, eat into real wages and profits and add further ammunition to the 'anti-state' parties of the left.

For the time being, these differences tended to simmer below the surface rather than break out into open debate, largely because the German bourgeoisie was so hard hit by the depression that expensive bread seemed a moderate price to pay for immediate relief, and it was hoped that the repressive measures of the anti-socialist laws would keep the masses in order. The catastrophic fall in prices and of turnover was a matter for grave concern. The average price of raw materials such as coal, iron, metals and building materials fell from 145 in 1873 to 69 in 1879, taking 1913 figures as 100. Many firms were to suffer heavy losses and wondered how long they would be able to survive.

The Concentration of Industry

Protective tariffs, however high, were clearly not enough to save industry from the consequences of the depression. Many industrialists agreed that in this crisis situation, those in big industry would have to stand together to survive. The formation of cartels seemed to be one of the more promising means of riding out the storm. Some of these cartels were successful, others never got off the ground, but there was general agreement that the cartel was a viable and desirable form of industrial organisation. Even massive organisations such as the Gelsenkirchner Bergwerks AG and its closely associated banker, the Diskontogesellschaft, began to discuss the possibility of forming a coal syndicate. There are clear indications of informal cartels in the period before the depression, but the economic crisis speeded up the tendency for a 'protective collectivism' in which industry sought the protection of the state in the form of protective tariffs and increased government expenditure on projects such as the railways, and formed agreements on how best to work together to survive the crisis. The attitudes of free-enterprise capitalism had gone, and the age of monopoly capitalism was dawning. Liberal notions of freedom from state interference and the healthy effects of free competition were discredited. Solidarity, collectivism and close co-operation with the state apparatus were now the slogans of the day.

The tendency to form large industrial conglomerates had been pronounced even before 1873, as had been the close connections between finance capital and industrial capital. The process is also structurally imminent within capitalism, as both Marx and Max Weber had argued, to the former as a result of the problems of capital reproduction within a capitalist economy, to the latter from the tendency towards rationalisation within industrial society. There can, however, be no doubt that the process was accelerated by the effects of the Great Depression.

Even a cursory glance at the statistics shows that during the depression the number of industrial companies declined in some sectors, whereas the number of employees increased, as did output. In Rhineland Westphalia, about 40 per cent of the mining companies ceased to exist as independent entities between 1873 and 1890, while production trebled and the number of miners increased 2.5 times. In branches of industry where a number of new companies were formed, the increase bore no relation to the far greater increases in output and in manpower. Within each branch of industry there was a rapid increase of the percentage of larger firms, as the smaller companies were unable to survive a declining market in which the giant corporations had achieved a commanding position by their ability to survive when margins were squeezed by falling prices.

Price cartels were formed in the cement industry and the puddle-iron works in 1882. Similar agreements were made in many sectors of industry in the late 1870s and early 1880s. Even liberal economists gave their blessing to these efforts, on the grounds that in exceptionally difficult circumstances industry had a right to protect its vital interests. The new and expanding industries, such as the chemical industry, were heavily cartelised, almost from the outset. In 1893 one of the most powerful cartels of all, the Rhineland-Westphalian Coal Syndicate, was formed, followed by an Iron Syndicate in the next year. The 1890s saw the final triumph of the cartels, but the foundations had been laid during the depression years.

Poverty, Prices and Profits

If the depression speeded up the process of industrial modernisation in the sense that it led to monopolisation and the attempt to overcome the anarchy of capitalist production, it also modernised industry in the sense that only the most effective and productive firms were able to survive. Hand-weavers, who still survived in an age of advanced industrial technology, were particularly hard hit. In 1873 there were 2,964 handlooms in Chemnitz, but by 1876 there were only 1,840. The productivity of labour was greatly increased, not only by the elimination of antiquated and unproductive firms, but also by forcing the workers to work more intensely. With high unemployment and the outlawing of the socialist unions and party, the working class had little chance but to accept a steady worsening of their position. With falling prices improving the real wages of those who were able to find steady employment at fixed wages, the main problem for the working class was unemployment. As firms cut back their work-force and the population continued to rise, unemployment reached appalling levels. In Berlin in 1879 more than 25 per cent of the industrial labourers were unemployed.

Unemployment, cartelisation, falling prices and the failure of many firms seemed to be an indication that German industrial capitalism was collapsing from a surfeit of success. The excess capacity which had been built up in the period of high investment and rapid technological change now found no outlets either at home or abroad. Once the railway-building programme began to slow down when the immediate transportation needs of the country had been met, this critical stimulus to the economic growth of the past was removed, and the railways no longer were able to absorb a large share of the country's industrial output. Whereas between 1870 and 1874 the railways absorbed nearly 24 per cent of net investment, by the end of the depression it had fallen to below 6 per cent. Contemporaries were perplexed by the fact that although industry had become so efficient and productive, there seemed to be no possible way of stimulating effective demand to meet the increase in productivity. Indeed, the more efficient industry became, the more demand was reduced. Industrial society, far from bringing prosperity for all, seemed about to be suffocated by its own excesses.

The depression, even in its first stage to 1879, did not result in a no-growth economy, but the rate of growth was reduced by about 50 per cent. Industrial growth continued at a higher rate than in agriculture, so that in the course of the depression Germany finally became an industrial country in the sense that the industrial sector created more wealth and absorbed more investment than agriculture. A stagnating agricultural sector was gradually overtaken by a slowly growing industrial sector. Within industry there was also a shift of emphasis, with a decline in the proportion of the production of consumer goods and an increase in the production of capital goods. Although the absolute preponderance of the capital-goods sector was not achieved until the 1890s, the structural change was clearly discernible in the course of the Great Depression. The position of industry over agriculture and heavy industry within the industrial sector was further strengthened by the export drive during the depression years which was remarkably successful for heavy industry and engineering in terms of volume, although goods had to be sold at dumping prices. By the end of the first period of the depression, Germany was a close challenger to the United States as the second-largest industrial exporting nation.

If industrialists were prepared to sell on the export market at prices up to 40 per cent below those that could be met on the domestic market, simply in order to keep their plants running, they were also selling on a falling market at home. During the first stage of the depression from 1873 to 1879, industrial prices fell by about 30 per cent. Coal prices fell by about 66 per cent, iron by about 60 per cent. Again the cause was the improved techniques of production which enabled industrial goods and raw materials to be produced in larger quantities and more cheaply. Given the high levels of previous investment, industrialists were very reluctant to cut back production, and in order to maintain profit margins they tended to produce even more commodities which then had to be sold at lower prices. Thus prices spiralled downwards and industrialists were unable to reap any benefits from the fall in the price of raw materials. Production costs were greatly lowered once the initial investment had been made and the process was immeasurably faster with the introduction of the Bessemer converter, but here again the relief was only temporary, for the price of Bessemer steel also fell steadily. Much the same is true of the Gilchrist Thomas system, introduced to Germany in 1879, which enabled the use of lower-quality ores.

Statistical information on industrial profits in this period is very sparse and unsatisfactory, but all the evidence suggests a decline in profits which could only partially be offset by skilful management and ruthless business practices. Undistributed profits in the boom years averaged about 142 million marks, but between 1873 and 1896 they fell to an average of 125 million. But during these years there were wide fluctuations and deviations from the average. With the fall in undistributed profits there was a corresponding decline in dividends, and indeed many companies were unable to pay any dividends at all in the worst years of the depression. Stock prices collapsed, and investors were understandably reluctant to buy stock even at prices which must have seemed attractively low. The result was that an excess of investment capital built up, so that the state or local government authorities had no difficulty in raising money and the interest rate was allowed to fall. The result of the movement of investors away from the stock market to the bond market was a noticeable rise in the value of bonds. The state thus could find ample supplies of cheap money, its hand was strengthened against Parliament, the conservative elements were bolstered and Bismarck's authoritarian system could disregard demands for more stringent budgetary control of the government. With the low yields on government bonds and the miserable performance of the stock exchanges, investors showed a much greater interest in foreign stocks and bonds. Thus German capital investment abroad grew steadily during the years of the depression.

Increases in the amount of foreign investment formed one reason for the growing balance of payments deficit during the depression. Another more important reason was the substantial increase in the amount of imported corn, even though in some years, such as 1885 to 1888, there was a marked drop from the trend. The rapid development of the American Midwest in the years after the civil war, the expansion of farmland in southern Russia and the Ukraine, the fall in the price of transportation and the completion of the railway network in Europe all served to increase the flood of cheap grain on the European market which threatened the ruin of German farmers who simply were unable to produce corn at a competitive price. The extraordinary achievements of American agriculture in overcoming the shortage of manpower by the use of the most advanced machinery were coupled with the rapid growth of the railway from Atlantic to Pacific. The rate at which it was built seemed incredible to Europeans; it was certainly one of the great engineering feats of the century, and it further reduced the price of American corn. The age of the sailing ship had passed, and the new steam ships were fuelled with coal, the price of which fell continually. Freight costs across the Atlantic fell by 80 per cent during the depression so that German agriculture was no longer protected by high freight rates but had to compete almost on equal terms with the American, Canadian and Argentinian producers. The result was that German agriculture stagnated, and was only able to keep up its levels of earning by means of the protective tariffs of 1879. From the time of the Great Depression the landed aristocracy became a protected species, supported by protective tariffs which ran contrary to the interests of the industrialists and of the vast mass of the German people, protected by the financial support of institutions such as the Prussian Land Commission and organised first in the 'Reformers', then in the *Bund der Landwirte* (Farmers' League) of 1893, which was to become one of the most outspoken and influential organisations of Wilhelmine Germany. Partly due to these efforts, agricultural prices did not fall quite as badly as industrial prices or the price of key raw materials. Taking the 1913 figures as equal to 100, agricultural prices fell from 95 to 77, whereas industrial goods fell from 136 to 77, coal from 116 to 49 and iron from 181 to 76 between the years 1873 and 1879.

Price fluctuations were very considerable in different branches of the economy, and within each branch. Available statistics are mostly open to serious criticism, and it is doubtful if a truly accurate picture of the movement of prices and wages in nineteenth-century Germany will ever be possible. On the other hand, certain trends are clearly discernible. During the boom years of 1871 to 1873 there was a distinct rise in real industrial wages. A booming industry was able to pay higher wages to attract skilled labour and to meet the demands of labour for wage adjustments to meet the cost-of-living increases. Higher wages increased the demand for consumer goods which tended to push prices up still further, which in turn fuelled fresh wage demands. After 1873 this process was reversed. Production was cut back, profits declined, the work-force was reduced in some sectors and prices and wages fell. Although the cost of living fell in the depression, benefiting all those on fixed incomes or wages, industrial wages tended to fall even faster. In general it would appear that real wages in industry fell during the first stage of the Great Depression from 1873 to 1879. In the next period until 1896, real wages climbed upward as industry began a slow recovery, with increased investment and expansion in some key sectors, such as chemicals and the electrical industry. Rising real wages encouraged further growth, but with the steady increase in population the output of consumer goods was spread more thinly, thus retarding the upward movement of real wages.

During the period of the depression the population of the Reich rose from 41.5 million to 52 million. This placed a further strain on the depressed economy, and although 2 million Germans emigrated during this time, the economy still had to provide for a 25 per cent increase in the population. Agriculture was unable to absorb this increase in the population, so that the movement of population towards the towns was further accentuated. The expanding industries were able to draw on an adequate supply of labour, but for many Germans the experience of the depression was of urban squalor and poverty which was only partly alleviated by the efforts of the 'welfare state' of imperial Germany. It is to the wider social and political impressions of the Great Depression that we shall now turn.

7 THE IMPACT OF THE GREAT DEPRESSION 1873–1895

The Political Consequences of the Depression

As historians compile and analyse the statistical data of the period, the picture of the Great Depression becomes ever more differentiated, complex and contradictory, to the point where it has been seriously suggested that the term 'Great Depression' is without any analytical value. As far as the experience of Germany is concerned, the simple dating of the Great Depression from 1873 to 1896, with a first period to early 1879, a brief period of modest recovery to January 1882 and a second period of depression to 1896, has some value as a means of sorting out the available material into manageable periods. It tends, however, to magnify the effects of the depression, to overlook the degree to which many key factors in the period such as the effects of overseas trade, changes in the terms of trade or the fall in prices were set in motion before the onset of the depression. But in psychological terms there can be no doubt that there was indeed a depression. The economic hangover after the heady days of the foundation of the Reich plunged businessmen into the darkest gloom. Contemporaries were unanimous in their opinion that times were bad and were getting worse, and that industrial capitalism fluctuated between times of prosperity, when the workers made outrageous demands and the prices of raw materials rose, and depression, when business was forced to cut its own throat with price reductions, production restrictions and low profits.

In large part this was due to the exceptional performance of the economy in the boom years since 1848. Temporary set-backs in 1857 and 1866 were only short interruptions in almost thirty years of high profits and rapid expansion. The depression showed that industrial capitalism was not necessarily synonymous with endless expansion and boundless prosperity. Nor was the structure of the German economy an unchanging and immutable fact, for it had to make major and often painful adjustments in order to accommodate itself to the changing world economic situation.

The years of the depression marked the triumph of big industry. It speeded up a process which had begun in the boom years when the joint-stock company, supported and sustained by joint-stock banks, became the characteristic form of industrial organisation. Smaller firms found it increasingly hard to compete and frequently were either forced into bankruptcy or taken over by one of the large companies. Although the number of small independent craftsmen and tradesmen actually increased during the depression years, particularly in the service industries, there was a steady decline in their number relative to the increase in population. Faced with falling prices and declining consumption, they were in a particularly difficult position. Their operations were too small to reap any significant economies of scale, they lacked the capital to purchase more efficient equipment, and thus many of them had to eke out a precarious existence producing and selling speciality goods. The social-democratic leader August Bebel earned his living in the depression years by selling doorknobs which he had turned by hand on his own lathe. Bebel's experiences confirmed his belief in Marx's analysis of the contradictions within capitalism, but others sought solace in wild irrational behaviour, in Red-baiting, anti-Semitism and in a crude and ill-articulated anti-capitalism. The reaction to the difficulties, failures and weaknesses of industrial capitalism in the late nineteenth century marks a pre-figuration of Fascistic ideas and the 'destruction of reason', in Lukács' phrase, that was to form the ideological background to the age of imperialism.

The historical record shows that bourgeois democracy provided the best framework for the industrialisation of countries in the nineteenth century. For all its shortcomings and injustices it at least promised in theory, though seldom in practice, an extension of individual liberties and freedoms as a worthwhile reward for the frightful upheavals and dislocations caused by the Industrial Revolution. In Germany the liberalism which some historians see as the necessary concomitant of industrialisation was weakened and distorted by the specific historical circumstances in which it developed. In many circles political liberalism was abandoned in the concentrated pursuit of economic gain, but the liberal idea survived and there were brief moments when it flourished. In many people's minds liberalism was equated with 'Manchesterism', with an industrial capitalism red in tooth and claw, bent on the heedless pursuit of private profit and the destruction of the certainties of the old way of life. As long as the system provided for general prosperity, and as long as a sizeable proportion of small businessmen and artisans had been able to hold their heads above water, the system had been accorded a degree of grudging acceptance. With the Great Depression, critics of liberal capitalism had an easy time stirring up the slumbering resentments and anxieties of a wide section of the population. In political terms the discrediting of liberal democracy was probably the major consequence of the Great Depression. As the depression followed immediately after a period of feverish economic activity, both the contrast and the causality were emphasised. A system from which many had made huge speculative gains was now denounced because the self-same speculators were beginning to make a loss.

The anti-liberal offensive took many forms and created many novel alliances in the course of the restructuring of political formations, economic interest groups and ideological platforms. As one sour conservative put it, those who had failed to get rich by swindling now hoped to get rich by protective tariffs. This was particularly true of the agrarians. Agriculture in Germany stagnated and the country became increasingly dependent on the world market to feed its growing population and to obtain the most favourable price for agricultural products. Protective tariffs enabled some 25,000 owners of large estates, about half of whom were Prussian aristocrats, to maintain their political influence, their economic power and their social status when, if things had been allowed to take their course, they would have become ruined economically and eventually politically powerless.

Life was indeed hard for the big landowners. The price of agricultural produce was falling, the rural population dwindling and thus higher wages had to be paid at a time when profits were squeezed and land values falling. The home market was increasingly flooded with cheap foreign corn, the traditional export markets having dried up. Very few of them, like the industrial magnates of Upper Silesia, were actively engaged in industry. Their economic and social status threatened by industrial capitalism, the long-term prospects of agriculture bleak and their political influence within the new Reich uncertain, the big landowners adopted a stance of severe anti-modernism, chauvinism and belligerent authoritarianism.

This politicisation and radicalisation of the land-owning aristocracy was part of a widespread phenomenon of the depression years. Public life became more intensely political than ever before as the weight of economic problems was felt by an increasingly wide circle of people who were angered at the seeming complacency of bureaucrats and politicians and their reluctance to deal with the pressing problems of the day. Few civil servants or politicians had any practical experience of the business world, coming mainly from the law schools of the great universities, and there was mounting criticism of their ignorance and indifference towards the economic problems that dominated men's thinking. 'Complacency' and 'lack of worldly wisdom' were frequent accusations made against the traditional administrative and political élites. Agrarians, industrialists, artisans and workers organised their own interest groups to demand relief from their immediate problems. Self-help and the pursuit of sectional interests took the place of discussions about political freedom, constitutional reform or the responsibility of Ministers. The political parties ceased to talk in general terms about social goals and abandoned their attempts to articulate an all-embracing ideology. They became the political mouthpieces of sectional interests. Agrarians and industrialists, merchants and bankers, artisans and workers all found themselves faced with acute and immediate economic problems. As a result, political consciousness was narrowed and focused on specific problems, discussions of the public good or of national integration were largely abandoned as the class struggle heightened and the social question became a class question. Between the demands for a socialist revolution or for a right-wing *coup d'état* a whole series of programmes for drastic social change were proposed which would bring relief to the immediate problems of one sector of society.

With the decline of old ideological and party loyalties, with liberalism as the most severe casualty, came the formation of a new class and interest solidarity. The old distinctions within the conservative party were forgotten, and the party rallied round the defence of agricultural interests. The conservative party thus became the political organisation of the land-owning aristocracy which, with its close ties to the upper echelons of the bureaucracy and the officer corps, gave to the class it represented a sense of direction and purpose which it had partially lost in the days of prosperity when it had seemed to many that some sort of accommodation with industrial capitalism and liberalism would have to be made. With this new formation the traditions of East Prussian liberalism, of free-trading agrarians with their admiration for Adam Smith and Kant, were lost forever. Kant's liberal and humane teaching became perverted into a mindless devotion to duty, the categorical imperative a high-sounding term for subservience and automatic obedience.

With this change in the attitudes of the conservatives came a systematic purge of liberal elements within the bureaucracy. A strictly conformist and ultra-conservative bureaucracy emerged from this process that was wholly committed to the autocratic quasi-dictatorship of Bismarck's Germany. This purged bureaucracy was given the task of implementing the social policy, the economic measures to stimulate the economy and the tariff legislation that were all necessitated by the depression. Thus, at a time when the state intervened more than ever before in the daily life of the country, its executive and administrative leadership was more reactionary and hidebound than at any time since the reform era after 1806.

The coalition of agrarians and industrialists as the political basis of the support for the new order of 1879 was also supported by a large section of the lower middle class who voted for the Catholic centre party or, if they were Protestants with a desire to appear respectable, the conservatives, and in some instances the anti-Semites. Those in opposition supported the independents (*Freisinnige*) or the social democrats, both of which parties made significant gains as the full anti-social effects of the new tariffs began to be felt.

The triumph of the conservative party in the Reichstag elections of 1878, in which they received the largest percentage of the vote that they were ever to obtain (26.6 per cent), was the most striking achievement of the political party that formed the basis of the pro-Reich forces. Conservatism in its German form was the political expression of agrarian interests, and it was therefore unable substantially to increase its share of the vote. Agriculture was increasingly less significant within the economy, and the numbers of those working the land declined relative to the total population. Conservatism was thus doomed to decline even though it had wide popular support from voters who remained constantly loyal to their party.

The conservative parties could count on about 1.5 million votes, so that a party of big landowners had become a mass party. This was the price that the old conservatives had to pay in order to have a voice in the pseudo-democratic institutions of imperial Germany. In their wake followed ex-liberals who had left their old party allegiance whether from conviction or opportunism, civil servants and army officers, small businessmen and artisans who looked for support against liberal capitalism, Protestant small farmers and some wild social revolutionary anti-Semites. As the position of agriculture became more precarious, the attitude of the conservatives became increasingly radical. Wild outbursts against the tyranny of interests and the usury of the banks, against commercial malpractice and the evils of the Jewish-capitalist-liberal spirit became increasingly common, and were used in the demogogic rabble-rousing propaganda that is in such a marked contrast to the old patriarchal, self-assured and snobbish attitude of the conservatives of the past. Those who had remained disdainfully aloof from the masses now made desperate appeals to the little men whose votes they so badly needed. The conservatives' ideology thus became an extraordinary mixture of aristocratic reactionary clichēs and petit bourgeois radicalism. Aristocratic landowners and small farmers who traditionally had eyed one another with the deepest suspicion now worked together in party politics and actively looked for the support of the plebs. But they were never wholly able to win popular support, for the nature of the interests that they represented made this impossible. Their influence was, however, immense on the state apparatus, and such popular following as they had strengthened their hand when they claimed to speak on behalf of the people against the claims of the 'enemies of the Reich'.

The collective efforts of the politicised agrarians ran parallel to the similar activities of the industrialists. The free competition of the market-place now gave way to collective agreements and concerted efforts to influence the political course of the Reich. Agrarians and industrialists abandoned their political isolation as they began to use the Reichstag in order to achieve their economic goals. Within the Reichstag the 'Free Economic Association' (*Freie Wirtschaftliche Vereinigung*) with members from the conservative parties, the national liberals and the centre party, formed the basis of the parliamentary majority for the protective tariffs of 1879. Within the groups the Catholics, whose experience of the *Kulturkampf* made them determined opponents of Godless materialist liberalism, played a vital mediating role.

The protective tariffs marked an end of the liberal economic policies of the bureaucracy. In the years of prosperity the state had slowly removed the remaining barriers to the creation of a free market economy and had restricted its interventionist role. Now, with the depression, there was an increasing demand for state intervention in the economy to protect it from foreign competition, to increase government spending to stimulate growth or at least to counteract the effects of falling production, and to secure the gains that had been made from the attacks of social revolutionaries and even liberal democrats. Economic liberalism had achieved great things. The Industrial Revolution had been completed, agriculture modernised, the wealth of the country greatly increased, but now was the time to consolidate and protect what had been achieved. 'Protective collectivism', in Hans Rosenberg's phrase, replaced the free-trading liberalism of the years of prosperity.

For its part, the state had strong motives for taking up the challenge. From 1873 the financial situation of the Reich and of the state governments grew steadily worse. Income from direct taxation dwindled as the economy continued in a depressed state. State-owned factories no longer made the healthy profits on which the governments had come to depend. The states were understandably reluctant to increase their matricular contributions to the Reich, for they too were feeling the pinch. In the face of these problems Bismarck outlined a thorough reform of state finances. A strong argument for higher tariffs was therefore to increase revenue from customs, revenue which went directly to the Reich government. Nationalisation of the railways was also suggested as a means of increasing revenue, as was the tobacco monopoly. With low interest rates and depressed share prices the nationalisation scheme seemed particularly attractive.

The finance reform could only partly be realised owing to the opposition of the states to having their remaining budgetary rights further curtailed, and the fiscal effects of the tariffs modified by the Franckenstein clause. The protective tariffs thus became the panacea for all Germany's economic problems. Protection of 'national labour' was the foremost duty of the state, high tariffs on grain being equated with sound conservative government, with the preservation of traditional values and as insurance against violent social change. Whatever the arguments in favour of protective tariffs in the 1870s as a short-term solution to the immediate problems of falling agricultural prices and foreign competition, there can be little doubt that in the long run they were disastrous. Industrial tariffs remained fairly low even after 1879, so that the foreign markets which were so essential for the sale of surplus production were not entirely cut off. Agricultural tariffs on the other hand were constantly increased, so that between 1879 and 1887 they rose fivefold. Even when the depression was over and the original rationale for the tariffs was no longer valid they were retained. The price that was paid was high indeed. Expensive bread, the protection and preservation of the most reactionary elements within German society, and the elevation of an irrational agrarian ideology to the status of an official state doctrine were all to have disastrous consequences and to provide potent ingredients in the witches' brew of German Fascism.

Whereas industry by 1879 was in a strong enough position to weather the storm, and industrial sectors of industry were even opposed to the idea of protective tariffs which they did not deem necessary, given that industry was no longer in Emil Kirdorf's words a 'frail flower', agriculture was protected against the implications of structural changes in the world economy. Agriculture had to adapt itself to the challenges of cheap foreign agricultural produce and of sophisticated, modern and specialised methods of scientific farming and rigorous accounting. The inefficient and backward would have to be allowed to go to the wall, the efficient and forceful would have taken advantage of low prices to extend and improve their estates, invest in new equipment and prepare for the time when in an improved economic climate they would have reaped the benefits. Protective tariffs, combined with preferential railway freight charges, tax relief and cheap credit, preserved the class of land-owning aristocrats and the social *status quo* within the Reich. At a time of rapid and fundamental economic change the social structure was placed in quarantine, and as a result the antagonisms and contradictions between a modern economy and an antiquated social structure grew increasingly acute. The increase and the continuation of the tariffs on agricultural produce were thus both economically and socially harmful. It helped the inefficient and unimaginative producers, and it insulated a powerful caste against the necessity of change. Thus it was not 'national labour' that was protected in 1879 but a small group of aristocratic landowners, and the cost of that protection weighed heavily on the vast mass of Germans who were obliged to pay a high price for their food and whose aspirations for a more flexible and equitable society were once again frustrated.

Bismarck's policy was an extraordinarily successful attempt to preserve the old elites of pre-industrial Germany and to ensure their dominance in the new industrial age. The land-owning aristocracy which provided the personnel and the *Weltanschauung* of the officer corps and of the bureaucracy was preserved and protected against the forces of industrialisation and universal suffrage. He had discredited the liberals and tied the Catholic centre party to his political band-wagon. He had overcome the particularist tendencies of the south German protectionists by granting them their economic demands. He had unified the Reich behind his economic policies, but he had done so by further alienating those who remained true to their liberal political principles and by strengthening the support given to the socialists, whose determined opposition to his reactionary and anti-social policies made them the rallying point for all those who demanded a fundamental change in the direction of German policy. The result was a growing and dangerous split between the 'friends of the Reich' (*Reichsfreunde*) and the 'enemies of the Reich'

(*Reichsfeinde*).

Even in 1871 many perspicacious contemporaries asked themselves what would keep the Reich together once the delirium of the unification of Germany had worn away and the country would be faced with the prosaic realities of daily politics. The problem of adjustment was made all the more difficult by the fact that the political excitement was heightened by the extraordinary economic activity of the years of the foundation. The hangover of 1873 was thus all the more painful. It was then all too apparent how heterogeneous was the composition of the Reich. Particularism, anti-Prussianism, ultra-conservatism, Prussian chauvinism, republicanism and socialism were all given a new lease of life. In the place of ruling with the support of an uneasy alliance of liberals, Bismarck attempted to rally the country behind the programme of protective tariffs. This also proved to be a somewhat troublesome marriage of convenience and could only be held together by the technique of what Wolfgang Sauer has called 'negative integration' – the clear delineation of those who were for the system from those who were against it. A common hatred of the *Reichsfeinde* was to hold this coalition of right-wing conservatives, right-wing national liberals and Catholics together. In the early years the Catholics had been designated 'enemies of the Reich', their loyalties were deemed to lie in Rome rather than Berlin, their Catholicism un-Prussian and un-German. But the *Kulturkampf* had misfired. It had strengthened the determination of political Catholicism, and had alienated those who felt that Catholicism was better by far than the atheism of the socialists. With the need to find a parliamentary majority for tariff reform Bismarck had no scruples in designating the Catholics as *Reichsfreunde* and abandoned his futile campaign against the Catholic Church. There was still an ample supply of enemies of the Reich: Poles and Jews, Danes and Alsatians, Guelphs and Greater Germans, but above all the independents (*Freisinnige*) and the social democrats. In some instances these groups were the victims of discriminatory legislation such as the 'Germanising' policy directed against the racial minorities, or the anti-socialist laws. In other instances the 'enemies of the Reich' were subjected to the discrimination of powerful groups. Jews were excluded from the officer corps, and thus found it virtually impossible to enter the upper ranks of the civil service or to move to high society. This division of German society into a *Gemeinschaft* of right-thinking Germans defending their value system against the attacks of enemies of the Reich was one of the most pernicious legacies of Bismarck's Germany. There was no question of a loyal opposition, that fundamental concept of bourgeois society, but rather of a 'cancerous growth', a 'foreign body', a 'parasite' within the body politic which sapped its strength and threatened its continued existence.

The years of the Great Depression saw an alarming revival of anti-Semitism, which Bismarck was prepared to use as part of his policy of 'negative integration'. The anti-Semitism of these years was in one significant way different from the traditional hatred of Jews; it became a political movement that was quite distinct from previous outbursts of hatred and violence, religious intolerance and cultural prejudice. Jews in Germany had made an enormous contribution to the life of the country. In the arts and the universities, as journalists and politicians of almost all parties, including the conservatives, as bankers and industrialists they had excelled. By contrast there were also many non-assimilated Jews, most of whom were extremely poor and who usually came from the east. They were often treated contemptuously or at best indifferently by their more successful co-religionists. Traditionally anti-Semitism had been expressed in religious terms and in outbursts against sinful usury. The anti-Semitism of the depression was quite different, it was the anti-Semitism of the industrial age that was to prove more virulent and powerful than anything that had gone before. The new anti-Semitism was based on economic, political and racial arguments and was thus more all-embracing and insidious than the earlier manifestations of race hatred. Racial anti-Semitism was simultaneously an attack on liberal society in that it denied the possibility of assimilation and of cultural pluralism. With its often intoxicating propaganda it was able to mobilise mass support and could thus form the basis of a 'democratic' assault on democratic society.

There is a clear correlation between economic depression and anti-Semitic outbursts. When times were bad agrarians and peasants, small shopkeepers and artisans and the embittered petit bourgeois blamed 'Jewish' finance capital for their miseries. The Jews became the scapegoats for all the shortcomings and difficulties of industrial capitalism in the throes of a cyclical depression. It was particularly on the land that the Jews were hated, for in many areas Jews dominated the business life of the community and with so many farms heavily mortgaged, their prominence in banks and credit unions was particularly resented. The leaders of the *Bund der Landwirte* were only too willing to use anti-Semitic propaganda in order to whip up popular support for their movement.

The new anti-Semitism was not simply the ideology of hard-pressed farmers or disgruntled petit bourgeois, it was also adopted by men of culture and intelligence. Wagner, Treitschke and Lagarde were the most prominent of the 'respectable' anti-Semites, but their views were shared by many civil servants and professors, professional men and politicians. They dressed up their aversion to the Jews in pseudo-scientific theories and in high-falutin' philosophical systems, and were careful to dis-associate themselves from the crude visceral hatred of the plebs. As guardians of German *Geist* and culture, they were determined to rid the schools and universities of this foreign spirit. Men like Theodor Mommsen who stood up against the growing academic anti-Semitism were deeply concerned that such ideas were but the civilised face of the brutal racial hatred of the disgruntled masses, and that far from preserving German culture with its strong tradition of cosmopolitanism and tolerance, they were helping to create the kind of unthinking and barbarous anti-Semitism that was so striking and disgusting a feature of Tsarist Russia.

The anti-Semitism of these prominent members of polite society was part of a modish cultural pessimism that was so striking a by-product of the depression years. Anti-modernism as an aristocratic and reactionary form of anti-capitalism could be easily combined with anti-Semitism which equated materialism, commerce and industry, the flashy behaviour of the parvenus, the competitiveness and uncertainties of industrial capitalism, and the demands of radical social and political change, with the 'Jewish spirit'. Seen in these terms anti-Semitism was a violent expression of the anxiety of all those who feared the social and economic changes that were bound to occur as a necessary result of industrialisation, an anxiety that had become particularly intense as a result of the hardship of the depression.

It is extremely difficult to see the anti-Semitism of the depression years in true historical perspective because of the looming horrors of the *Endlösung*. Was the programme of the United Anti-Semitic Parties of 1899, which called for the solution of the 'world problem' of the Jews by having all Jews rounded up and then destroyed, simply the mad outburst of a fringe movement that was losing support in the years of prosperity, or was it a significant step forward to the mass murder of the Jews by the German Fascists? Were Bismarck's attacks on the Jewish money behind his political enemies, his attacks on the Jews as being the best propagandists for anti-Semitism, or his insults of the progressive politician Lasker ('stupid Jew-boy') or the Minister Friedenthal ('Semitic shit-in-the-pants') merely outbursts of aristocratic prejudice and electioneering, or did they show that anti-Semitism was a deep-rooted and growing political force? In terms of its immediate political impact, anti-Semitism had very little effect. In 1893, when the movement was at its height, 16 Reichstag members came from the anti-Semitic parties and 7 members of other parties associated themselves closely with this group. This group made a lot of noise, but was unable to influence legislation. What concerned many liberal and social-democratic politicians was that anti-Semitism was a wild and irrational force that could not be controlled even by those who tried to use it cynically for their own ends, as Bismarck did in 1884 when preparing for the Reichstag elections. It was not possible to debate or discuss with anti-Semites, the best that could be hoped was that the movement would die of its own accord. To a large extent this is exactly what happened. When the economy recovered after 1896 anti-Semitism lost much of its immediate potency. But the scapegoat role was revived during the First World War and had become an essential part of the ideological baggage of the extreme right.

These outbursts of political anti-Semitism were the most striking examples of the paranoia of the depression years, but even the movement for protective tariffs with its ideology of the 'protection of national labour' had a similar irrational moment. Protection was seen as a necessary shield against a world of enemies, an attitude that was all the more absurd given the fact that by 1879 industry had shown remarkable resilience and had managed to hold its own, even on the world market, and in such an uncomfortable economic climate. Behind Bismarck's slogans was an iron determination to strengthen the authority of the government and his own personal rule. Protection was a means to that end, and the real or perceived need for protective tariffs was not of itself a sufficient cause of the major changes in the direction of German policy that Bismarck instigated in the late 1870s. The uncertainties and anxieties of the depression years were exploited by Bismarck for his own political ends. The reforms further reduced the budgetary rights of the Reichstag, and as military expenditure was by far the largest item in the Reich budget, this meant that in effect the Prussian army was almost exempt from the scrutiny of Parliament. The army as the bastion of aristocratic, Prussian and ultra-conservative principles was thus one of the main beneficiaries of the protective tariffs of 1879.

With the Catholics now elevated to the status of 'Friends of the Reich' and with Bismarck's reluctance to go too far with political anti-Semitism, the socialists were designated as the prime enemies of the Reich. The modern German labour movement was also in many ways the child of the depression. Until the formation of the Socialist Workers' Party at Gotha in 1875 the socialists had been badly divided and had little popular success. With the Gotha conference the socialists were soon to become a mass party taking a larger share of the popular vote than the free conservatives or the progressives. The party benefited from the heightening of the class struggle, from the economic crisis, and from the widespread feeling that something drastic had to be done. The party's somewhat timid practice was disguised from all but the most diligent experts in socialist thought by rousing revolutionary rhetoric, massive assaults on the evils of capitalism and a somewhat romanticised picture of the socialist state to come. Marx and Engels might have been appalled at the Utopianism and the inconsistency of much of this thought, and decried the influence of Lassalle and the French apostles of co-operative labour on the new party, but to the German bourgeoisie the party was a united and revolutionary band of dedicated enemies of the established order and morality. They overlooked the fact that the party was far more interested in municipal drainage and questions of taxation than it was in revolution and the destruction of capitalism.

Nevertheless there can be no doubt that the socialist party was fired by a new urgency during the depression years. There were a handful of revolutionaries in the party, mainly wild-eyed anarchists who were soon expelled, but the vast mass of the rank and file stood behind the leadership in demanding a fair deal for labour. Not socialist revolution but an end to the treatment of the working class as second-class citizens, not the dictatorship of the proletariat but decent living and working conditions, improvements rather than radical change were what the party demanded. But even this was enough to stamp the socialists as enemies number one of the Reich, as un-German, as 'fellows without a Fatherland'.

By 1877 the industrialists of the Saar had formed an organisation led by Stumm, the 'King of Saarabia', which called for the lock-out of all socialist workers. The industrialists of the Ruhr were quick to follow suit. With rising unemployment they could afford to take a harsh line, and the socialists found it difficult to counter these attacks. Bismarck was quick to climb aboard the anti-socialist band-wagon. Social democracy, he announced, was responsible for Germany's current economic ills. Its agitation undermined business confidence and was thus the direct cause of unemployment. Socialism would have to be destroyed if Germany were to survive.

This ferocious anti-socialist policy, which reached a climax with the anti-socialist laws of 1878, were in large part directed not against the socialists themselves but the liberals. When Hödel attempted to assassinate the Kaiser, Bismarck announced with glee: 'Now we have them!' When asked if he meant the social democrats he immediately replied, 'No, the liberals.' Socialist-bashing was a dramatic way of demonstrating his break with the liberals and of cementing the new alliance of conservatives, right-wing liberals and Catholics. At the same time the anti-social nature of the proposed tariffs, which necessarily led to high food prices and heavier indirect taxation, a regressive tax hurting those with low incomes the most, was likely to radicalise the socialist movement. The 'red peril' was thus both a piece of deliberate political manipulation and a distinct possibility. The denial of certain fundamental rights, such as freedom of speech, freedom to form associations and freedom of movement was a massive attack on liberal society, the motives for which were political rather than economic, even though the arguments used were usually economic. Bismarck was looking for a violent resolution of the political and social problems of a society that was suffering from the strains of a prolonged depression. It was bitter medicine that had to be sweetened with social policy so that the pretence of the 'protection of national labour' could be maintained and so that the change of course of 1879 appeared as something more than a selfish attack on the working class.

The anti-socialist laws and the social policy of Bismarck's Germany were the outcome of a revival of the 'social question' which had plagued men's minds in the years before 1848, but which had been pushed somewhat into the background of the collective consciousness during the relatively prosperous years since the revolutionary year. Liberal economic policy and the removal of restrictions on individual movement, the abolition of old economic restraints and the introduction of universal manhood suffrage, a bloodthirsty and aggressive foreign policy and finally the excitement of the foundation of the German Empire in 1871 had diverted men's minds from fundamental questions of domestic politics. In the early years of his career as Minister President Bismarck had maintained a stance of benevolent neutrality in the social question, lifting certain restrictions that still irked the working class, such as the anti-union clauses of the

Prussian Industrial Ordinances (*Gewerbeordnung*). His hope was that the working class would grow to accept the essential benevolence and good intentions of the state and gratefully accept its place in an autocratic but well-meaning state. The rich man would be in his castle, the poor man at his gate, but the poor man would be guaranteed certain minimum requirements, the rich man made aware of his social obligations.

Even Bismarck's moderate attitude towards the labour movement was hopelessly anachronistic and doomed to failure. A patriarchal attitude towards the working class was no longer acceptable in an age of universal suffrage and mass parties. Only by accepting as legitimate the claims to formal equality could Bismarck have avoided the confrontation that divided German society so badly that under the stress of war and defeat the entire structure collapsed. But it was very difficult to claim that the attitude of the state towards social democracy was dictated by the movement of the business cycle. For Bismarck the decisive experience was the opposition of the socialists, led by Liebknecht and Bebel, to the annexationist policies of the Prussian government during the Franco-Prussian war. Bismarck had been impressed by Lassalle and had hoped that some co-operation would be possible with the Lassalleans with their Hegelian notions of the moral superiority of the state, their naïve faith in universal suffrage, and their bureaucratic and centralised party structure; but Bebel and Liebknecht's outbursts against the war 'removed the scales from his eyes' and showed him the true nature of socialism. Since socialism was opposed to the national purpose, then all-out war would have to be declared on the enemies of the Reich. Socialism became all the more of a danger when the Gotha conference produced a united party and when the depression radicalised the movement. Although the anti-socialist laws could not be renewed in 1890 because of a change in the political alignments in the Reichstag, the socialists were still treated like pariahs and exotic schemes for a *coup d'ētat* and for military operations against the socialists were widely discussed.

Bismarck's Social Policy

If Bismarck began to think of the socialists as murderous communards he did not altogether abandon the carrot in favour of exclusive use of the stick. The aim of his social policy was to undo some of the harm done by the anti-socialist laws, to relieve some of the immediate hardship caused by the depression, and last but not least to take much of the wind out of the socialists' sails. Bismarck would give the state that sense of moral obligation which Lassalle had argued was its true purpose and thus undermine the social democrats' position, for the party was still heavily influenced by Lassallean ideas. In his choice of methods Bismarck consciously followed the French rather than the English model of social policy. He had little sympathy for the English Tories' efforts to improve factory inspection and ensure certain minimum standards in working conditions. The Chancellor wanted to have nothing to do with restrictions on child labour, on the employment of women, on the statutory regulation of the working day or the introduction of minimum wages. The factory inspection act of 1871 was left as a torso, and Bismarck showed no inclination whatever to become the German Shaftesbury. On his own estates he flaunted the existing regulations in a manner that his managers found somewhat alarming, for he felt that industry should not be hampered in any way by such rules and regulations, particularly at such a difficult time of depressed domestic markets and fierce international competition. On the other hand, he had long been an admirer of Napoleon III whose efforts to turn France into a nation of *rentiers* dependent on the state he felt to be the most effective form of social policy and the best prophylactic against revolution. If the state were to guarantee protection against illness, accidents and old age and be prepared to offer help to co-operatives and to the savings of the little men, then the population would not risk losing this security by following those revolutionaries who promised the working people an earthly paradise. There was nothing, in Bismarck's view, like the prospect of a nice little pension to turn people into good conservatives.

However grandiose the scheme might have sounded when Bismarck introduced it bit by bit into the Reichstag, the practice was less inspiring. Germany was so far behind England in the control of labour conditions and behind France in social security that something had to be done. In spite of the massive propaganda efforts of the government which were to make Bismarck's system of social insurance the envy of the industrialised world, it was in fact a hastily patched-up affair, a desperate attempt to make up for the complete failure of the government in the field of social policy. The scale of the operation was modest, and the benefits very small. The steadily employed and healthy worker, precisely the type of man that was attracted by the social-democratic party, received no benefits whatever until he became sick, injured, unemployed or old. The steady growth of support for the social democrats showed clearly that the policy was a failure. The true proletarian was given little protection against unsafe and unhygienic working conditions, or against excessive working hours. He had no right to form associations or unions, he was severely hurt by indirect taxation and all this at a time of unusual depression. He had no reason whatever to feel grateful to Bismarck for his largesse, and those who were protected, mainly the permanently unemployed, the destitute and the infirm, had little political influence or energy. The employers benefited in that welfare became a state rather than a private concern, and they were freed from many of the tiresome judicial obligations to their workers which they found such an irksome aspect of the old system.

The first of these measures was the Health Insurance Bill of 1883, which provided for sickness benefits from the third day of an illness for a maximum of 13 weeks. The scheme was administered through various voluntary associations such as the Local Health Organisations (*Ortskrankenkassen*) or the Miners' Association (*Knappschaften*). In most instances the worker paid two-thirds of the contributions and the employer the balance. At first the scheme only applied to factory workers, miners, and some white-collar workers. It was then extended to cover other categories of workers. But the scheme was by no means comprehensive. By 1885 only 10 per cent of the population was covered by the Health Insurance Act, and payments averaged out at a mere 11 marks per member.

Accident insurance, which had first been introduced in the Reichstag in 1881, was finally adopted in 1884. The insurance was administered by co-operative associations of the employers (*Berufsgenossenschaften*), and the employers had to bear the full cost of the premiums. Payments began in the fourteenth week after the accident, when the health insurance benefits were no longer paid. Accident insurance benefits amounted to two-thirds of average earnings, and a particularly progressive aspect of the scheme was that it was a no-fault insurance that was paid almost automatically without any legal wrangles. Lifetime pensions and widows' benefits were also provided by the scheme.

The final piece of social legislation, and the one that was closest to Bismarck's intentions, was the Disability and Old Age Pension Act of 1889. The disability pension was paid to those who had been in the scheme for at least four years, old age pensions paid at age 71 after 24 years of payment. The pensions were extremely modest. By 1900 they averaged 155 marks per annum. By no means all workers were eligible for the scheme. Payments were shared equally by the employers and the employees, but the state subsidised the scheme by direct grants of

50 marks per annum toward each pension.

Being neither universal nor generous, the social insurance schemes were resented by both employer and employee. To the employers the scheme was regarded as an intolerable burden at a time of economic hardship and a fearful waste of public money. To the employees the premiums were burdensome and the benefits inadequate. On behalf of the social democrats Bebel attacked the legislation in the Reichstag on the grounds that it was not universal, that the employers did not bear the full cost of the contributions, and that the scheme was not centrally administered by the state. Certainly these modest efforts at reform were quite insufficient significantly to ameliorate the condition of the working class and did nothing whatever to undermine the social democrats. But on the other hand they were superior to anything in Britain or France, where the working class suffered even worse conditions.

To a large extent these measures were insurance against the consequence of poor working conditions and the lack of any adequate system of factory inspection. It was not until the early twentieth century that proper legislation against the exploitation of child labour was introduced as part of a systematic extension of Bismarck's social legislation. The old spirit lingered on. Social insurance was not seen as a means towards the emancipation of mankind from the indignities of unnecessary hardship and suffering. Social control rather than emancipation was the guiding principle. Men like Stumm, for example, enthusiastically instituted an exemplary social service for his workers and their families, but the very idea that the recipients of these services should have any say in their organisation or operation would have filled him with horror. For him, industry had to be run as a military operation, and like a good general he felt that his men had to be well looked after, decently housed, adequately fed and provided with medical services when required. Social policy was thus not a set of measures to help the working class, but rather to help the employers.

The Depression and Industry

Bismarck's social policy that accorded so well with Stumm's 'master in my own house' attitude towards industrial relations was also an adequate expression of the structural changes that had taken place within the German economy in the course of the Great Depression. Protective tariffs in 1879 had given the class structure of imperial Germany a new lease of life and had saved the land-owning aristocracy from the necessary consequences of the profound changes of the world's agricultural system. But no amount of legislation could alter the fact that Germany was becoming an industrial nation in the sense that industry generated more income, employed more people and was growing faster than the agricultural sector. At the same time a significant change of emphasis was taking place within industry. In 1873 the consumer-goods industry had played the dominant role, and in the course of the depression heavy industry took over the lead. With this change in the structure of industry went an increase in the significance of the large industrial firm. Small firms were driven out of business not only by the exigencies of the depression, but also by the consequences of this growing emphasis on heavy industry, and the effects of the new tariffs.

The consumer-goods industry relied on cheap imports of raw materials and a healthy foreign market for its products. Now this sector had to pay more for raw materials, found it increasingly difficult to export and had to sell on a depressed domestic market. The heavy industrialists on the other hand, with their efforts to form syndicates and cartels, their close association with the government and the Reichstag and their powerful interest groups, were far better placed to withstand the effects of the depression. The huge industrial conglomerates, working closely with other similar formations, were headed by a small group of immensely powerful men who, along with the leading bankers, formed the economic élite of imperial Germany. These men were the *grands bourgeois* of Germany whose life-style reinforced the position of the land-owning aristocracy at a time when economically and politically they would otherwise have been in absolute decline.

There had been a chance in the 1870s, just as there were to be further chances in 1919 and 1945, to break the political power and influence of the land-owning aristocracy, but Bismarck would not betray the interests of his class and indulge in a dangerous democratic experiment. But the costs of maintaining this class in such a position of strength were very high. It involved the heightening of the class struggle by the process of 'negative integration' which bound the aristocracy and the big bourgeoisie together in a common front against the emancipatory efforts of the working class. The result was an increasingly antagonistic society in which efforts at reform were regarded with justifiable cynicism. The frustrations and anxieties that such a society produced were to feed the irrational and anti-modernist ideologies of the period, and to provide a powerful force behind German imperialism.

8 IMPERIALISM

The Beginnings of German Imperialism

As the depression dragged on there was a mounting chorus of voices demanding a German colonial empire so that industry could find new markets, the unemployed find work, and the country given a sense of national purpose which seemed to have been lost in the gloom of continual economic stagnation. Men like Ernst von Weber, who had spent time in Africa, argued that without a colonial empire a modern industrial state would be unable to overcome its chronic crises of over-production and would eventually be faced with a bloody social revolution in which the propertyless would take their revenge on the propertied. This argument set the tone for the widespread discussion of the colonial question in the late 1870s and early 1880s. There was general agreement that given the lasting crisis of over-production which many felt was so serious that capitalism itself was unlikely to survive, and since repressive measures had done nothing to lessen the 'Red peril', colonial expansion was the only salvation. Thus familiar arguments from the classical political economists on the limits of capitalist expansion and the need for new markets to offset the imbalance between supply and effective demand were combined with social imperialist notions of the deflection of internal tensions away from their objective source in the hope that socialist revolutionaries could somehow be converted into flag-planting colonial adventurers. Imperialism was thus intended to complete the job that the anti-socialist laws and the protective tariffs of 1879 had failed to do – to protect Germany against the rising tide of social democracy and industry from the problems of over-production.

The colonial enthusiasts soon formed a number of interest groups that were to have a considerable impact. Western industrialists called for colonies to ensure a good return on capital, to stimulate industry and trade and to protect the country against the perils of a socialist revolution. In Berlin professors and journalists made similar pleas. In 1882 the German Colonial Association (*Deutsche Kolonialverein*) was formed on the initiative of Freiherr von Maltzan who had written an influential series of articles in the *Augsburger Allgemeine Zeitung* on his experiences during an extended tour of Africa, and who had some close connections with leading figures in industry, particularly with the chemical firm BASF. Leading members of the association included Johannes Miquel, the banker and industrialist Guido Henckel von Donnersmarck, and the Reichstag member Hohenlohe-Langenburg. This new association proved to be more vital and attractive than any of its predecessors. Many of the smaller colonialist groups either joined the association or worked closely with it, often having members on the executive committee. The membership came largely from middle-sized industrialists, the professions and merchants, but among them were men of considerable influence – Siemens, Hansemann, Krupp, Kirdorff, Haniel, Stumm, Pless, Treitschke, Sybel, Schmoller and Ranke, to name but a few. The association thus represented precisely those forces that Bismarck had brought together in the defence of 'national labour' under the banner of protective tariffs.

Up to this time Germany had made some first steps towards the creation of an informal empire by expanding overseas trade, establishing naval stations and branch offices of banks and trading companies. In the Far East German shipping predominated in Chinese waters, and a naval station was established for the Prussian navy in Yokohama in 1867. After the foundation of the Reich a number of banks made their first unsuccessful attempts to found branch offices in China. During the Franco-Prussian war there were demands for the seizure of parts of the French East Asian empire to form the basis of further German expansion in the area. Cochin China or Saigon were suggested as suitable booty. But Bismarck was not prepared at this stage to run the risk of antagonising Britain, particularly as the German fleet was still very small and insignificant. In the following years the Germans extended their trading network in the Pacific, although Berlin refused to support any of the efforts to lay formal claim to areas such as North Borneo. With both the United States and Britain pursuing a policy of imperialist expansion in the area the Germans had to tread warily, often finding that their carefully negotiated treaties with local chieftains were rendered null and void when either of the two great naval powers intervened. Nevertheless German interests had considerable success, particularly in Samoa, and the Berlin government was careful to point out that Germany was only interested in trade, not in the formation of a colonial empire. The Reichstag majority opposed any state support for Germany's informal empire, as the debates on the Samoa question in 1880 showed, and Bismarck was therefore unwilling to lend his support for any schemes such as Hansemann's colonial project in New Guinea. Increased foreign trade was one thing, but the government was not yet willing to support the formation of new colonies, the more so as the Reichstag was clearly opposed to any such moves.

German businessmen were also very active in Latin America. By the late 1860s two-thirds of Mexican foreign trade was in the hands of German interests, the British having lost control of the situation by supporting the Emperor Maximilian and his right-wing régime against the Mexican revolutionaries. The Germans were also active in the other Latin American countries, but the amount of business was still rather small-scale, and even in Mexico the Germans tended to work as intermediaries for British and French firms so that Latin America never accounted for a significant proportion of German foreign trade. As late as 1913 Latin America only accounted for 7.6 per cent of German foreign trade and about 10 per cent of Germany's foreign investments. German influence was felt in Latin America more by emigration and by the important role played by military advisers than by trade, commerce and investment.

The government showed a similar attitude towards demands for German colonies in north Africa, for Bismarck was always concerned with the reaction of Britain and France to any over-hasty move by the Germans in an area where their interests were very much at stake. Again German businessmen were active throughout Africa and the Middle East, a few German consulates were established in Africa and the occasional naval vessel made a visit to show that the government stood behind the German traders.

Government Intervention

With the onset of the Great Depression the principal aim of German overseas policy was to stimulate exports so that industry could find adequate outlets for its excess capacity. Bismarck was particularly concerned to expand the consular service and to make sure that it was more effective in furthering Germany's economic interests abroad. Although commercial attaches were not attached to embassies and consulates until the Weimar Republic, increasing emphasis was placed on the economic activities of the foreign service and there can be little doubt that part of the success of Germany's export industry was due to the efforts of these carefully selected civil servants who were chosen more for their familiarity with the business world than their adeptness at the more traditional diplomatic skills.

Efforts by the government to stimulate the export trade were not confined to the more effective exchange of information through diplomatic channels, as Bismarck was determined to give active support to enterprises involved in foreign trade. The banks, whose foreign branches had mostly been closed down at the beginning of the depression, were anxious to get government support and exemption from the rules and regulations governing joint-stock banks. But the price they demanded was too high, and some senior civil servants would not agree to allow some of the banks exemption from the normal provisions of the law, even though the Chancellor was quite prepared to turn a blind eye. The reluctance of the banks to indulge in risky overseas ventures and the opposition of the Ministry of Finance to the suggested irregularities resulted in no new foreign banking ventures, and business and commercial circles complained that foreign banking was a British monopoly. It was not until 1886 that the 'German Bank Overseas' (*Deutsche Ueberseebank*) was founded, mainly on the initiative of the Deutsche Bank. Its first branch was opened in Buenos Aires.

A more promising approach seemed to be the subsidisation of shipping lines, a policy which had already been implemented in most of the great trading nations, including the home of free trade – Britain. Some doctrinaire German free-traders opposed the idea out of principle, others saw no reason why Hamburg shipping should be given the help that was denied to equally deserving candidates for state support. Opposition in the Reichstag to such proposals was so strong that it was not until 1884 that a Bill was introduced calling for a subsidy for shipping to the Far East and Australia. The proposal was eventually accepted in a modified form in the following year when the Reichstag majority accepted the argument that after twelve years of depression, with no end yet in sight, the state would have to do something to stimulate the economy. The most profound heart-searching took place within the ranks of the social democrats. There were those who stuck by the principle of 'not one *groschen* for the system', while others argued that given the high levels of unemployment in the shipyards, the shipping subsidies would help the working class. Some socialists denounced the subsidies as an imperialist levy, while others welcomed any measures that would encourage employment. Finally the majority of the party supported the shipping subsidy, and the social democratic party thus made an important step in the direction of accommodation with the existing system. 'Revisionism' was thus in part a child of the depression.

For the first eight years both the shipping lines and the shipyards registered heavy losses, and some of the most unprofitable routes such as those to Samoa and Tonga had to be abandoned. Critics of the entire scheme saw their worst fears confirmed, but were roundly condemned by their opponents for their 'shopkeeper's mentality'. By the end of the depression the subsidised lines were beginning to make handsome profits, and there was steadily growing activity in the shipyards until Germany was soon to become one of the world's greatest shipbuilding nations. Although the short-term effects of the subsidies might have been a trifle disappointing to some, within a decade it was obvious that they were a success and all but the most determined critics were silenced.

Africa

Shipping subsidies seemed to many to be a step in the right direction, but insufficient on their own to lead to economic recovery. Something more dramatic and exciting was needed. Looking to Britain, where the effects of the depression were not nearly so severe, they saw the obvious answer – India. India became in the eyes of the German imperialists a fabulous Eldorado on which the wealth and might of the British Empire rested. If only Germany could find its own India the Reich would be as prosperous and as powerful as its great rival across the North Sea. During the depression years there was much talk of a 'German India' in the Far East or in central Africa that would provide new markets for German goods, a home for the excess population and a vast reservoir of wealth. Imperial propagandists rivalled one another in painting highly romantic and exaggerated visions of a German Empire which would form the basis of the country's future prosperity.

The beginnings of Germany's African empire were somewhat more prosaic. Friedrich Fabri, travelling in the area between the Orange River and Portuguese Angola, brought the word of God and German weapons to the natives and was soon obliged to ask the German Foreign Office for protection when tribal war broke out, and the British refused to guarantee the safety of the Germans in the area. Fabri was forced to declare bankruptcy, the Foreign Office being unwilling to become too heavily involved in this rather unpromising area.

Another German adventurer, F.A.E. Lüderitz, was also busy smuggling weapons in the area south of Walvis Bay. He too asked for German protection, but once again Bismarck was reluctant to become too heavily involved in the formation of expensive and troublesome colonies in Africa and was not prepared to do anything more than send a naval vessel to the area at irregular intervals as a gesture of support. The British government promised to keep an eye on German interests provided that the distance from Walvis Bay was not too excessive. At this time Lüderitz had no clear ideas where the German area of influence was to be located and the British wanted precise details. Thus in the spring of 1883 an expedition was mounted and the area of Angra Pequena was bought from the local chief for £100 and some guns. Lüderitz hoped to exploit the mineral resources of the area, but Fabri, perhaps a trifle embittered after his bankruptcy, argued that he did not have sufficient capital to embark on ambitious mining schemes. Bismarck was concerned about Lüderitz's efforts to establish a regular colony under the German flag, as he was claiming sovereignty over Angra Pequena. Lüderitz was informed that he could make himself sovereign over the area if he so wished, but that the German government did not want to become involved. Lüderitz was undaunted and continued to buy up vast tracts of land. In November 1883 for a mere £500 he bought the coastal strip from the South African border to the 26th parallel. An encouraging report from the captain of the German ship *Nautillus* that had been sent on a visit to Angra Pequena led the Foreign Office to suggest that Lüderitz might try to purchase all the coastal land up to the Angolan border. But the greater the area that Lüderitz controlled, the more difficult became the question of sovereignty. Did it reside in Lüderitz, in the local chiefs or would the whole area have to become a German protectorate? Bismarck preferred to vest sovereignty in 'Lüderitz the First', who would be given the limited protection of the German government. In this manner he hoped to avoid the trouble and the expense of a formal colony.

The Kingdom of Lüderitz the First was hardly a viable solution to the problem because South Africa and Britain were both suspicious of German intentions and regarded south-west Africa as being within their sphere of influence, even if they were not prepared to establish a formal colony. The establishment of an English protectorate over Bechuanaland was clear indication that the British government was intent on containing German expansion in southern Africa and wished to frustrate Lüderitz's schemes to link one African coast to another. At the same time Fabri's remarks that Lüderitz lacked the capital to exploit the area proved to be quite true. A company was formed in Germany, the German Colonial Company for South-West Africa (DKGSWA) in which investors included Bleichröder, the Diskontogesellschaft, Mendelssohn, Oppenheim, the Dresdner Bank and the Deutsche Bank, and bought out Lüderitz's interests. Lüderitz did not live long enough to enjoy his new-found wealth, for he drowned shortly afterwards on an exploration. The distinguished investors in the new company were soon to be bitterly disappointed, for the mineral resources of the area proved to be rather more modest than had been touted, and the company's only consolation was that it had undertaken a heavy burden for the glory of the German Reich rather than for the profit of investors.

Although South-West Africa became a formal German protectorate in 1884, the colony did not prosper. The DKGSWA sold most of its holdings to a British company, and the German government showed small interest in a colony which was of such little economic importance. It was not until the early twentieth century, when the discovery of diamonds and copper excited the interest of investors, that the colony began to show some signs of economic activity.

Lüderitz's other schemes for African colonies were even less successful. Little came of the grandiose plan of a German colony in Zululand forming the eastern end of a trans-African German colony in which the anti-British Boers would co-operate with their fellow Teutons and the Germans would supplant the British as the colonists of central Africa. The Boers showed little enthusiasm for such schemes, and Bismarck was prepared to abandon the entire scheme when the British government protested. Thus the schemes for German colonies in Zululand and Santa Lucia Bay were used by the Chancellor as bargaining counters with Britain when the Sudan crisis and the problems of Afghanistan were placing the British government in an exceedingly difficult position.

In West Africa, from Liberia to the Congo, German firms were engaged in the highly lucrative trade in palm oil. Among these firms the Woermann shipping firm was the most successful. Woermann tried to persuade Bismarck to establish a German colony in the Cameroons in order to secure this valuable market. There was some urgency in the note he sent to the Chancellor in 1883 because there were British moves to incorporate the Cameroons into the empire which, although opposed by Gladstone, might one day materialise. Failing that, either France or Portugal might be tempted to seize the area. Woermann had powerful allies. He was a director of the Diskontogesellschaft and supported by the Hamburg Chamber of Commerce which had abandoned its strict free-trade principles under the impact of the depression and now called for a naval base on Fernando Po and a colony in the Cameroons. As in Angra Pequena, Bismarck was not yet prepared to support the idea of a colony in the Cameroons, but he was anxious to do everything possible to encourage German trade in West Africa. A coaling station on Fernando Po and a satisfactory understanding of German rights in the area by the other imperialist powers was as far as he was prepared to go.

Increasingly strained relations between London and Berlin made it impossible for such a policy to work, and it soon became clear that if the Germans did not establish a protectorate over the Cameroons and Togo the British would hoist the flag. Bismarck was thus obliged to give way to the demands of those who insisted that a colony was needed in West Africa if German trade in the area were to continue to thrive. He was also unable to convince Woermann and the other West African traders to take over responsibility for the administration of the new protectorates under the terms of a charter company. To many left-wing liberals and most social democrats the suggestion that the German taxpayers should pay the enormous cost of administering colonies in Africa was another blatant example of class politics. At least three-fifths of German exports to West Africa was *Schnaps*, most of which was produced in the distilleries of the Prussian Junkers. The distilleries were already given handsome subsidies and tax relief as well as export premiums. The export of *Schnaps* had already increased enormously during the depression. Now the Chancellor, owner of four distilleries, was asking for further assistance for this pampered industry. Anti-colonialists were joined by missionaries who painted lurid pictures of the effects of alcohol on the Africans and both were attacked by those who argued that with the economy in such a depressed state there was no time for such sentimental arguments and pious denunciations of *Schnapspolitik*. Spirits continued to be exported in large quantities to the German colonies in West Africa and Germany's power and influence in the area rested in large measure on this trade.

Woermann and the West African Syndicate, which had been formed by a number of leading Hamburg firms, showed no interest whatever in taking over any of the administrative functions of the colonies, and spent much of their energy in finding ingenious ways of avoiding payment of any taxes or duties that were applied to the area. Frequent native uprisings against German rule were brutally crushed by naval units and gradually an administrative and military establishment was created, the cost of which was carried by Berlin. The syndicate itself collapsed within two years, so that the government had to accept the inevitable and the colonies were ruled directly from Berlin.

If Lüderitz and Woermann were the leading figures of the colonisation of West Africa, in the east Karl Peters led the pack. Peters had founded the Society for German Colonisation (*Gesellschaft für Deutsche Kolonisation* – GfDK) in 1884 when as an impatient young man of 29 with overbearing ambition and desire for self-aggrandisement he had broken with the Colonial Association, which he accused of inaction, and proclaimed himself the champion of the new German Empire. Peters had spent two years in London and, like so many Germans of his generation, he combined a profound respect with a deep loathing for Britain and the British Empire. He was convinced that British wealth and the stability of British society rested on the empire, and felt that without a similar empire Germany was condemned to lead a 'proletarian existence' among the nations of the world. Peters' imperialism combined a rabid chauvinism and racism with social Darwinism and a large measure of personal ambition. Suffering from severe ego weakness, he over-compensated by his assertive and strident behaviour in the singularly unattractive manner of so many of the upper classes of imperial Germany, a mode of behaviour which was regarded as 'dashing' (*schneidig*) and which is so brilliantly satirised in Heinrich Mann's novel, *Der Unterthan*.

Peters at first thought of becoming the new Treitschke, having gained his doctorate in history in 1879, but he soon became impatient with the idea of working his way up into the professoriat and from thence into the Reichstag. Having melodramatically toyed with the idea of suicide, he decided instead to secure his place in German history (later he upped the ante to world history) by becoming the German Clive or Warren Hastings. His short-term aim was a German colony stretching from the Zambesi to the Nile and he was intoxicated by the vision of his triumphal entry into Cairo as a second Napoleon. These were the ravings of a disturbed and even pathological mind, and with the best will in the world it is difficult to find anything attractive in Karl Peters. His cruelty, anti-Semitism, racism and bloated ambition were all greatly admired by imperialists and later by Fascists, but more balanced minds can do little more than extend sympathy towards the diseased and look for the social determinants of such vicious and brutal behaviour.

Whereas both Lüderitz and Woermann were businessmen who could speak with a certain authority on the need for securing overseas markets, Peters had no direct experience of the business world, and although he spoke at length about the need for secure markets Bismarck was not attracted by his fanaticism, and preferred rather more sober businessmen. Many Foreign Office officials found his personality repulsive. The GfDK was undaunted by the lukewarm reception accorded to its ideas in official circles. Wild plans for a spectacular expedition were discussed. South America, the Congo and Angola were suggested until it was finally agreed that the colony should be on the east coast of Africa, opposite Zanzibar.

The Foreign Office told Peters that he could not count on their support, and the German consul in Zanzibar was instructed not to give Peters any encouragement and to warn him again that the Reich did not intend to establish a protectorate in east Africa.

Peters pressed on regardless, signing a series of fraudulent treaties with local chiefs until he claimed control over 140,000 square kilometres of land in the area of Usagara. He then returned to Berlin in early 1885 and began a campaign to bring the entire area under the protection of the Reich. In order to make the proposition as attractive as possible to the Chancellor, he suggested the formation of a 'German East African Company' (DOAG), based on the model of the East India Company, that would be responsible for the administration of the territory. With the hinterland under German control and with the powerful position of the established Hanseatic merchants in Zanzibar Peters argued that German influence could predominate in East Africa. Bismarck was prepared to accept these arguments and Peters was given an imperial letter of protection, a form of royal charter for his enterprise. The British were alarmed at German plans to colonise the Usagara, for the importance of the area in controlling the trade routes from central Africa to the coast was obvious. The Sultan of Zanzibar protested against what he regarded as a violation of his sovereignty over the area. But as long as the British government was fully occupied with problems in other parts of the area, and as long as Bismarck continued to reassure and placate the Sultan, there was little that either could do to stop the Germans. Indeed both the British and the Germans found that they had a common interest in resisting the Sultan of Zanzibar and his efforts to bolster what remained of his authority in east Africa. Bismarck was quick to underline the need for a common front against 'fanatical Muslims and cannibals'. The result of this policy of co-operation was most satisfactory for the Germans. The Sultan was held in check and the British gave way to German demands. The main problem was to place the DOAG on a sound financial footing. In early 1887 the company was reconstituted, Peters was in effect thrown out of the company, having earned the well-deserved reputation of being a financial incompetent, and capital began to come in from a number of well-known banks and industrial enterprises. But that was not the end of the company's difficulties. The Arab traders in east Africa were suspicious of the Germans and regarded them as potentially dangerous rivals. The black Africans, provoked by the brutality and rapaciousness of the DOAG representatives, revolted and drove the Germans from the rural areas until they were besieged in the ports of Dar-es-Salaam and Bagamoyo.

The attempt to rule an east African colony by means of a charter company had failed. The alternatives seemed to be either to fight a full-scale colonial war or to abandon the attempt altogether. A colonial war would be costly and contrary to Bismarck's views on how to stimulate foreign trade by imperialist ventures. On the other hand, to give up would be a serious loss of prestige, especially after the long and careful diplomatic negotiations that had resulted in Germany's potentially favourable position in the area. German warships lopped shells rather ineffectually into some of the port towns whilst a major expeditionary force was prepared, ostensibly to eradicate the slave trade. With a helping hand from the Pope, who denounced the slave trade, and thus encouraged the Catholic centre party to vote in favour of the funding of a punitive expedition to east Africa, Bismarck was able to secure parliamentary approval for military operations. Those who voted for the measure talked of the civilising mission of the Germans in Africa, of the crusade against slavery and of German honour which was at stake. More cynical souls felt that the profits of the DOAG were of somewhat greater concern. But these carping voices were soon silenced, the expedition was sent at a cost of over 9 million marks and with great brutality restored law, order and civilisation to the area.

Karl Peters' further escapades in east Africa led to some rather tense situations with the British authorities. Bismarck was anxious to maintain good relations with Britain and announced that the friendship of Lord Salisbury was worth more to him than 'twenty swampy colonies in Africa'. Bismarck dismissed Peters as a criminal, William II called him a stupid idiot, but even Peters' antics in east Africa did not stop the signing of the Heligoland-Zanzibar agreement in the summer of 1890, which was the high point of Anglo-German relations. The German east African colony had been used skilfully to reach an accord with the British, but the cost had been very high. Once again the Reich had to take over the cost and responsibility for the administration and protection of the colony, to put up with Peters and his tiresome adventures, and to undertake military operations to pacify the native population.

The 'informal Empire' approach was much more successful in the Congo where, although there were no German colonies, Germany's economic interests were carefully guarded. Of the firms trading in the Congo, Woermann's was the most important, sending the traditional

Schnaps and weapons, the mainstay of Germany's civilising mission in Africa, in return for palm oil, rubber and peanuts. Woermann's main concern was that German trade with the Congo should not be hindered in any way and he was particularly concerned about the Anglo-Portuguese agreement of 1884, which Woermann and the Hamburg senate wished to have replaced by an international agreement securing free trade in the Congo. Portuguese customs duties on German goods were a serious threat to the continuation of a prosperous and growing trade with the Congo, and the Wilhelmstrasse was bombarded with petitions from concerned businessmen and chambers of commerce who stressed the importance of the Congo market. Bismarck had every sympathy for these appeals for an open door in the Congo and based his diplomatic strategy upon them.

At the conference which met in Berlin in November 1884 to discuss the Congo, Bismarck's main concern was to establish free trade in the area. Initially he had imagined that the conference was desirable in order to restrain the territorial ambitions of the British, and he had been so successful in enlisting the support of the French against the British that they had even been prepared to abandon their protectionist stance. At the conference, however, Bismarck soon discovered that his fears of the British were largely unfounded, and that French attachment to protectionism was greater than he had imagined. Germany and Britain found themselves united in seeking to extend the free-trade area beyond the immediate area of the Congo, whereas the French and Portuguese opposed any such moves. Bismarck grew increasingly impatient with the endless discussions over questions of sovereignty and the recognition of Leopold II's 'International Congo Association'. For him the only concern was that the Congo should be a free-trade zone in which Germany could continue to sell guns and spirits in spite of the rather half-hearted humanitarian objections of the British delegation. In these terms the Congo conference was a success. A compromise was finally reached on the sovereignty issue and the Congo basin became a huge free-trade area, an open door to the African continent, and the Germans were determined to exploit the possibilities of a free-trade zone from coast to coast through the centre of the African continent.

The Pacific

Whereas in Africa the colonial enthusiasts had had some success, the nightmare of the Samoa débâcle was a restraining influence on further adventures in the Pacific. At first Germany's attention was focused on

New Guinea. The British Foreign Office was not particularly concerned about German schemes, and Gladstone and his colonial secretary, Lord Derby, had no ambitions to increase British colonial holdings in the Pacific. The Australians demanded the annexation of that part of New Guinea that had not already been annexed by the Dutch. The German planters were thus concerned that the British government might give way to pressure from the British colonists in Australia and that the fate of their highly lucrative plantations, which were based virtually on slave labour, would be uncertain. The disgraceful exploitation of labour, and the high death rate of the workers, meant that the principal concern of the plantation owners and the German officials in the Pacific was for an adequate supply of labour which they feared might be interrupted by the colonising activities of other powers. The humanitarian objections of those who spoke up against the treatment of native workers were dismissed as sentimental fulminations by idealists who refused to see that the commercial prosperity of Germany was of prime importance and that the Pacific islanders were in some mysterious way benefiting from their contact with western European culture. A further consideration was that when and if the projected canal through Panama was built, the importance of the Pacific would be greatly enhanced.

A 'New Guinea Consortium' was formed, largely at the initiative of Adolph van Hansemann and Bleichröder, in order to exploit the possibilities of the Pacific and to press for the annexation of eastern New Guinea. Under their leadership, the consortium had little difficulty in attracting the support of a number of influential figures in the business world. The consortium had strong support in government circles, including Kusserow in the Foreign Office, who was related to Hansemann and who, it was revealed in the Reichstag, owned land in New Guinea, and also Herbert Bismarck, who urged his father to support the formation of a charter company for New Guinea. Hansemann, having by highly dubious means convinced the other major German firm operating in New Guinea to join in with his New Guinea company, could claim to represent all German commercial interests in New Guinea, and promised to establish an orderly administration in the new colony at the company's expense. In return for this undertaking Hansemann was granted an imperial charter. Once again an experiment to run a colony through a private company was a failure. The New Guinea Company failed to make a profit from its investments and asked the Reich to take over the administration of the colony. In 1898 the company ceded its rights to the Reich in return for a rather modest compensation.

In Samoa the situation was very confused, with the German, British and American consuls busy jockeying for position without any clear instructions from their governments. A conference in 1886, held in Washington, failed to settle these outstanding problems, but there was a general agreement to live and let live for the time being. A continuing civil war in Samoa was used by the German consul to strengthen Germany's position in the islands, even though he was clearly far exceeding his instructions from Berlin. German marines took part in the fighting and were badly mauled. Washington replied by sending naval vessels to Samoa, and rousing speeches were made in Congress calling for the protection of America's insterests in the Pacific. A conference was hastily called in 1889 to meet in Berlin in order to defuse the situation. Samoa was in effect controlled by a triumvirate of America, Britain and Germany, although the fiction of an independent kingdom was maintained. The arrangement suited Bismarck's schemes, for a co-protectorate was likely to be a less costly and troublesome arrangement than a formal German colony, and German economic interests thrived in Samoa.

Germany had co-operated with Britain over Samoa, and could count on British support in the Carolines, where Spain was threatening to impose her customs system. German interests in the Carolines, particularly the firm of Robertson and Hernsheim, which Hansemann had effectively swindled over Samoa, were anxious to establish German rights over the Carolines and stop the islands falling into the hands either of the Spanish or of the British after the continued demands of the Australian colonists for further annexations in the Pacific. A German warship, the *Iltis*, was sent to Micronesia to show the flag and to warn off the Spanish. The *Iltis* arrived after a Spanish vessel on a similar mission had also been to Micronesia. Spanish public opinion was outraged and violent demonstrations were staged in Madrid, and the German press retaliated with blistering attacks on the disgusting conduct of excitable Mediterranean peoples.

There were those, like Robertson and Hernsheim, who argued that trade with Micronesia was essential, but many other businessmen feared that German intransigence in the Carolines would lead to reprisals by the Spanish government, and they could convincingly show that trade with Continental Spain was of far greater significance than any future commerce in the Pacific was likely to be. The Spanish bought enormous quantities of German spirits, more than could possibly have been unloaded on the natives of Micronesia, and the trade was steadily growing in spite if the depression. In these circumstances Bismarck was quite prepared to allow Spain to claim sovereignty over the Carolines in return for an extension of the extremely favourable trade agreement for a further six years.

In order to secure this agreement Bismarck enlisted the services of the Pope, and Leo XIII was delighted to do exactly as the Chancellor desired. The Pope not only secured the compliance of the Spanish to Bismarck's plan, but also his intervention was extremely embarrassing to the centre party, a fact that was exploited to the full by the Chancellor who never missed an opportunity to deal a blow to political Catholicism. Germany was given complete freedom of trade in the Carolines as well as the right to maintain a naval station. When the Spanish were driven out of the Pacific as a result of the Spanish-American war, the Carolines were added to the German colonial empire.

The Nature of Bismarck's Imperialism

German imperialism in the age of Bismarck was a response to the economic and social problems caused by the Great Depression. The traditional free-trading policy had been abandoned in favour of the protectionism of 1879 when the alliance of agrarians and industrialists had been cemented and the state began a deliberate policy of anti-cyclical intervention in which the careful stimulation of foreign trade played an important role. Bismarck had no ideological predisposition to colonialism. Colonies for him were expensive, tiresome and potential sources of friction with the European states. It is hardly surprising that the Chancellor of a Germany that had been formed by war, and which occupied a central position in Europe, should remark that his map of Africa lay in Europe. His colonialism was dictated in large part by his desire to stimulate Germany's foreign trade and to lessen the economic effects of the depression. The German colonies were improvisations, and Bismarck overcame his reluctance to setting up protectorates by comforting himself with the thought, however unrealistic it was to be, that if the colonies did not work out satisfactorily they could always be abandoned.

The formation of the alliances of 1879 coincided with an upswing in the business cycle so that the full implications of the new interventionist approach to economic policy were not immediately felt. By late 1882 the full effects of the second depression were apparent. Although in real terms this second wave was less severe than the first, in psychological terms it was shattering, for it followed after a period of amelioration and it also seemed to indicate that the protective system of 1879 was not working according to the expectations of its proponents. The development of new markets overseas seemed to be the only way out of the crisis of industrial over-production that plagued the developed nations of the world. The industrial states began a new round of economic rivalry which was intensified by the enormous increases in industrial productivity combined with the concomitant problems of over-production and under-consumption, a rivalry in which the interventionist role of the state apparatus was to be vital. The age of imperialism had arrived.

In Germany the new phase of state intervention in the workings of the economy began with a series of *ad hoc* measures. The steam ship subsidy, improvements of the consular and diplomatic services, and tax and customs reforms were all used to try to improve Germany's performance as an exporting nation and to help the country out of the consequences of the depression. As a 'reluctant imperialist', Bismarck only accepted the need for formal protectorates when his policy of the 'open door' failed and when he feared that if Germany did not move then another imperialist power would take over the territory concerned and place hindrances in the way of German trade.

Colonies were seen more as potential markets for German goods rather than sources of cheap raw materials. They were thus seen as springboards to the vast market of central Africa and the Pacific. At times Bismarck had an almost fantastic vision of the potential size of such markets which in his more sober moments he realised were only likely to have a marginal value, even though that marginal value might have been of critical importance. To his critics he answered that colonies had to be regarded as long-term investments, like undeveloped land or a new coal seam, and that the profits would begin to come at a later date; but again he would moan that colonies were expensive and wasteful, and that the German dream of Africa as its India was a foolish illusion.

In attempting to stimulate the economy by means of colonial expansion, the German government was using one of the few tools at its disposal. Protectionism had not been sufficient, and indeed it had caused a number of acute social problems as a result of the sharp rise in the cost of living. With an imperfect understanding of the monetary system and with a pious belief in the value of the gold standard which the new Reich had introduced in 1873, there was little chance of using monetary policy to help pull the economy out of the depression. Nor were the state governments prepared to spend large sums of money on public projects in order to fill the order books of needy industrialists. Colonialism therefore seemed to be one of the most promising ways out of the problems of depression.

Bismarck's imperialism was not dictated by the exigencies of foreign policy or by his own profound imperialist longings, as some historians have suggested, but resulted from the economic problems of an expanding capitalist economy that found itself in a chronic crisis of over-production and which was looking for ways out of this lengthy depression. The particular circumstances of the German experience of economic growth seemed to make the need for foreign markets all the more pressing. Germany had grown rapidly from a position of relative backwardness and its growth had been unstable and uneven. The structural changes that were taking place within the economy, away from the agricultural to the industrial sector, and within industry to heavy industry, caused severe disruptions. As its industrial sector grew, so foreign markets became increasingly important, and in the circumstances of a world-wide depression the need to maintain these markets was critical. As the other leading industrial nations had also greatly increased industrial output, there was a growing competition in international trade and a strong tendency towards the dog-in-the-manger attitude of 'preclusive imperialism', the cutting off of potential markets that might be of benefit to a trade rival. But there were also important political considerations behind Bismarck's imperialism.

In foreign politics Bismarck hoped to manipulate colonial rivalries in order to distract attention away from the problems of Germany's position in central Europe, and at home by means of a policy of social imperialism antagonisms and hostilities could be directed away from their objective source by pursuing a policy that would excite the imagination of a large number of Germans. Seen in these terms, Bismarck's imperialism was a diversionary strategy, but even this policy was dictated by economic considerations. A lessening of the tensions between states, the establishment of clearly recognised spheres of interest and the acceptance of the position of Germany in Europe, and the defusing of domestic political conflicts were all seen as necessary preconditions for the economic recovery of the country. The assertion of Germany's place among the community of nations, the strengthening of Bismarck's Bonapartist rule and the completion of the 'revolution from above' could be achieved in large measure by a successful imperialist policy. Thus economic and political considerations were combined in a close relationship so that it is seriously misleading to discuss German imperialism in these early stages as a purely political ruse. On the other hand, imperialism was not the automatic response to a cyclical crisis of over-production. Imperialism provided a means of integration in an antagonistic society by neutralising political antagonisms by economic and political means.

As the magical success of 1871, the victory over France and the formation of the German Empire began to pall, Bismarck looked for another mission that would revive the enthusiasm and excitement of the 'years of the foundation'. Manipulative foreign policy in Europe was of limited efficacy, and the 'war in sight' crisis had given Bismarck something of a fright and had shown him the limits beyond which he was unwilling to go. As he remarked to Holstein, first came the victories, then the *Kulturkampf* and then the colonies. Thus in the election campaign of 1884 imperialism was used as a weapon against the critics of the régime who were denounced as feeble little men who were not up to the challenge and adventure of colonial ventures on which the future prosperity of the Reich would be based. Friedrich Engels, writing from London to his friends Bernstein and Bebel, was quick to point out the role of the 'colonial swindle' in the election in which the loudly proclaimed Congo conference, which was held in Berlin, played a central role. This colonial enthusiasm was sharply spiced with anti-British slogans to provide a tonic to chauvinistic sentiments. The policy was a triumphant success for Bismarck. The opposition parties were badly mauled in the election and the popularity of colonialism to the electorate clearly demonstrated.

Ultra-nationalism, a blind patriotism, the search for an appropriate scapegoat, social Darwinism, racism and anti-Semitism were expressions of the frustrations and aggressions of the depression era. They were manipulated and used as means of strengthening the political domination of the authoritarian Bismarckian system. Imperialism legitimised this rule and channelled these dark and irrational drives into paths that could be controlled and deflected. But once having conjured up these pernicious spirits, it became increasingly difficult to control them. The genie could not always be persuaded to return to the bottle.

As long as Bismarck was able to hold together what Eckart Kehr called the 'agrarian-industrial condominium', these forces could be held in check and used to crush the aspirations of the working class and of all the progressive elements within German society. But how long could Bismarck maintain his dictatorial rule, the semi-feudal agrarians hang on to their dominant position, the emancipatory longings of the masses be frustrated? The cost of social conservatism became increasingly high, and the tensions it was designed to overcome grew apace.

It is exceptionally difficult to draw up the balance sheet of Bismarck's imperialism. Exports to the colonies only accounted for about 0.1 per cent of the value of German exports and never even reached 1 per cent before 1914. Imports were similarly insignificant. The relationship of imports from the colonies to total imports was about the same as exports, and averaged something like 0.1 per cent. Investments in the colonies were also but a small fraction of total foreign investments. By 1905 only 2 per cent of German foreign investments were in the colonies. Nor did the colonies absorb the excess population. A mere 6,000 German citizens lived in the colonies in 1905, most of whom were civil servants and military personnel.

With these modest returns it is hardly surprising that the German banks showed little enthusiasm for the colonies and were very reluctant to invest much money in them. Far greater profits were to be found in investment and railway-building in other countries rather than in the colonies. Isolated individual companies made handsome profits from the colonies but the expense to the Reich government was very high indeed.

The marginal effect of the colonial market on German industry at the present state of empirical knowledge is impossible to assess. It might be that some firms were able to maintain a satisfactory rate of production and avoid further sharp reduction of domestic prices because they had new colonial markets that could absorb excess production, but detailed studies of the experiences of individual firms are needed before any confident statements can be made. On the basis of available evidence it seems unlikely that the colonies did much to counteract the effects of the depression because the scale of investment and trade was so small. There is sufficient evidence, however, that Bismarck realised that any economic benefits from the colonies would be in the long term, and that the talk of the vast wealth of Africa was a hopeless exaggeration.

In social imperialist terms the policy was slightly more successful. A substantial part of the German socialist movement came to accept imperialism as both natural and desirable, and Karl Kautsky provided a 'Marxist' justification for this point of view in his writings on 'ultra-imperialism'. It also became apparent that a significant sector of the German working class profited directly from imperialist policies. The formation of a 'labour aristocracy', providing the mass for the revisionist policies and practice of the social-democratic party, helped to destroy the revolutionary élan of the working class and helped to reconcile the socialists to the existing order. Only the left wing of the party, led by Rosa Luxemburg, fought a determined struggle against this view of imperialism, and even though Rosa Luxemburg's own views on the nature and dynamics of imperialism were seriously deficient, her contention that imperialist policies were undermining the revolutionary and emancipatory role of the proletariat was undeniable.

Bismarck's imperialism, in which the interventionist role of the state to overcome dysfunctionalities in the economic system became increasingly important to the point where it was to become the new form of legitimisation for the system of social domination, was but the early phase of German imperialism. In its mature form German imperialism more closely meets the criteria that Lenin laid down in his classic pamphlet, *Imperialism, the Highest Stage of Capitalism*. The economic life of the country was marked by the decisive role played by the monopolies. Bank capital had merged to a considerable degree with industrial capital. The export of capital rather than goods was of particular importance. International combines of capitalists were formed and the territorial division of the world by the greatest capitalist powers was completed. Bismarck certainly preferred foreign investment and overseas trade to colonisation, and most German bankers and industrialists agreed. Colonies were part of a strategy of protecting private capitalist profit which had only limited success. The imperialism which Lenin described, and his theory was based in large part on the German experience, was the imperialism of a new stage of capitalist development which in turn had resulted from the effects of the depression in intensifying the monopolistic tendencies within capitalism. The exploits of intrepid adventurers in pith helmets which had excited the imagination of an entire generation were of trivial significance compared to the manipulations of international finance, the massive foreign investments and railway-building projects. German imperialism was much more than colonialism, and its main thrust was to be in Europe and the Near East rather than Africa and the Pacific. It was not until almost twenty years later that sufficient investments had been made to make the German colonies into anything approaching a viable economic undertaking, and even then their importance to the German economy was marginal.

9 RYE AND IRON

Agriculture During the Depression

The social Darwinist and racist doctrines of imperialism were also expressions of the profound *malaise* caused by the structural changes within German society during the course of the Great Depression. The census returns on professions of 1882 showed that a narrow majority of Germans earned their living from the land, but by 1895, when the next such census was taken, 20.2 million worked in industry, whereas 18.5 million worked on the land. By 1895 the population of the German Reich was 52 million, and had thus almost exactly doubled since 1816. This increased population had been largely absorbed by the urban areas and by an expanding industrial economy. The population of the rural communities had remained virtually constant, the excess population being forced off the land to look for work in the towns.

In general this movement of population away from the agricultural areas to the towns and cities was also a movement of the population from the east to the west. Attracted by the possibilities of higher wages and of greater opportunities, and no longer bound by feudal obligations, the eastern land labourers moved west to the industrial centres. This created a certain shortage of labour in the east, a shortage that was intensified by the very success of the agricultural sector in increasing productivity by improving techniques and making better use of the land by crop rotation. As the level of mechanisation of agriculture was still relatively modest, the agrarians were obliged to rely increasingly on casual labour from the east, mainly from Poland. The growth of seasonal labour at harvest time, in the hop fields and also in the construction industry, when work gangs were formed to build roads, canals and railways, was one of the striking features of the Industrial Revolution in Germany. The problem was made all the more noticeable by the fact that a large number of the casual labourers were Polish. Bismarck had tried to contain this mounting flood of foreign workers by expelling Polish labourers from Germany, but the measure had little effect and was abandoned by his successor, Caprivi. By the outbreak of the First World War there were at least one million Polish casual labourers working in Germany.

The ruthlessly exploited Polish labourers, housed in barracks on the large estates, hired on short-term contracts and paid in hard-earned cash, were striking examples of the change that had taken place in German agriculture. Max Weber, in his famous inaugural lecture at Freiburg in 1895, spoke of the 'death struggle of feudal agriculture', the end of patriarchal relationships on the land, and the formation of a harsh capitalist regime with the proletarianisation of the labourers and the creation of a new class of nomadic labourers. The contrast between this modern capitalist practice and the quasi-feudal ideology of the agrarians and their dominant position within German society was symptomatic of the profound contradiction between the social structure and the development of the forces of production which was to make Germany such a seriously imbalanced and antagonistic society. The position of the Polish labourers on the land was a dramatic illustration of this situation. They were hated and reviled and they were hostile and resentful towards their employers, but German agriculture could not survive without them. In southern Germany where Czech, Slovak and Ruthenian labourers worked on the farms, much the same conditions applied.

The increasing dependence of German agriculture on foreign labour gave rise to demands for a population policy aimed at the expulsion of the Poles from the east and for the colonisation of the area by German farmers. These demands were articulated in alarmingly violent racist language and the implementation of such policies was an early form of the barbarity of Fascist racial programmes. Bismarck remarked that the Good Lord had made the wolf the way he was and that men could not be blamed for shooting him. The Polish aristocrats who owned land in Prussia he likened to a trichina which had to be destroyed. Bismarck pursued a systematic policy of Germanisation. German was made the official language even in areas where there was a large Polish majority. Schools had to be conducted in German. Laws were passed which made it increasingly difficult for Poles to own land, and Germans were actively encouraged to settle in the east. The agrarians were quick to see the advantages of such a policy. Of the billion marks that were spent on the 'Germanisation of the land' a large proportion went into the pockets of the Junkers, who used their fervent patriotism and nationalism to free their estates from debt by means of cheap credit. With the 'expulsion law' (*Aussiedlungsgesetz*) of 1886, many Poles, even though they were living on Polish territory that had been annexed by Prussia, were forced to leave. Some 32,000 Poles who could not demonstrate that they had German nationality were driven out in a campaign which combined anti-Slav with anti-Semitic hatreds. Over 25 per cent of the expelled were Jewish. The policy of direct expulsion rather than Germanisation was later to be championed by the *Hakatisten* or *Ostmarkenverein* (Eastern Association) formed in 1894 by Hansemann, Kennemann and Tiedemann (hence the name '*Hakatist*') which was one of the most outspoken and virulent of the pressure groups in imperial Germany. The racism and the *Lebensraum* theories of the *Ostmarkenverein* were an ominous prefiguration of National Socialist ideology.

Two major facts stood in the way of the successful realisation of these anti-Polish policies. Ten per cent of the population of Prussia was Polish, and the expulsion of over 2 million citizens was rather more than even the most extreme chauvinists could contemplate, and even the expulsion of 1886 had been severely criticised, not only by humanitarians from the left but also by conservatives who felt that this was an unjustified and alarming attack on the principles of the inviolability of private property guaranteed in the constitution of the Reich. The other factor was that agriculture could not do without seasonal labour, and the authorities were not prepared to close the borders to Polish workers.

Between 1886 and 1916 more than 21,000 small farms were created in the east as part of a programme of 'internal colonisation'. These holdings averaged about 10 acres and were considered sufficient to maintain a family. The creation of these small holdings was an attempt to ameliorate the consequences of the emancipation of the peasantry after 1806 and to counteract the effects of the capitalisation of the large estates. Although this effort has been widely praised in the literature on the economic history of German agriculture, it seems to have been of marginal significance. It was no longer possible to halt the progress of industrialisation and the establishment of capitalist relationships on the land. Agricultural wages increased at a far slower rate than industrial wages. In absolute terms the amount of money for agricultural wages declined steadily throughout the period of the depression and up to the outbreak of the war. By the turn of the century the birth rate on the land declined to the point that it matched the lower birth rates of the industrial areas. The agricultural sector declined in wealth and importance and was kept going by increasingly large subsidies that went to the larger estates. The work of the settlement commission (*Ansiedlungsgesellschaft*) did, however, do something to slow down the rate of social change on the land and protect the smaller farmers from the full effects of technical change and the concentration of production.

The social problems of agriculture were in a sense a measure of the agricultural sector's success in meeting the challenge of a rapidly expanding population and the growth of the industrial sector. Increases in productivity had triumphantly disproved the dreary predictions of the Malthusians, who had foreseen mass starvation and deprivation. The productivity of the land had inc sed about threefold during the period that the population had doubled. The completion of the railway system meant that the increased production could be brought quickly and cheaply to the large markets and to the seaports, thus reducing waste and costs. In 1876 Carl von Linde invented the compression refrigerator which was to prove so enormously important for the storage and transportation of perishable foods. The continuing improvement of fertilisers and the triumph of scientific agriculture were further to help agriculture meet the heavy demands placed upon it.

The mechanisation of agriculture also continued at a steady pace. Most of the new machinery was still horse-drawn, even on the large and capital-intensive estates, but steam engines were increasingly used to drive standing machinery such as threshing machines. Small farmers who were unable to afford new and expensive machinery frequently joined together in co-operatives to buy machinery, or rented the equipment from the manufacturers. It was not until the end of the century that electric power was available to many farms, but farmers were quick to realise the value of cheap electric motors to drive relatively simple pieces of machinery such as butter churns, pumps, shredders, threshing machines and circular saws.

Industrial and agricultural improvements complemented one another with the introduction of the Gilchrist Thomas system which produced a waste that was rich in phosphates, the 'Thomas powder' which augmented the raw phosphate which was imported largely from Algeria. By 1890 synthetic nitrogen was slowly beginning to replace the more expensive saltpetre from Chile and guano from South America. By the outbreak of the war the researches of great chemists such as Birkeland, Eyde, Bosch and Haber had made possible the mass production of nitrates for agriculture by catalytic synthesis.

From the 1860s an increasing importance was placed on education for farmers. The agricultural colleges and schools were expanded, their curriculum improved and the results of the most recent research made available to the farmers, often by means of visiting specialists who suggested possible improvements appropriate to local conditions. This *Wanderlehre* (mobile teaching) had started in the Rhineland in the middle of the century, spread throughout southern Germany in the following decades and was gradually introduced to the other German states in the course of the century.

This great improvement in the technical knowledge of farmers was the direct cause of the introduction of improved crops and the development of hardier and more productive plants. The development of new corn types, such as 'Rimpau's early bastard', the colourful name of an improved wheat discovered by Rimpau in 1889, greatly improved the productivity of German agriculture by producing hardier strains that yielded more per acre than the earlier types. Ferdinand von Lochow's Petkus rye, produced in 1880, became the standard type for Germany's main grain crop. Farmers now no longer grew their own seeds but bought them from farms specialising in the latest strains. Rigorous standards were applied to seeds and supplies were regularly inspected by officials from the local agricultural colleges. The first seed control station of this sort was established in Saxony in 1869. The result of these measures was a steady improvement of grain crops and the speedy dissemination of new seed types throughout the country.

The improvements in seeds and plants were further enhanced by advances in the treatment of plant diseases, the introduction of pesticides and an increase in the knowledge of different soil types. The application of scientific methods to farming can also be seen in animal-breeding. Few improvements in cattle-breeding were possible without accurate statistics on average milk yields of cows. It was not until the 1890s that statistics were collected, usually from the large farms, on milk yields. Breeding was greatly improved by following the example of the race-horse breeders. In England there had been a racing calendar since 1727 and the General Stud Book of 1793 listed all thoroughbreds, establishing a standard that was accepted throughout Europe. A similar stud book for shorthorn cattle was introduced, again in England, in 1822. The careful compilation of pedigrees and accurate information on every breed of farm animal were gradually introduced in the course of the nineteenth century and the suspicions of the farmers towards what at first appeared to be unwarranted interference with their breeding programmes was eventually overcome.

The higher degree of the division of labour which developed in the course of the century with the advent of seed farms, specialised breeders and new techniques is also shown in the growing dependence of German agriculture on the import of feed grains, mainly from

Russia. Critics of the course of agricultural development were appalled at Germany's dependence on foreign sources of supply for essential foodstuffs, and indeed the First World War caused a very serious disruption of agriculture once these supplies ran out. Others welcomed this increase in the international division of labour as being a stage in the development of the mutual dependence of nations, and therefore of peaceful co-operation.

In 1884 the Swabian Max Eyth founded the German Farmers' Society (*Deutsche Landwirtsgesellschaft* – DLG). By 1896 when Eyth retired, the society had 12,000 members and was playing a vital role in the dissemination of the latest knowledge throughout Germany. The society was based on the experience Eyth had on the efforts of the Royal Agricultural Society to promote British agriculture, for he had worked for a company producing agricultural machinery in Leeds for some time. The DLG was the most vital and important agricultural organisation in imperial Germany, and completely eclipsed Bismarck's 'Agricultural Council' (*Deutsche Landwirtsrat*), which had been formed in 1872. Unlike many such organisations, Eyth could proudly claim that 'more sweat flowed than beer', and the society continued to play an important role in German agriculture until it was disbanded by the Nazis in 1933.

The increasing specialisation of agriculture and the development of a true world market for agricultural produce had a profound effect on the development of German agriculture and its place within the European and world markets. The development of the great agricultural countries such as the United States, Australia, New Zealand, Argentina and South Africa, linked to Europe with a cheap, efficient and swift transportation system, meant that Germany could no longer rely on its export of commodities like wool to the British market. The British woollen industry imported the cheaper Australian wools, and even the German manufacturers preferred Australian wool, which they used to produce cheap textiles to undercut their British competitors. Faced with this situation, German farmers gradually reduced their stocks of sheep, even though they had greatly improved the strains and produced fine-quality wools and meat, starting in the late 1860s. Farmers switched over to the more lucrative production of calves for veal and were quick to realise that by abandoning sheep-farming they could increase the productivity of their land by reducing the acreage under fallow and producing feed crops for their cattle. The deeply engrained dislike of lamb and mutton among German consumers was such that there was little hope of producing sheep for the table, which alone would have justified an attempt to produce quantities of speciality wools for the luxury market.

Germany ceased to be a wool-exporting country by 1870 and other industries were also ruined by new international competition. German flax and hemp, the raw materials for the canvas which Germany exported, could not compete with sisal from the tropics and jute from India. Vegetable-oil crops were abandoned with the introduction of petroleum and the invention of margarine which used palm oil, soy oil and peanut oil from the tropical countries. Yet most serious of all was the threat to German agriculture posed by American corn. The socialist leader Wilhelm Liebknecht was delighted. He told the delegates to the Brussels conference of the Socialist International that American corn would be the ruin of the German small farmers, who would be driven from the land and forced into the ranks of the industrial proletariat. Reactionary peasants would thus become socialist militants, and American competition was the best possible guarantee for the triumph of socialism. There were many on the right who feared that Liebknecht might indeed be correct, and a fierce debate began on the likely effects on society of economic change and continuing industrialisation.

Trade Relations with Russia

The immediate problem was not so much the United States as Russia, for here economic and political considerations conflicted. After the wars of unification Bismarck had based his foreign policy on an understanding between the three great conservative powers, Russia, Austria-Hungary and Germany. At the Congress of Berlin Bismarck had felt obliged to opt for Austria-Hungary when the Russo-Turkish war had placed an intolerable strain on Russo-Austrian relations. Thus Bismarck's conservative alliance was undermined by Balkan rivalries, but also by the commercial policy of the Reich during the Great Depression. German agrarians demanded, and got, protective tariffs against Russian corn and feed grains. Russian industrialists demanded similar protection against German industrial goods, which was achieved by demanding payment of customs duties in gold. The *Verein Deutscher Stahl- und Eisenindustrieller*, supported by the *Zentralverband* and backed by a massive newspaper campaign, called for a new trade agreement with Russia that would take their interests into consideration. The German government, acting in the interests of the agrarians rather than the industrialists, met the Russian threat by increasing customs duties on agricultural goods from Russia so that the new tariffs of 1885 reduced the import of Russian wheat and rye by 50 per cent within the first year. The Russians were unwilling to retaliate because the Russian aristocracy opposed high tariffs on industrial goods which merely helped the industrial bourgeoisie and increased the price of goods that they wished to import.

Bismarck was concerned to maintain good relations with Russia, at least for the time being, and was alarmed at the signs of a possible trade war between the two countries. For this reason he opposed those who wished to further Germany's imperialist ambitions in the Balkans, and in the 'Reinsurance Treaty' of 1887 tried to patch up the relationship with Russia without alienating the Austrians. But this highly contradictory treaty was not enough to smooth over the growing antagonisms between the two countries in the economic sphere. Henckel von Donnersmarck wrote to the Chancellor on behalf of German industrialists, demanding the exclusion of Russian securities from the German market only two days before the Reinsurance Treaty was signed, and this memorandum was followed by a massive press campaign against Russian securities which resulted in an instruction to the Reichsbank that Russian securities could no longer be used as collateral for loans. Shortly afterwards, in December 1887, the tariffs on rye and wheat were increased once again.

Thus Russian agrarians were angered at the high German tariffs and Russian industrialists were demanding protection against German industrial goods. German agrarians wanted even higher tariffs and the industrialists complained that the Russian market was being closed to them and that the government was not doing enough to support German interests in the building of a railway to Constantinople, or taking adequate financial measures against aggressive Russian commercial practices. At a time when relations with Russia were getting steadily worse, France was plunged into the Boulanger crisis and the possibility of a European war was deliberately exaggerated by a press campaign mounted by the armaments industry. The Ludwig Löwe company was even trying to sell weapons to Boulanger, showing that industry would stop at nothing in the attempt to find new markets. Bismarck hoped to defuse the situation, to avoid heightening international tensions which would simply encourage the war-mongering military under the chief of the general staff, General Waldersee, and push the young Kaiser William II completely into the military camp. Although Boulanger was discredited so that the threat from France disappeared, Bismarck found himself unable to satisfy all the major centres of power within the Reich. The agrarians were on the whole pleased with his tariff policies, but the industrialists disliked the high tariffs on foodstuffs and prohibition of advances against Russian securities (*Lombardverbot*), the military disliked his pacific policy, his anti-socialist legislation could not be renewed in the Reichstag, and the Kaiser was anxious to emerge from the shadow of the grand old man of German politics and would not hear of the suggestion of a personal dictatorship by Bismarck.

Caprivi's Tariff Policy

With the dismissal of Bismarck and the appointment of Caprivi, the 'Chancellor without a perch or a blade of grass' (*ohne Ar und Halm*), the alliance between industry and agriculture, between rye and iron, threatened to collapse. Between 1890 and 1894, when the trade cycle again hit a low point, the struggle between agriculture and industry entered a new phase. The immediate problem in 1890–1 was a sharp rise in corn prices, which were particularly high in Germany because of the tariffs. Prices were pushed up still further by producers holding on to their stocks in the hope of getting even higher prices and by the Russian crop failure. To the industrialists the answer had to be a lowering of agricultural tariffs which would not only bring down the price of food but also stimulate the export market for German industrial goods. The resulting discussion over Caprivi's trade agreements was marked by a growing conflict between agrarian conservatives and the industrialists over the question of whether protection was still desirable.

The first of the Caprivi trade treaties was with Austria-Hungary. There were slight reductions in the German tariffs on Austrian agricultural produce, although the import of livestock was still forbidden, and Austria-Hungary similarly reduced its tariffs on German industrial goods. The treaty underlined the special relationship with Austria which was the cornerstone of Caprivi's foreign policy and marked a slight retreat from the extreme protectionist position of the agrarians. Similar modest adjustments in tariffs were made in the treaties with Belgium and Italy.

On 10 December 1891 Caprivi explained the thinking behind these treaties in a major speech in the Reichstag, which was the outstanding performance in his brief political career. His central argument was that protection had failed to overcome the problem of industrial over-production, and indeed had made it worse. Germany was faced with the choice of exporting men or industrial goods, and he insisted that by expanding the export market by means of long-term trade agreements the economy could be revived and the expanding population would no longer be forced to emigrate. Corn tariffs benefited a small number of farmers but were a heavy burden on the consumers, particularly those with low incomes. Two-thirds of the population earned less than 900 marks per annum so that the social cost of the corn tariffs was very high. As Germany was unable to meet its own requirements for foodstuffs it was essential that it establish good relations with the food-producing nations and not engage in tariff wars with countries on which it was dependent. The Chancellor dismissed the argument that love of Fatherland, Kaiser, Church and family depended on the maintenance of high corn tariffs and described the privileged economic status of the Prussian Junkers as a piece of unjustified special pleading.

In general those who wished to see the dominant position of the land-owning aristocracy attacked welcomed the treaties and the Chancellor's speech. Socialists, progressives, Catholics and even national liberals welcomed the treaties. An influential group of conservatives, whose spokesman was Robert von Puttkamer, accepted the treaties on the grounds that a patriotic sacrifice should be made by the agrarians in order to maintain the alliance with Austria, but argued that restrictions on the free movement of labour and the introduction of bimetallism would be an appropriate compensation for the generosity of the agrarians. Other conservatives were horrified at these ideas. Although such a prominent reactionary as Puttkamer could not be accused of harbouring liberal thoughts, it was suggested that the sacrifice that he was demanding was nothing short of the abolition of agrarian society and the triumph of the industrial bourgeoisie and, even worse, the victory of the forces of democracy. Germany would go the way of England, the great estates would become the weekend retreats of Ruhr barons and the country would be delivered up to the whim of the Reichstag majority.

In spite of the fierce criticisms of the agrarians, the majority of Germans welcomed the trade treaties. The treaty with Austria was accepted by 243 votes to 48 in the Reichstag and the agrarians had to accept their defeat. They were, however, determined to continue the fight, for the trade treaties coupled with excellent crops resulted in a dramatic fall in the price of corn, and the majority of the agrarians feared that if the trend continued agriculture would be ruined and only the highly efficient, modern and specialised estates would be able to survive. Even that was problematical, for refrigeration made possible the mass import of meat from Argentina, butter from New Zealand, and fruits from throughout the world. Farmers were partly able to meet the challenge of falling prices at a time when costs were still rising by taking out large mortgages. The crisis certainly weeded out a number of inefficient producers but the question remained whether, if the crisis continued, even the more efficient would be able to survive. With the fall in the price of corn in 1892 the agrarians became increasingly critical of the government and many began to call for militant political action. Feeling deserted by the government, they decided to win influence in the Reichstag by fielding their own candidates for election, lobbying members and openly criticising the government. What Frank Wedekind with bitter irony described as the 'meek horde of agrarians' organised themselves in 1893 into the Farmers' League (*Bund der Landwirte*), which was soon to become one of the most outspoken and influential interest groups in imperial Germany. Within a year the League had 200,000 members.

Although lacking the financial resources of the great industrial interest groups, the Farmers' League had a more coherent and all-embracing ideological position and was more successful at mobilising popular support. The League was rigorously centralised under the leadership of experienced politicians, and had an impressive following in the provinces. It was able to influence the selection of candidates in both the conservative and national liberal parties to the point that it was able to play a decisive role in the lower houses in both Prussia and Saxony and to form an impressive power bloc in the Reichstag at least until 1912. Its militant ideology of neo-conservatism, extreme nationalism, anti-Semitism, social Darwinism and its apparently middle-class values enabled the old conservative party to gain mass support in the industrial age and thus to survive in the age of plebiscitary politics. Its profound cultural pessimism, rabble-rousing political techniques and *völkish* nationalism was another striking prefiguration of Fascist manipulative techniques. Although acting in the interests of the big landowners, the League had many contacts with other groups, and associations with industry, the professions and, above all, the small farmers, who found the League's ideological position irresistibly compelling.

The Farmers' League first went into action against the Rumanian trade treaty of 1893. A prominent leaguer, Freiherr von Wangenheim, warned that German agriculture was indispensable, but that the Chancellor was not. The old familiar arguments were trotted out. Any reduction of agricultural tariffs would lead to the destruction of traditional German society, for the rural areas supplied loyal recruits to the army and were the seedbeds of decent conservative thought. To vote for the treaty was to vote for anarchy, democracy and socialism. The treaty was finally approved by the Reichstag, but the majority in favour had been reduced to a mere 24 votes. It had now become perfectly respectable for conservatives to attack the government, vilify the Chancellor and to imply that Caprivi was in some sinister way allied to the socialists and radicals, who were bent on undermining the basic values of German society. In their determination to defend their own interests the agrarians lost all sense of proportion and their wild and immoderate attacks on industrial society threatened to destroy the careful alliance between the agricultural and the industrial sectors which had been the basis of Bismarck's politics since 1879.

The debates over the Rumanian treaty were a prelude to the even more hectic differences over the new trade agreements with Russia. The agrarians produced a flood of pamphlets, newspaper articles and resolutions denouncing the proposed reduction of agricultural tariffs in the treaty and attacking the Chancellor for a policy which they claimed would merely benefit the socialists and the democrats. Industry was confident that it had the Chancellor's support, and thus kept relatively quiet and exerted influence through the commission of enquiry established by Caprivi to discuss the terms of the proposed treaty. The Reichstag debates on the treaty were very heated, with Caprivi under almost constant attack from the conservatives for reputedly attempting to undermine the basis of German civilisation and military might, but the Chancellor gave a spirited defence of his policies and in turn attacked the agrarians and the Farmers' League for their immoderate and shabby tactics. The treaty was finally accepted by 205 votes to 151, although the right was quick to point out that without the support of the socialists and the radicals, the Chancellor would have been defeated.

The treaties were economically a success, although they did not have the political effect that Caprivi had hoped. Tensions between Russia and Germany were certainly diminished, but the Franco-Russian military convention was completed during the negotiations for the trade agreement. Economic relations between Russia and

Germany were greatly strengthened by the treaty. German industry was able to push the British aside in the Russian market. Trade relations between Germany and Russia were normalised and the tariff warfare of the preceding period was abandoned. The *Zentralverband Deutscher Industrieller* was delighted with the treaty, although the association was sharply critical that the Chancellor did not attack the social democrats and had to rely on their votes to get parliamentary sanction for the trade agreements. For the time being the association was prepared to support the Chancellor, for it needed Caprivi's trade agreements and his determination to stand up against the agrarians in order to overcome the problems of the cyclical crisis. On the agrarian side all-out war was declared on the Chancellor. The conservative *Kreuzzeitung* thundered that 'from now on we must devote our energies to a war of annihilation against capitalist liberalism and everything that supports it'.

In spite of these attacks on the Chancellor by the agrarians, some were generous enough to admit that Caprivi had not totally neglected the agricultural sector. Miquel's tax reforms blatantly favoured the owners of large estates, had little effect on the smaller farmers and had raised taxes somewhat on the industrial bourgeoisie. Restrictions on immigrant labour were lifted somewhat so that the agrarians were able to get an adequate supply of cheap labour and resist the upward trend of wages. The Junkers were given preferential rates for freight on the railway system. Caprivi had also abolished the identity pass system by which duty was paid back if foreign grain was exported within a certain period. Under the new system, farmers could import foreign grain duty-free if they exported their own grain and, given the structure of the world grain market, it amounted to the granting of an export subsidy. Farmers were now able to export large quantities of grain, particularly to Scandinavia. Although this was highly profitable, it made nonsense of the agrarians' insistence that Germany's military security was dependent on agricultural self-sufficiency and their attacks on corn imports as unpatriotic.

Caprivi was keenly aware of the dangers of the militant agrarian movement, and was convinced that Germany's strength lay in her industrial potential. Yet although he was the most far-sighted of imperial Germany's Chancellors, he was without any effective political support. The agrarians saw him as their enemy, and their aggressive behaviour made this a self-fulfilling prophecy. Although Caprivi had lowered tariffs, the industrialists denounced him for being too conciliatory towards labour and for wanting to continue with Bismarck's social policy. The petit bourgeoisie felt that they had been abandoned to the ravages of industrial capitalism and attacked him with irrational, anti-Semitic and anti-modernist slogans taken from the ideological outpourings of the increasingly fashionable ultra literati. The liberals were disgusted with his conservative educational policies, whereas the left dismissed his social policy as empty tokenism. Imperialists were disappointed by his lack of enthusiasm for overseas adventures, militarists annoyed by his reduction of the term of service to two years and his attack on the excessive power of the military attachés. From the right came strident demands for a social reactionary course, and warnings that the murder of the French president Carnot was the beginning of a wave of anarchist terror that would sweep Germany if the government failed to take steps to crush the left. In October 1894 Caprivi, having lost the confidence of the Kaiser, who no longer wished to be the 'social emperor' and was now listening to the siren calls of the extreme right, was obliged to resign and Chlodwig Hohenlohe was appointed Chancellor, an ancient front man for the ultra-reactionary 'king' Stumm.

Caprivi had gone, but his treaties were to remain in force until 1905. Although it is impossible to determine how far the success of the treaties was due to the general improvement of the world economic system as the economies of the major industrial nations pulled gradually out of the depression, it would seem that on balance they were a success. Certainly there was an impressive reduction in the number of Germans emigrating which cannot be explained solely in terms of the increasing lack of opportunity in the United States for ambitious immigrants. Germans continued to leave the rural areas, but tended now to settle in the towns as industry was able to absorb a number of new workers. The new tariffs did not lead to lower revenues from customs for the increased volume of trade actually pushed up revenues to unprecedented heights, just as Caprivi had predicted, and this increase far outstripped increases in population. Industrial production and foreign trade both made impressive gains and the increase in exports to the treaty nations was particularly noticeable. Exports to Russia, for example, increased by 370 per cent by 1900. To the exporting industries Caprivi became something of a hero, and a propaganda campaign was launched to continue the work of the trade treaties.

The agrarians' arguments that the Caprivi trade treaties would ruin German agriculture turned out to be quite unfounded. Grain production increased markedly, and exports thrived with the abolition of the identity passes. Meat production also increased rapidly, owing in part to the lower price of feedstuffs from abroad and partly because of increased domestic demand as real wages began to rise. In an expanding economy it was possible for there to be an increase in grain imports and at the same time an increase in domestic production. With the introduction of a *de facto* export premium much of the increased imports, particularly from Russia, simply made up for the grain that was exported. The fact that Germany was not able to meet its own agricultural needs was not due to Caprivi's treaties but rather to the structure of the entire German economy. Bülow's experiments with the reintroduction of protective tariffs showed that tariffs could not reverse this trend.

Falling grain prices and increased foreign competition tended to bring down land prices, particularly on the large estates. For decades the Junkers had managed to maintain artificially high land prices and had failed to rationalise the money management of their estates. This, rather than the influx of cheap foreign corn, was probably one of the main reasons for the agricultural crisis in Germany. The high level of indebtedness on the larger estates in the east was thus due in large part to the disastrous policies of the past rather than the failure to modernise and rationalise the productive side of farming. Smaller farms and estates in the west, which were also faced with the problem of falling prices for agricultural products, did not have the same level of indebtedness. Falling land prices and increased indebtedness were undoubtedly causes of the mounting radicalism of the agrarians, as can be seen in the propaganda of the *Bund der Landwirte*, but once again it is illogical to place the sole blame for this situation on the Caprivi treaties, even though it is an immensely significant historical fact that the agrarians felt that Caprivi and his free-trade policies were to blame. The settlement commission continued to pour money into the Junker estates so that land prices were never allowed to collapse, and the Bülow tariff which the agrarians hoped would help solve the problems of indebtedness had little effect on land prices.

Agrarians versus Industrialists

The period of Caprivi's chancellorship, which coincided with the third cyclical downturn within the Great Depression, thus saw another round in the struggle between industry and agriculture which threatened to destroy the alliance of 1879. Industrialists were very concerned with the possible consequences in domestic political terms of the trade treaties, and at first were lukewarm and even critical of the Chancellor. The 'Long-name Association', for example, sided with the agrarians against the Chancellor in 1891, feeling that a lowering of agricultural tariffs was a small compensation for the abolition of the anti-socialist laws and the possible alienation of the agrarians. Gradually, however, as the crisis persisted, industry was no longer prepared to allow its consideration for the immediate needs of agriculture to stand in the way of possible new markets abroad, particularly in Russia, which had become exceedingly difficult ever since the customs war which began in 1887. The growing split between the industrialists and the agrarians was a matter of grave concern to the ruling élites, and the slogan was now 'Consolidation' (*Sammlungspolitik*), the effort to restore the alliance of 1879.

The struggle between the agrarians and the industrialists was also reflected in the great academic debate which raged throughout the period between political economists of the conservative and the liberal persuasion. For the conservatives, Adolf Wagner was the star performer. He was a professor at Berlin University from 1870 until his death in 1917, his lectures eagerly attended by politicians and civil servants as well as by his students, many of whom were to carry on the tradition of his thought. Beginning his career as a conventional free-trader Wagner became, shortly after his arrival in Berlin, one of the most outspoken critics of industrial capitalism from a conservative perspective. He was disgusted by the squalor and poverty in which the Berlin workers were condemned to live and he argued that a system based on greed and unscrupulous business practices would have to be severely restricted and regulated by state intervention if the Reich were to be saved from materialism, atheism and socialism. Wagner believed that a healthy society would have to keep industrialism in check, which was only possible by strengthening the role of the state as the regulator and controller of social and economic forces.

Adolf Wagner and his fellow critics of industrial society, Max Sering and Karl Oldenberg, argued that industrial states were dangerously dependent on agricultural states for supplies of food, which in turn was a major source of the instability which was characteristic of all the developed capitalist states. They argued that as there was a tendency for all states to industrialise, sources of agricultural produce would diminish, and therefore the industrial states would find it increasingly difficult to feed their expanding populations. They painted a grim picture of Germany excluded from markets in Russia, the United States and Britain by high protective tariffs, and forced to compete in what was left of the world market with countries like Japan, whose low production costs made them dangerous competitors. Along with this depressing picture of mass starvation, economic isolation and the complete loss of national freedom, went thundering denunciations of the alienated and soulless existence of the urban worker, the loss of moral values and sense of duty which they felt were the necessary and permanent consequences of industrialisation and which they contrasted to a romanticised picture of the old, virtuous and satisfying rural values. It was a short step to take from these views to a violent anti-Semitism of the type that was becoming increasingly fashionable in cultural pessimist circles, and Adolf Wagner associated himself with Adolf Stöcker's Christian Socialist movement which was the best-known and most influential anti-Semitic organisation in the 1890s.

Industrialisation was also blamed for the prevalence of neo-Malthusian ideas which were also denounced as an offshoot of 'Jewish and French rationalism'. Large healthy families on the land were contrasted with miserable small families in the urban areas, but as an increasing proportion of the population lived in towns and as the rural population began to imitate the town-dwellers and limit the size of their families, there was cause for alarm. The existence of Polish immigrant labour was taken as sufficient proof that unless this trend was reversed, Germany would be swamped by the Slavonic hordes and German *Kultur* would disappear under this barbarian invasion. Germany would no longer have the men to maintain an army to defend it against its enemies, and recruits coming from urban areas where they came in contact with dangerously seditious ideas were morally depraved and physically inferior. Industrialisation thus led to the moral and physical degeneration of the race, the weakening of national defence and the destruction of social cohesion.

Gradually the political economists adopted an extreme reactionary position, in part because their critics from the right, like Stumm, mistook their condemnation of the evils of industrial capitalism and their talk of 'state socialism' for some insidious form of Communism. They began to yearn for the good old days before the Industrial Revolution when the guilds controlled production and a healthy peasantry had given the country its robust character. Rationalism was condemned as a cold and sterile system and contrasted to the mystic virtues of peasant life. They bemoaned the demise of the small independent shopkeeper and denounced the new department stores which caused an increasingly uneven distribution of wealth and the destruction of individual initiative. The special rights and privileges of the Junkers they defended on the grounds that this class produced the officers and civil servants whose devotion to public service and whose patriotism and valour guaranteed the strength and independence of the country. Their selfless devotion to duty was contrasted with the rapacious materialism and selfish vulgarity of the industrial bourgeoisie.

In countless public lectures and articles the political economists argued that the fatal trend towards full industrialisation could be reversed by the implementation of high tariffs on agricultural goods and by bimetallism. By these means it was hoped that Germany could become a truly autarkic state. Originally Wagner had accepted the contention of the classical political economists that the gold standard would regulate exchange rates and create an equilibrium in the balance of payments, but he soon came round to the view that Germany on a gold standard was defenceless against the manipulations of the silver-standard nations. Gold then became associated in his mind with dubious deals on the stock exchange, the triumph of industry and the domination of the world markets by the British. Bimetallism became the panacea for Germany's financial difficulties and the future salvation of German agriculture.

The great opponent of Wagner and the conservative political economists was the Munich professor for political economy, Lujo Brentano. Although a convinced free-trader and an enthusiast for the industrial state, Brentano believed that the state would have to intervene with adequate social legislation to protect the interests of the working class, and he also believed in the right to strike – a view that placed him to the left of the liberal camp. Other prominent figures on the pro-industrial side included the social-imperialist ideologue Friedrich Naumann, the ex-Minister of Commerce from Austria, Albert Schäffle, and, to a more limited extent, the great historian of German agriculture, Theodor von der Goltz. The most profound and far-reaching of the pro-industrialists was undoubtedly the sociologist Max Weber, who was a shrewd critic of the agrarians and whose analysis of the disastrous effects of their disproportionate power and influence has proved to be of exceptional interest and benefit to later generations of historians from Eckart Kehr to the present day. These critics of the Wagner school argued that the autarkic agrarian state would be unable to survive in the modern world. Its best talents would emigrate abroad. It would be hopelessly weak in times of crop failure and bad harvests. It would be without sufficient foreign reserves. Self-sufficiency was a hopeless illusion in a world in which economic interdependence was a striking and ever more pronounced feature. High protective tariffs would drive up the price of food to absurd heights, and further depress the living standards of the industrial workers. Thus the conservatives' programme would exacerbate the very conditions which they denounced in the modern world. Brentano suggested that the solution lay in the re-distribution of wealth in favour of the industrial workers and in the provision of cheaper food by tariff reductions.

Whereas the conservatives blamed all Germany's problems on the trade treaties and the lowering of tariffs, the liberals insisted that there were important sectors of German agriculture that were doing very well and that one of the main reasons for the problems of eastern agriculture was the ridiculously high level of indebtedness, due in large part to excessive speculation in the period of prosperity. High levels of indebtedness, combined with unnaturally high land prices, made it impossible for the average farmer to invest sufficiently in modern equipment and fertilisers so that German agriculture was not increasing its productivity at a satisfactory rate.

In the course of this debate it gradually became clear that the argument was not really about economics at all, but whether or not it was desirable to preserve and shore up the social structure of the Reich and to preserve the unique position of the land-owning aristocracy. Max Weber was particularly fascinated by this problem as he analysed the way in which the German bourgeoisie affected the style of life and the mentality of the aristocracy. This 'feudalisation of the bourgeoisie' was sufficient to make the industrial middle class abandon its immediate economic advantages in the interests of a common alliance against the demands for democratic change and fundamental social reform. To the conservatives industrial society was too risky a gamble, for they took the socialists at their word in thinking that it would almost inevitably lead to a socialist revolution, or at least to the creation of social problems that could not be mastered. Liberals like Lujo Brentano and Max Weber dismissed the Marxist analysis and insisted that increased industrial wealth, imperialist ventures abroad and the strengthening of Germany's industrial economy would provide the sole way of overcoming the social problem and confounding the socialists. The liberals were confident that industrial society could be mastered and that it was the key to German power. The conservatives feared that it would unleash forces that could not be restrained. The common ground between them was fear of the left and a determination to strengthen the place of Germany in the world. This was to form the highly contradictory and explosive basis for *Sammlungspolitik*.

With the dismissal of Caprivi, the industrialists could still not be won over to support the 'Kanitz plan', which involved nationalisation of grain imports, bimetallism and a reform of the stock exchange. On the other hand they were anxious not to sever all their links with the agrarians and shared a common dislike, although from a different perspective, of the ex-Chancellor's politics. Co-operation between industry and agriculture was to be founded on a common front against social democracy and in bombastic imperialism. The architect of the alliance was Johannes von Miquel, who had unique connections not only with industry and banking, in which he had had a brilliant career before becoming Prussian Minister of Finance in 1890, but also with the agrarians. The Kaiser was also anxious to revive the cartel, having lost his enthusiasm for being the 'social emperor', and he was now determined to build a secure majority for the naval programme.

Sammlungspolitik began to take shape in 1897 with Cabinet changes that brought Bülow from the Rome Embassy to the Wilhelmstrasse, Tirpitz to the Admiralty, and the dismissal of the Caprivi-ites Boetticher, the deputy Reichschancellor and Minister of the Interior, whose position was taken by the conservative Posadowsky, and Marschall, who was forced to make way for Bülow. In November 1897 the first meeting of the Economic Committee (*Wirtschaftlicher Ausschuss*) took place in Berlin. The committee was made up of representatives of the *Zentralverband*, the Chambers of Commerce and the *Deutscher Landwirtschaftsrat*, with further members appointed by the government. The committee at once set about discussing the revision of the trade treaties and its majority was clearly protectionist, prompting the export-oriented industries to denounce this alliance of 'cabbage Junkers and chimney-stack barons'. The exporting industries were alarmed at the renewed talk of the 'protection of national labour', that tired slogan of the Bismarck years that had come to mean little more than expensive bread and the feather-bedding of the agrarians. Industrialists from the electro-chemical, armaments, tobacco and light engineering branches combined with commercial interests to criticise the committee and its one-sided representation of the tariff question. They joined together to form the Trade Treaty Association (*Handelsvertragsverein*) in November 1900. Although the association was to gain impressive support, its formation was left too late and it was unable to combat the powerful alliance of protectionist industry and the agrarians.

This alliance was by no means quite as smooth and united as Miquel had hoped. The agrarians were determined to push up the tariff as high as possible, and were prepared to make their support of the government dependent on promises that the tariffs would be substantially increased. Thus the agrarians only voted for the great naval Bill of 1898 when they were assured that the grain tariffs would be increased, and in the following year they would not support the building of the Mittelland canal which they had already turned down in 1894, on the grounds that the government was not protecting their interests in a satisfactory manner and would not make any guarantees about the new tariffs. In spite of rather rash promises to the agrarians for a shipping route from Berlin to Stettin, the building of a canal from the Vistula to the Oder and an extension of the Spree canal, the new Chancellor, Bülow, was unable to push through the canal Bill on a third attempt in 1901, even though the Kaiser had expressed his fury at the conservatives for their behaviour in 1899, and had dismissed a number of senior civil servants for voting against the Bill; the Bill had to be withdrawn.

The new Chancellor, Chlodwig Fürst zu Hohenlohe-Schillingsfürst admitted in his first major address to the Reichstag that he had no programme. The heavy industrialists, led by von Stumm-Halberg, had a very distinct programme, which involved an all-out attack on the social democrats. The resulting Bill in the Reichstag, the 'Revolution Bill' (*Umsturzvorlage*) was the first Bill to be debated in the new Reichstag building, which was completed in December 1894. But Stumm and his supporters had seriously misjudged the climate of the times. It was no longer possible to solve the social question by such violent means, and Stumm was attacked by such figures as Adolf Wagner and Adolf Stöcker, neither of whom could be accused of harbouring any affection for the left. The *Umsturzvorlage* was abandoned but the extreme right-wing course of the 'Stumm era' continued. In 1896 Berlepsch was dismissed from his post as Minister of Trade, and this man, whose name was associated closely with Bismarck's social insurance system, complained that he had been driven out by the pressure of heavy industry which was known to be opposed to any concessions to the workers. His successor, Ludwig Brefeld, was well known to be the creature of the heavy industrialists. The failure of the repressive Stumm politics made almost inevitable the rise of 'world politics', the particular

German form of imperialism. In 1896 there was a wave of demonstrations commemorating the victory of 1871 over France, which were answered by the social democrats sending a telegram to their French comrades on Sedan Day condemning war, chauvinism and such deliberate attempts to heighten international tension.

10 WORLD POLITICS AND MITTELEUROPA

The Imperialism of the 1890s

With the failure of Stumm's heavy-handed tactics and the emergence of the world economy from the depression, by 1896 there was a growing determination to overcome the problems of domestic politics by imperialism or, as Wilhelm Liebknecht had put it, 'to export the social question'. The process of bringing the undeveloped parts of the world into the capitalist system, which had begun as the industrial states attempted to find ways out of the depression, was now virtually completed and the resulting tensions from the colonial era caused the deadly arms race which was to be one of the most disastrous characteristics of the age of imperialism. The developed states now began to struggle for the control of the strategically important areas of the world, such as the Middle East, the Balkans or South Africa, where economic and military considerations became closely entwined. With the resulting tensions and the prospect of a major European or even world war the importance of frontier districts such as Alsace-Lorraine, Poland or even the Ukraine became increasingly significant as states began to worry about sources of raw materials and the maintenance of an adequate domestic market in the event of war. The imperialism of 'world politics' thus sprang from the exigencies of the German economy, the powerful heavily industrialised late-comer demanding its place in the sun, and from the political and social problems that resulted from that stage of development. It was the classical imperialism of a developed capitalist economy, but it contained within it a strong social imperialist movement.

The task of patching up the alliance between the cartels and the agrarians was eagerly taken up by Johannes Miquel, a man of exceptional talent with a varied career behind him. He had been a socialist sympathiser and was acquainted with Karl Marx, but had renounced this early enthusiasm for left-wing ideas and became mayor of a number of large cities, a bank director and prominent man of finance, and then a leading parliamentarian. Miquel was determined to revive the alliance of 1879, prepare the way for the negotiation of new tariffs, form a sufficient majority for the ambitious naval building programme and continue the struggle against the social democrats in a somewhat more subtle manner than that selected by Stumm and his cronies. But in rapidly changing conditions this task was far from easy.

The process of syndicalisation, cartelisation and monopolisation which was so characteristic of the German experience continued apace in the post-Bismarck era. On New Year's Day 1894 the Rhenish-Westphalian Coal Syndicate, with Emil Kirdorf of the Gelsenkirchner Bergwerks-Aktien-Gesellschaft as chairman, was started. By 1904 the syndicate controlled 98 per cent of Germany's coal production. This was only possible by using ruthless tactics against the small producers who were eventually faced with the choice of joining the syndicate or being ruined, and also by making considerable concessions to the industrial magnates like Krupp and Thyssen, who were guaranteed unlimited supplies of coal at favourable prices in return for placing their own coal-mines in the syndicate. In the chemical industry Carl Duisberg tried to follow suit, insisting that cartels and trusts had to be formed in times of prosperity in order to guarantee the highest possible profits and so as to be ready to offset the effects of any downturn in the business cycle. The problems of forming a trust in the boom years before the war were exceedingly difficult to overcome and it was not until much later that the IG-Farben trust could be formed.

Another important new organisation in this period was the Industrialists' Association (*Bund der Industriellen*) formed in 1895. Unlike the Zentralverband with its close associations with heavy industry, the Bund represented the interests of light industry which was concerned about export markets and keeping down the price of raw materials. Spokesmen for the interests of the *Bund*, of whom the most prominent was Gustav Stresemann, were bitter about the powerful role of the trusts and cartels and passionate protagonists of imperialism, which they saw as a means to break out from under the overwhelming domination of heavy industry. Both the *Bund* and the *Zentralverband* had their own employers' associations which had been formed from the amalgamation of many such organisations. Finding that they had common interests as employers in combating the economic influence of the unions and the political influence of the social democrats, they partially amalgamated in 1913 to form the Association of German Employers' Associations (*Vereinigung Deutscher Arbeitgeberverbände*).

Within an economy marked by increasing concentration the banks continued to play an important role. On the one hand, the success of the great cartels and trusts made it possible for industry to rely less heavily on the banks for capital, but they were far from being independent. The close association between bank capital and industrial capital remained, and the banks maintained a lively interest in firms which they had founded or in which they had a substantial stake. In many instances the banks were very much the senior partner. The great industrial concerns could plan their long-term investment programmes, and think in terms of new projects, products and techniques, but without the support of the banks none of these plans could be realised. Unlike Britain, where the high rates of industrial profits made it possible to meet the long-term needs of industry by insider financing, and the banks were used for short-term financing to maintain satisfactory liquidity or to meet immediate needs, the lower rate of profit, the heavy demand for capital, lower absolute income, lower savings and the general shortage of capital in Germany meant that the banks played a vital role in the supply of badly needed capital. The banks, being so heavily committed to industry, were determined to secure their industrial investments and also the investments of their clients who were looking for secure havens for their investment capital. The relationship between the great banks and big industry in Wilhelmine Germany is highly complex, and one that has not yet been studied in sufficient detail, largely because of the lack of archival material. It is clear that the success of some of the great concerns made it possible for them to become slightly more independent from the great banks and they were no longer the executants of the economic and industrial policies of the great banks. Furthermore the enormous debts of some industries were sometimes used as weapons against the banks, the fate of both debtor and creditor being so closely bound together.

This general shortage of investment capital meant that Germany had little capital available for the promotion of imperial ventures, whether formal or informal. Most of the investment capital available was ploughed back into industry. Thus at a time when the British were beginning to neglect investment in their own industry, from the early 1870s onwards, and preferred to invest in the colonies or in areas of economic influence, the Germans were painfully but busily laying the groundwork for their future spectacular success in the new industrial techniques. While British industrial productivity was beginning to slip, Germany was rationalising, expanding and improving output. Thus, relative to Britain, the Germans were strengthening their position, so that when the world economy recovered from the depression Germany was to be in a much better position to challenge the British in the export markets of the world. The change from the informal to the formal empire was in part due to the declining strength of Britain as an industrial power in the face of the growing competition of its Continental and transatlantic trade rivals. As long as Britain had an unchallenged industrial dominance throughout the world an informal empire was the most effective, cheapest and most flexible form of imperialism. As competition became more severe and free trade was gradually abandoned, the 'imperialism of free trade' had also to be replaced by the classic imperialism of the 'highest stage of capitalism'. Britain now had to rely increasingly on the formal empire to overcome the problems of its declining importance as an industrial power. Without the close co-operation between banking and industrial capital, without a high degree of vertical or horizontal integration, and with distinct limitations on the capital market, the British economy found it increasingly difficult to meet the challenge of the United States and Germany. In the British Empire the structural weaknesses of the metropolitan economy were reproduced, and thus imperialism acted as a brake on the development of the productive forces. By contrast the new industrial states were to flourish, their economies were better organised to meet the challenge of the new situation, and their combined dislike of British imperial splendour helped them to work together to destroy British dominance in the world market.

Bismarck's imperialism was part of a deliberate interventionist policy to stimulate the economy, which was suffering the effects of the low point in the business cycle, and to find new markets for goods that could no longer be sold in the traditional markets. It was hoped that, given the particular characteristics of the Germany economy, it might be possible to counter the effects of the depression by means of an informal empire or, if absolutely necessary, by the creation of formal colonies.

In addition to this use of an imperialist policy as an anti-cyclical device was the strong social imperialist motive, the desire to overcome the contradictions between the old traditional élites of the army and bureaucracy, the agrarians and the Church and the new élites of industrial society. Industry and agriculture, government and parliament, bourgeois and proletariat, progress and restoration were in sharp conflict, and it was hoped that these tensions could be directed outside the country by an ambitious imperialist policy. Imperialism would cement the alliance between rye and steel, industrialist and agrarian, the new and the old. It would be the prize for the success of *Sammlungspolitik*.

This theory of social imperialism, which is fundamental to most of the recent research on imperial Germany in the Federal Republic, is seriously flawed and often misleading. It cannot be denied that there was a strong social imperialist motive in the politics of Bismarck and his successors, and it has proved most fruitful that this moment within German imperialism has been stressed. The problems begin when the subjective desires of the politicians are confused with the objective realities of capitalist reproduction. Social imperialism was a powerful manipulative ideology, a useful means of crisis management, but in the final analysis it was a miserable failure. The conflicts and tensions within German society intensified, and the imperialist policies made them even more severe. The growing significance of the world market was both a necessity to the German economy and in sharp contradiction to the 'solidarity protectionism' of the agrarians and their supporters.

Bismarck's social imperialism was subject to both economic and political restraints. Imperialism was limited by the economic weaknesses and shortcomings which it was designed to overcome, for 'depression imperialism' lacked the powerful dynamic of the later imperialism. Politically Bismarck still intended to pursue a conciliatory policy to preserve the European *status quo*, and was not prepared to run the risk of allowing a major international crisis to result from some quarrel over the colonies. Under Caprivi industry was freed from the constraints of the Bismarckian system by the trade treaties and was able to profit from the upturn of the world economy. German manufacturing industries were quick to exploit the possibilities of the markets of eastern Europe and the Balkans, and at the same time the volume of overseas trade was greatly increased. The counter-offensive by the agrarians and heavy industrialists who attempted to restore the policy of 'solidarity protectionism' resulted in the imperialism of *Weltpolitik* being based on a contradiction between the dynamics of an expanding industrial economy and the political exigencies of the ruling elites, who were determined to preserve their own privileged position and to protect the domestic market against the challenge from abroad. *Sammlungspolitik* was thus undermined by the conflicts between free-traders and protectionists, between heavy and light industry, and thus lacked the legitimising effect without which domestic conflicts could not be overcome. The resulting frustrations and aggressions gave to the imperialism of *Weltpolitik* its particular vehemence and lack of consistency.

Whereas Lenin insisted that the characteristic of the new imperialism was the export of capital rather than goods, German imperialism was seriously restricted by the shortage of capital. The support of French and Belgian capitalists was frequently needed to assist German foreign ventures, and when after the Agadir crisis of 1911 the French withdrew this support, Germany was faced with an acute capital shortage. Between 1908 and 1911 German banks could count on about 1 billion francs to support their foreign investments. Turkey, Russia and the Balkan states were able to buy German industrial goods and weapons that were purchased with French money. From Latin America to the Baghdad railway German and French interests worked together for mutual benefit. When the vital financial support of the French was withdrawn the demands for a formal empire became more strident, for open-door imperialism no longer seemed to guarantee Germany the foreign markets and the sources of raw materials that it so badly needed. As the world had already been largely divided up, there was little prospect for a successful policy of formal imperialism. The only viable alternative seemed to be *Mitteleuropa*, a Europe dominated by Germany. But once again the forces opposing such a policy were too strong and the result was a strengthening of the Entente and mounting tensions in the heart of Europe.

Although co-operation between German and French financial interests in ventures in third countries was of long standing, and in spite of the many close links between banks in the two countries, it was not until the late 1890s that French capital was invested directly in Germany on a large scale. In late 1897 French banks offered long-term loans that were quickly snapped up by the German banks. With the German economy booming at least until the end of the century, and with the severe shortage of capital, the German market was an attractive prospect to French investors. Relations between the two countries had improved, German interest rates were higher than in France, and the French were quick to fill the gap in the capital market left as British investments dwindled, in part because of the mounting crisis in South Africa and the German Emperor's sympathetic attitude towards Kruger. Although some French commentators feared that such investments would serve to strengthen France's great rival and the recession of 1901 prompted gloomy predictions of an imminent '*krach allemand*', German bonds continued to interest French investors. In the downswing of the business cycle from 1901 to 1903/4, German industry remained calm and continued to invest heavily in new plant and equipment in preparation for the predicted upswing.

Industrial securities continued to attract investors, but the bond market was seriously depressed. Government indebtedness in Germany was considerably greater than in either France or Britain, due largely to excessive military expenditure and an inadequate income from taxes.

As the conservatives opposed any proposals for fundamental financial reform, the government had to rely largely on revenue from customs and indirect taxation and attempted to make up the short-fall by issuing new bonds. As the banks were under no obligation to invest part of their assets in government bonds, the loans were seriously undersubscribed even when the interest rates were pushed up. As the demands of industry, governments and municipalities for capital exceeded the rate of growth of capital formation, it is hardly surprising that there was little capital left over for foreign investment. This deficit financing and expansion of the money supply helped promote economic growth which was fast enough to postpone repayment problems. Helfferich estimated that 85 per cent of German capital investments were made at home, and subsequent scholarship supports this view. Britain and France were investing nearly half their national savings abroad in the decade before the First World War. In real terms the differences are not quite so great. In 1914 German foreign investments amounted to about 35 billion marks, compared to 40 billion marks for France and 75 billion marks for Britain. Although such figures should be regarded as very rough estimates, they are indicative of the remarkable growth of the German economy in this period and also of the critical importance of foreign investment for Germany, without which its performance could not have been so impressive. About two-thirds of German foreign investments were in industrial enterprises, most of which gave a satisfactorily high return. By contrast, about half of France's foreign investments were in government bonds, yielding an average of 5 per cent. Unlike British investments, which were largely in the under-capitalised parts of the world, German investments were concentrated in Europe with heavy commitments in Turkey and north Africa.

Although foreign investment by Germany played a relatively small role, it was sharply criticised by the agrarians who feared that it would reduce the availability of capital in Germany, drive up interest rates and worsen their position as a debtor class. In February 1911 the agrarians' spokesman, Kanitz, was demanding drastic measures against the influx of foreign securities which he claimed were a constant drain on German capital. The counter-argument, that the export of capital stimulated the export of goods and thus would improve Germany's trading position, was not one that was likely to impress the agrarians, and as governments and municipalities began to suffer from a shortage of funds, it was easier to convince the officials in the Ministry of Finance that foreign loans were a potential danger. The fact that foreign investors, particularly the French, were attracted by German bonds was hardly a compensation, for such bonds were quickly sold at the first signs of any change in the political climate. The Agadir crisis of 1911 resulted in French banks avoiding the German money market and the problem of capital shortage became acute.

This shortage of capital and the need for French financial support for imperialist ventures from the Baghdad railway to exploits in South America is clear indication of the insecure basis of German imperialism. The deep suspicions of the agrarians and heavy industrialists of foreign capital, suspicions which were often spiced with anti-Semitism, resulted in the growing isolation of Berlin and the great banks from the international money market. Informal imperialist expansion was frustrated by this lack of capital and there was a growing demand for a formal empire that would secure adequate sources of raw materials and sufficient overseas markets. Capital shortage, particularly after 1911, resulted in inadequate financial and military preparations for war at a time when mounting international tensions, exacerbated by the particular virulence of German policies, made a war more likely than ever. Germany was obliged to play the role of an under-imperialist power, acting on behalf of American interests in Mexico after the revolution, combining with American capital in China and North Africa, and working alongside the British in the Portuguese colonies. The result was an extraordinary confusion and lack of direction in German policy. German financial interests in Mexico were in direct conflict with the policies of the Foreign Office. Financial interests concerned to get British support for foreign ventures had little sympathy for the naval building programme, not only because it was a constant drain on existing capital resources, but also because they were anxious to maintain their ties with the London market.

The uneven development of the world economy further heightened the tensions of a divided world. Germany was increasingly dependent on exports of industrial goods to countries that were potential enemies: England, France, Russia, Belgium and the Netherlands. These exports were in turn not possible without a steady supply of raw materials and foodstuffs from overseas, supplies that increased fivefold in the twenty-five years before the outbreak of the world war. By 1913, 60 per cent of exports went to Entente countries, and 68.1 per cent of imports came from them. By contrast only 12.2 per cent of exports went to allied countries, and a mere 8.4 per cent of imports came from them. The dynamism of the German economy resulted in a growing rivalry in overseas trade as the competition of German goods was felt even within the British and French colonial empires. Of the great industrial nations only Germany was able to increase its share of world trade, securing an almost monopolistic position in the chemical industry, particularly dyestuffs, electrical goods and precision instruments, and overtaking Britain in a number of key markets, including Russia and Scandinavia. With rising prices at home and a reduction in real wages after 1911, the export drive was further stepped up, resulting in the growing contradiction between the exigencies of the economy and the sectional interests of the agrarians and their protectionist allies. Blocked by protectionists at home and abroad, frustrated by the internal political and social tensions of the Reich, and exacerbated by a mounting economic nationalism, the pressures built up within Germany to the point that war seemed the only possible way to overcome the seemingly insoluble problems of an antagonistic society.

Extensive empirical research is needed before the precise nature of these contradictions can be clearly delineated. The simplistic dichotomy between 'heavy industry' and 'manufacturing industry', one protectionist and the other free-trading, which features in much of the historical writing on the period can no longer be seriously upheld in its pristine form. On the other hand the fundamental contradictions between the practices of the iron, steel and coal interests and manufacturing industries with their vital need to increase exports cannot be denied by placing undue stress on the lack of unity among the manufacturing industries, the diversity of their professional organisations or the problem of precise definitions. The complexity of the problems and the resulting tensions account for the frustrations and the lack of direction in German imperialism. The dynamics of Germany's economic growth pushed in the direction of the expansion of overseas trade and foreign ventures and the creation of an informal empire, but this was frustrated by the preponderant social and economic power of the less developed sectors of the economy and by the mounting international tensions. As the forces of production were restrained by an outmoded social structure, it was hoped that the situation could be mastered by a heavy dose of imperialistic, militaristic, chauvinistic and anti-socialist propaganda. But this wild and irrational ideology could not in the long run mask the objective realities of the situation, and its very aggressiveness, far from giving to the nation a sense of common purpose, served to cloud the issues and to confuse and frustrate those it was intended to placate and control.

These problems were exacerbated by the protectionist Bülow tariff, and became critical after 1911, whereas the relative free trade of the

Caprivi trade agreements tended to favour the 'informal' imperialism which best suited Germany's economic structure. The question of the direction which that imperialism was to take remained open. In his inaugural lecture at Freiburg, Max Weber had said that the unification of the German Empire in 1871 would simply be regarded as a youthful prank, were it not to form the basis for German world-power policy. This view reflected the opinion of the academic community, of the economists, historians and the 'socialists of the chair', who believed that Germany had the strength and the moral right to form an empire that would be the equal of the great imperialist powers of 'Greater Britain', 'All-Russia' and 'Pan-America'. The proponents of the 'Fourth Empire' thought in terms of overseas colonial expansion, and most were content to accept the existing borders in Europe. At this stage the idea of *Mitteleuropa* was seen largely in terms of customs agreements with neighbouring states, proposals which understandably alarmed foreign commentators who rightly saw them as schemes to establish the European hegemony of Germany. *Weltpolitik* and *Mitteleuropa* were thus seen as complementary ideas, slogans that could attract widely divergent sectors of the German bourgeoisie. Some hoped that imperialism would overcome the social and political contradictions within the state, give a sense of common purpose to German policy and preserve the *status quo*. Others saw it as a means to overcome the domination of political and economic life by the agrarians and their supporters and thus make possible the liberalisation and democratisation of society. Some hoped that imperialism would provide the means to satisfy the needs and aspirations of the working class. Above all, imperialism would assert the independence of the German nation and provide clear evidence that the Reich had come of age.

The thrust of this policy was away from England, to end the dependence on the British money market, on Reuter's news service, on British communications networks and, most important of all, to build up a German merchant marine protected by a large German navy. Although the naval building programme only accounted for less than 2 per cent of total iron and steel output and directly profited a mere handful of armaments firms, the programme was welcomed as a means of guaranteeing German economic interests and of giving to the nation a sense of true national purpose. The more pronounced this social imperialism became, the louder were the denunciations of England. This gave rise to a further contradiction, for Germany could not risk a war with England at a time when the navy was under construction and yet *Englandhass* ('hatred of England' in Kehr's phrase) was needed to fuel the programme.

Yet to challenge England entailed strengthening the industrial base, forcing exports to overcome the crises of over-production and modernising the economy. Such a scheme formed the basis of Caprivi's *Mitteleuropa* policies which had been so roundly denounced by the conservatives for being anti-agrarian and anti-Prussian. Hohenlohe agreed with Posadowski's gloomy predictions that Caprivi's commercial policies were undermining the monarchy and leading Germany along the path to republicanism, but he was at a loss to see how Germany could become a great power as the conservatives demanded without some fundamental changes in the social order. There was much talk in government circles of a possible European war, but there was general agreement that it would be almost impossible to stage such a war without Germany appearing as the aggressor. Alternatives seemed to be more colonial acquisitions, the naval building programme, or even a *coup d'état* to revise the constitution and crush the forces of social change. The *coup d'état* was unlikely to gain the support of the federal states and might prompt foreign intervention. Tirpitz certainly saw the naval programme as a means to counter social democracy and to provide the mass support needed for a dynamic imperialism, but at least in the early years as Secretary of State for the Navy he had little sympathy for the agrarians, whom he regarded as a doomed social class.

Miquel's *Sammlungspolitik* was thus without a clearly defined set of objectives and without a carefully considered programme of action. A continual sniping by conservatives at 'international capitalism', at *Weltpolitik*, and even at the 'hideous fleet' was hardly an adequate substitute for a genuine political platform. Demands for bimetallism, for the nationalisation of grain imports as proposed by Kanitz, or an attack on commerce by means of the Stock Exchange Act of 1896 had no real hope of success. The new edition of Bismarck's cartel of 1897, the industrial and agrarian condominium directed against the proletariat, had to be kept together not merely by calls for the protection of national labour against political and economic radicalism, the slogan for the Reichstag elections, but, as Miquel insisted, by an active and bombastic foreign policy. The agrarians were still suspicious of the naval programme, and tried to make their support conditional on the acceptance of the Kanitz proposals for control of grain imports under the slogan '*ohne Kanitz keine kähne*'. They continued to oppose the proposals for the *Mittellandkanal* running from the Rhine to Berlin, which they feared would cause the German market to be flooded with cheap foreign grain, and they persisted with their demands for bimetallism. Whereas many agrarians took an extreme intransigent attitude towards the commercial treaties and their proposed revision, the more moderate were prepared to accept Miquel's assurances that his prime concern was with the domestic market, and they were prepared to co-operate with the Economic Committee which had been formed to discuss new trade agreements.

Weltpolitik was thus not merely a political response to improved economic conditions as the economy entered a new period of rapid expansion, but was deliberate prestige politics designed to overcome, deflect or disguise the tensions and contradictions within a class society, and was part of an attempt to frustrate the process of political and social emancipation. The effects of industrialism were to be neutralised without mounting a full-scale attack on the industrial state as some extreme conservatives demanded. This attempt to square the circle was doomed by the fundamental contradiction between the development of the productive forces and the social and political structure of Wilhelmine society. It is for this reason that *Weltpolitik* followed an erratic, wild and uncertain course, lacked a solid political base, and in the long run served to exacerbate the contradictions it was designed to overcome.

Although the fear of social upheaval was quite genuine and was a powerful integrating force behind *Sammlungspolitik*, it is also difficult to see *Weltpolitik* as a direct response to pressure from below for social, political and economic change. 'Social imperialism' is not of itself an adequate explanation of the phenomenon. In fact the period from 1897 was one of relative quiet on the labour front. Militants in the steel and coal industries were still active, and strikes were not infrequent, but these sectors were hardly typical and labour relations were on the whole harmonious. The social democrats were becoming increasingly reconciled to capitalism, and the party was revisionist in practice though not in theory. It became obvious to all but the most purblind conservatives that some concessions would have to be made to the modern world, for the industrial state was there to stay. Wilhelmine Germany was a seriously divided and antagonistic society as can be seen from the almost pathological behaviour of certain factions, and from this it follows that *Weltpolitik* was bound to favour the sectional interests of certain groups more than others, for all its pretence of being a national policy. In an antagonistic class society no disinterested policy is possible so that the question of the *cui bono* of any such policy has to be asked. Once this question is raised the fundamental concerns of the agrarians that were so often disguised by their immoderate and ill-considered language become apparent. *Weltpolitik* was indeed a triumph of the cartels and trusts, of the hideous fleet and the military machine; it marks the fusion of industrial and economic problems with certain key structures within German society and thus in a profound sense marks the 'industrialisation' of society.

The industrial complex of the second industrial revolution was characterised by a high degree of cartelisation and monopolisation and by an increasing degree of state intervention in the workings of the economy, usually in the interest of those giant firms which dominated the industrial scene. During the years of the depression the state apparatus had gained considerable experience in the use of customs duties and tariffs, subsidies and taxes, transport rates and export premiums to control, stimulate and direct the economy. Far from being exceptional measures to meet a crisis situation, as some liberal economists imagined, they were endogenous to a developed capitalism, a necessary means to bring some semblance of order to the anarchy of capitalist production. The experience of the long depression did much to discredit the ideology of liberal capitalism, particularly in Germany where there was no strong tradition of classical political economy outside the socialist camp, and the new slogans were stability, preservation of the system, balance and the avoidance of industrial and social conflict. For the time being Germany lacked the instruments of effective intervention in the economy. The Reichsbank was highly conventional in its policies and limited in its field of action. Financial policy was imperfectly understood and there was no adequate control of the financial institutions of the Reich by the government agencies. Thus the main field of action was foreign trade, and hence the endless debates on tariffs and trade agreements from Caprivi to Bülow, for this was the principal means of economic control and of government intervention.

Even a cursory examination of the main outlines of German overseas and foreign trade policy reveals the bias of these policies. They profited the agrarians, the industrialists in heavy industry and the bureaucratic and military élites, and by driving up the price of basic foodstuffs they harmed the vast mass of the working people of Germany. August Bebel, the social-democratic leader, was perfectly correct in stating that protective tariffs were the best possible means of creating social unrest and furthering the cause of socialism, and as long as intervention in the economy was so blatantly in the interests of one privileged sector of society, it could never secure that stability which theoretically was its rationale and its justification.

The anti-British emphasis of *Weltpolitik* was as much a reflection of these political and social problems as it was a matter of economic rivalry. Bismarck had feared the liberalising effects of any close association with Britain, and the brief interlude of the reign of the 'liberal' Kaiser Frederick II with his English wife had alarmed conservative circles and served as a vivid reminder of the dangers of liberalism, constitutional monarchy and parliamentary democracy. It is hardly surprising, therefore, that the Germans sympathised so strongly with the Boers and their struggle against the British. A pious and bigoted people of simple farmers led by a hirsute patriarch was locked in a life-and-death struggle with capitalist exploiters and their Jewish henchmen. Here was a battle between virtue and vice, between simplicity and greed, between morality and a gross materialism. But, as always, this pro-Boer enthusiasm was tempered by divergent economic interests. On the one hand there was the attractive spectacle of the co-operation of the Boer republic with the German colonies in Africa, with a German-built railway from Pretoria to the east coast of Africa, but on the other hand the Boers were suspicious of German motives and refused the hand that was offered to them. The Kaiser told the Boers that Germany was the 'maker of the world's cannons', but they preferred to order their rifles from Schneider rather than Krupp, which was seen both as an insult to German industry and as a particularly hard blow at a time of intensified rivalry between French and German arms manufacturers. German bankers were quickly disillusioned with the Boers who favoured the Nobel Dynamite Trust, and under the leadership of the Deutsche Bank they mobilised German industrial interests in South Africa, the holders of gold shares, the *Kölnische Zeitung* and the *Norddeutsche Allgemeine Zeitung*, and mounted an anti-Boer campaign.

As Holstein wrote, echoing similar sentiments by Miquel, Bülow and other leading politicians of the time, Germany needed a clear foreign political triumph in order to overcome the political problems at home. He saw three possibilities for the success of such a Bonapartist policy: a European war, brinkmanship in world politics (*weltgeschichtliche Hazardspiel*), or territorial acquisitions overseas. The Boer War failed to produce any such results, and the next attempt at such prestige politics was in China between 1897 and 1900 where the role of the navy was to play an important part in German considerations. Whereas the Boers had shown little enthusiasm for Krupp's weapons, the Chinese statesman, Li Hung Chang, a man whose corruption was notorious even in Imperial China, had given Germany a written guarantee in 1886 of a weapons monopoly, and in the following years the influence of Krupp in China grew steadily. It was under Krupp's influence that the Germans decided upon Kiouchou as a naval base for, although it was quite unsuitable for such a base, it was close to important sources of coal and the German Admiralty was eventually forced to accept the argument that the fleet needed an industrial base as much as it needed ideal naval bases. Kiouchou was a success. Bülow wrote: 'Our external prestige has been enhanced and the general feeling at home has become quite different,' and it was perhaps the most striking achievement of a year in which Germany's position was strengthened by Fashoda and by the agreement with Britain on the Portuguese colonies. Yet for all the talk of a 'free hand' or even of Continental alliance, Germany was far from being the *arbiter mundi*, as William II felt in his more expansive moments, and was indeed in imminent danger of falling between the stools. Bülow complained that Germany lay like a slab of butter before Britain's hot knife, Holstein feared that any alliances that Germany might enter would increase the risk of war, and Tirpitz repeated that Germany was passing through a period of particular danger whilst the fleet was being built.

The Mobilisation of Popular Support

The imperialism and militarism of the 1890s was marked by the growing importance of the interest groups that mobilised mass support for imperialism and the navy programme. The first of these new groups was the Pan German League (*Alldeutsche Verband*) formed in response to widespread dissatisfaction with the Heligoland-Zanzibar agreement of 1890, which was seen as a betrayal of Germany's colonial interests and which soon developed an ideological position that was a clear prefiguration of Hitler's Fascism. Along with a virulent racism and anti-Semitism, an extreme imperialism and a belligerent nationalism, went often contradictory demands for a large overseas empire and the extension of *Mitteleuropa* under German leadership. The *Alldeutsche* were not a collection of exotic fanatics; among the 73 members of the executive committee of the organisation were some of the most respected and influential men in Germany. The organisational genius of the league, Alfred Hugenberg, was also chairman of the executive committee of the *Zentralverband* and also of the Mining

Association (*Bergbauliche Verein*), positions of enormous power and influence which he gained largely by virtue of his post as chairman of the Board at Krupp's. G.L. Meyer, the chairman of the Association of Iron and Steel Industrialists, Dr Reismann-Grone, the editor of *Rheinisch-Westfälischen Zeitung*, which was the semi-official mouthpiece of heavy industry, and the leader of the free conservatives, von Kardorff, were all on the committee, along with prominent industrialists like Emil Kirdorf, Duddenhofer (the explosives manufacturer) and Leuschner (Mansfeld Mines), as well as a number of prominent academics and economists. Standing for the particular wishes of heavy industry and articulating a customs, financial and social policy that accorded with those wishes, and led by some of the most prominent men of Rhine, Ruhr and Upper Silesia, the *Alldeutsche* could never hope to gain mass support for their programme. The association was more than a mere clique of heavy industrialists, but it would be equally mistaken to dismiss it as a petit bourgeois organisation, for the social basis of its membership and the appeal of its ideology was necessarily too narrow for it to have the impact of later organisations such as the Navy League (*Flottenverein*). Representative of a powerful sector of Wilhelmine society and with its close associations with the political parties of the right and with the military and naval élites, the *Alldeutsche Verband* was to have exceptional influence which was to continue with the formation of the extremist *Vaterlandspartei* in 1917, the German National Peoples' Party in the Weimar Republic, and finally with the National Socialists, whom they came to see as the heirs to their policy of world power in the years before the First World War.

The *Flottenverein* of 1898, formed to provide mass support for Tirpitz's naval programme, was the largest and most successful of the interest groups of imperial Germany. Some feared that in spite of the success of the Germans in China, the Reichstag would not accept the naval estimates and the Kaiser in his wilder moments revived his notions of a *coup d'état* in order to force his will on the people. The *Flottenverein* was therefore organised with the close co-operation of heavy industry in order to give the naval programme a pseudo-democratic legitimacy. The success was overwhelming, so that the Navy League could presume to speak with almost the same authority as the duly elected Reichstag. The *Flottenverein* had a large number of newspapers and magazines at its disposal, could rely on the enthusiastic support of prominent academics such as Max Weber, Lujo Brentano and Gustav Schmoller, and the innocent enthusiasm of a generation of sailor-suited children. The navy league inspired the deferential petite bourgeoisie, excited the enthusiasm of the protagonists of industrial society and warmed the hearts of chauvinistic conservatives. It seemed to provide the platform for mass support not only for the navy but for *Sammlungspolitik* itself. It soon became the largest organisation in imperial Germany, larger in terms of membership than even the Social Democratic Party (SPD), which was its closest rival. Even those who had serious reservations about *Sammlungspolitik*, such as the business élite of Hamburg, were prepared to support the naval programme because it brought profits and jobs to the shipyards, and it was only when the dangerous effects of the anti-English thrust of the programme became clearly apparent that they began to have serious reservations about the policy. For the time being Tirpitz was able to fool his contemporaries with his fraudulent 'risk theory', whereby he claimed that the purpose of the naval programme was to make the German navy strong enough that England would not risk a naval attack and that it was therefore purely defensive. He was so successful with this argument that he succeeded not only in calming his anxious critics but also in pulling the wool over the eyes of many later historians, among them scholars who had no sympathy for Tirpitz and his schemes. Within the Reichstag a majority could be found for the naval programme by means of the Economic Committee which had been formed by Miquel, and in which representatives of the agrarians and of industry discussed the forthcoming renegotiations of the trade agreements. Thus the naval building programme with its fundamental domestic and foreign political ramifications was closely linked with the question of tariffs and the question of the industrial versus the agricultural state.

Proponents of an unhistorical empiricism still insist that the German battle fleet was built simply because the forceful and ambitious Tirpitz wanted to build ships. According to this version, the naval programme was the result of departmental egotism. Sailors like ships, therefore they try to build as many as they can. Such a simple-minded view in no way accords with the known facts. The navy was built in order to destroy the British navy and secure Germany's position as a world power, although Tirpitz was not a proponent of an aggressive naval war but planned a strategy of counter-attack in which the British navy would be destroyed in its initial attack in the North Sea. The navy programme was also part of the social imperialist strategy of imperial Germany, although it was as such a miserable failure, creating more problems than it was able to solve. Industrialists were to profit, workers to get jobs and the petite bourgeoisie to enthuse over the navy. The aim was to create, in V.R. Berghahn's words, a 'Naval Caesarism' strengthened by the pseudo-plebiscitory effect of the *Flottenverein* that would stabilise the social system against the pressure of parliamentarism. The striking technology of the fleet could thus be used to preserve the anti-modernist forces within German society, and domestic political tensions and contradictions could be deflected by the national task of building a great navy. The navy and the world power it would bring were to be the Utopian goals that would replace the social vision of the militant working class or the political aspirations of the liberal bourgeoisie.

Tirpitz's master plan had many serious weaknesses. The tremendous cost of building massive battleships of the sort that Alfred T. Mahan had insisted were the key to sea power placed an intolerable strain on the financial resources of the Reich, and it meant that less money could be spent on the army. Although many army officers were enthusiastic supporters of the naval programme there was a feeling in some quarters, particularly among the young and ambitious general staff officers who were pressing for a larger army, that the army was getting short-changed, and that the way to world power lay through victorious war in Europe rather than a risky encounter with the British navy on the high seas. The agrarians with their close ties with the army and their suspicion of modern industry had certain reservations about the navy. The *Kähne* were built, but they did not get their *Kanitz*. Privileges and concessions were thrown their way to gain and hold their support, but they still regarded the navy with some suspicion. Although the navy copied the attitudes and habits of the army officer corps with its aristocratic ethos, it was still regarded as unpleasantly bourgeois and even by some extremists as 'liberal'. Similarly the mass support of the *Flottenverein* seemed to some to be alarmingly democratic in tone. The agrarians used the naval programme to gain concessions in the Bülow tariffs of 1902, but they still regarded the navy as a bourgeois weapon. In terms of the social origins of the naval enthusiasts they were perfectly correct to do so, and the programme undoubtedly did much to win over the liberal bourgeoisie to the imperialist ambitions and the reactionary political system of imperial Germany. When a leading liberal, Friedrich Naumann, could claim that Christ had spoken that the navy should be built, anything was possible, and it must have seemed that Tirpitz's powerful brew had worked its magic. Yet for all the enthusiasm for the fleet, the naval programme was not sufficient to overcome domestic political antagonisms, and the aggressive intent of Tirpitz's policies helped forge the 'encirclement' of Germany by strengthening the Entente. Even though by 1914 the German navy had almost reached the 2:3 ratio for which Tirpitz was aiming, the navy proved almost useless during the war and Tirpitz was obliged to resign, devoting his restless energies henceforth to the extreme radical politics of the *Vaterlandspartei*.

11 THE ECONOMIC FOUNDATIONS OF PRE-WAR POLICY 1900–1914

The Bülow Tariffs

The initiation of the naval programme coincided with discussions on the renegotiations of the trade agreements. Under *Sammlungspolitik* and within the Economic Committee (*Wirtschaftlicher Ausschuss*) heavy industry and the agrarians had a predominant position. Small industries that were relatively labour-intensive and thus concerned about the effects of high grain tariffs on the cost of labour, and the export-oriented industries such as chemicals, machinery and electrical goods formed the Trade Treaty Organisation (*Handelsvertragsverein*) in 1900 in the vain hope of winning heavy industry away from its alliance with the agrarians. Heavy industry was extremely annoyed that the agrarians constantly opposed the plans for the Mittelland canal, voting against the canal Bill in the Prussian lower house in 1898 and again in 1899, but the attacks on the heavy industrialists by the representatives of light industry and exporting industries helped to keep the alliance of heavy industry and the agrarians together. A major concession to the agrarians was the meat inspection Act of October 1900, which banned the import of sausages and canned meat, envisaged a ban on the import of foreign meat from April 1903 and made it possible to stop the import of livestock at any time. The meat inspection Bill was strongly criticised by consumers, who were faced with the prospect of an immediate rise in meat prices and even by some representatives of heavy industry who feared the effect of these measures on international trade. Even Bülow, who became Chancellor in October 1900, feared that excessive grain tariffs as proposed by the agrarians would ruin relations with other countries and provide further ammunition to the social democrats. On the other hand, Bülow knew that he could not function as Chancellor without the support of the agrarians and that therefore some compromise would have to be reached.

The *Handelsvertragsverein* was bitterly disappointed when Bülow told the Prussian lower house that agriculture needed better protection, but such vague statements were not enough to pacify the agrarians, who continued their opposition to the canal Bill and showed very little enthusiasm for *Sammlungspolitik*. With the *Sammlung* falling apart its architect, Miquel, whose sympathies for the agrarians over the canal Bill were widely known, was dismissed. Bülow was determined to find a solution to the tariff question in spite of the intransigent attitude of 'those gentlemen with Polish names'. The new Minister of Commerce, Möller, insisted that the only way that the increasing German population could be fed would be by a healthy export industry, and that although concessions would be made to the agrarians they would have to be kept within reasonable bounds. This was in line with the Chancellor's thinking. By means of a leak to a Stuttgart newspaper Bülow let it be known that the proposed new tariffs would be increased to a minimum of 5.50 marks per 100 kilos for wheat, 5.00 marks for rye and oats and 3.00 marks for barley. The *Bund der Landwirte* was furious, and continued its demands for a general 7.50 mark tariff, whereas 'free-traders', particularly in the *Deutsche Handelstag*, felt that the Chancellor had found a happy medium. Within the Reichstag the social democrats and liberals confronted the national liberals, the centre party and the conservatives while the extremist supporters of the *Bund der Landwirte* continued to attack the proposals from the right. At the committee stage the agrarians were able to increase the proposed government rates and even had the gall to propose a reduction of the pig-iron tariff, a suggestion which was a deliberate slap in the face of the heavy industrialists. This threat proved to be effective, for the *Zentralverband* agreed to an increase to 6.00 marks for the wheat tariff and the agrarians dropped their agitation against pig-iron. But the *Sammlung* was still seriously weakened by continuing arguments over tariffs. The German economy was suffering the effects of the world economic slump and a general move towards protection. Each sector wanted to protect its own interests but denounced the similar activities of others as selfishness. The ideologues of *Weltpolitik* feared that protectionism would negate the social and economic advantages of imperialism and turn into a system of 'state dotations' to a declining aristocracy intent on frustrating the modernisation of Germany society. Even attitudes towards the naval building programme began to change. Tirpitz, for all his suspicions of the agrarians and in spite of his 'modernist' convictions, realised that he could not do without the political support of the agrarians and therefore came to accept their position. Hanseatic merchants had been prepared to accept a fleet which they imagined would provide support for a liberal commercial policy, but they quickly became disillusioned when they realised that Tirpitz was building a battle fleet which was bound to alienate Britain and create the kind of tensions that would make successful overseas trade all the more difficult. In the Reichstag there appeared to be a deadlock between the government's proposals and the recommendations of the Reichstag committee, but there was also a growing feeling in conservative circles, both in industry and in agriculture, that the quarrels over the tariff had gone on too long and were threatening the alliance which few were prepared to jettison. The time had come for compromise. Kardorff's proposals were quickly accepted, somewhat to everyone's surprise and delight, by a two-thirds majority on 14 December 1902.

Table 1: Proposals for Grain Duties

	Rye	Wheat	Barley	Oats
Existing rates	3.50	3.50	2.00	2.80
Government Bill	5.00	5.50	3.00	5.00
Reichstag Committee	5.50	6.00	5.50	5.50
Bund der Landwirte	7.50	7.50	7.50	7.50
Kardorff compromise	5.00	5.50 [malt	4.00	5.00
		[feed	1.30	

Duty was per 100 kilos.

Reaction to the new tariffs was one of general relief that the compromise had been reached rather than any genuine enthusiasm. Industrialists complained that by reducing the duty on such items as pitchforks, ploughshares, sickles and agricultural machinery the government had shown that it shared the animosity of the agrarians for industry. The *Bund der Landwirte* announced that in the forthcoming elections it would only support candidates who would pledge to continue the struggle against industry. But the moderate agrarians and the vast majority of the industrialists were prepared to live with the tariffs, and the *Zentralverband* announced that it would continue its support of the policy of the 'protection of national labour'. The German people, however, were strongly critical of the new tariffs. In the Reichstag elections of 1903 the social democrats were big winners, gaining 25 seats. All of the parties that had voted for the Kardorff compromise lost votes. Moderate politicians blamed the 'demogogical presumption of the *Bund der Landwirte*', as Hutten-Czapski put it, but the real reason for the dramatic swing in public opinion was the rise in the cost of living which was the direct result of the new tariffs.

In spite of the clear rejection by the electorate of the new tariffs the Reichstag of 1903 still had a majority in favour of the tariffs, which would also provide the majority to ratify the new trade agreements once they had been negotiated. For the government the major problem was the negotiation of the new agreements with the foreign governments rather than the attitude of the new Reichstag. Austria presented no great difficulty, for half of Austria's exports went to Germany and agricultural exports from Hungary were falling as the Dual Monarchy industrialised. The most that was likely to happen would be a modest increase in the Austrian industrial tariff which would probably not alarm German industrialists unduly. Negotiations with Russia were likely to be much more difficult. If the *Bund der Landwirte* and their increasingly rowdy anti-Semitic followers had their way and the grain tariff was pushed up still further, relations with Russia would become extremely strained. Even the minimum rates of the Kardorff compromise bound the hands of the German negotiators and could hardly be reconciled with the request of the German export industries for a lower Russian tariff on industrial goods. The Russians announced that they intended to increase industrial tariffs, but the pro-agrarian Ministers, such as Posadowsky, Podbielski and Miquel's successor Rheinbaben, complacently argued that the Russians would have to accept whatever the Germans demanded, an attitude which filled the moderates at the Foreign Office with despair, for the prospect of a long and protracted tariff war with Russia was hardly encouraging.

As the German ambassador in Vienna had feared, the Austrians raised the duties on a number of industrial goods, including such new-fangled devices as motor cars. Bülow was furious at what he felt was a deliberate attempt to disrupt the negotiations, and the agrarians were encouraged to press their demands for prohibition of the imports of live animals from Austria. Negotiations with Austria were suspended, but there was a growing feeling in Berlin that an ally could not be so shamelessly bullied by the agrarians and that an agreement would have to be reached.

Although the negotiations with Austria had become deadlocked, agreements were quickly reached with a number of other countries. Although Germany increased the duty on foreign wines, concessions on fruit and vegetables as well as on some manufactured goods resulted in an agreement with Italy that satisfied both parties. Negotiations with Belgium were quickly completed. After two weeks of negotiation in Nordeney between Witte and Bülow the agreement with Russia was signed in July 1904, the Russians unable to hold out against German demands any longer with the war with Japan taking their full attention, and their reluctance was overcome by a 500 million mark loan from the

German government. To many Russians the treaty was a piece of shameless blackmail carried out when Russia was helpless. The trade treaty with Russia was undoubtedly a major factor in the worsening relations between the two countries. Germany's agricultural policy, dictated by the desires and needs of the East Elbian aristocrats, led inevitably to the anti-Russian thrust of German policy. In 1904 and 1905 this did not seem too serious, for Russia was also alienated from England, but the persistent anti-Russian policy of the agrarians did much to push Russia and England together and was a major contributory factor to the formation of the anti-German alliances.

Agreement with Austria had still not been reached and Bülow realised that if he gave in to the agrarians the alliances with Austria would be seriously endangered at a time when the Russo-Japanese war had made international relations extremely sensitive. On the other hand, if he was too conciliatory to the Austrians he risked losing conservative support in the Reichstag, would be unlikely to be able to push through the modified canal Bill and would even be placing the whole future of the *Sammlung* in question. An arrangement was finally reached with the Austrians which was acceptable to the Reichstag in spite of the complaints of Kardorff that some of the justifiable requests of the agrarians had been ignored, and by industrial circles who saw the treaty as yet another hand-out to the agrarians. Once the treaty with Austria was concluded all seven trade agreements were presented to the Reichstag on 1 February for approval. The tariff majority voted for this package and the social democrats and *Freisinnige Vereinigung* (independents) voted against.

The agrarians, although making their ritual murmurs of discontent, profited considerably from the new trade treaties, largely because of the free interchangeability of the import certificates which showed the amount of duty paid on exported grain and which could then be used to pay the import duty on grains entering the country. The East Elbian landowners were quick to see the advantages of this system and used the certificates from exported rye for imported barley for feed. The difference ton for ton was 37 marks of direct subsidy to the agrarians, and the result for the consumer was a further rise in the price of flour products. The Junker was able to import his raw materials, such as fertilisers, free of duty and could sell his rye on the most favourable market. Other farmers specialising in animals or poultry were hurt by duties on feed grains. Thus the tariff on eggs was 2 marks per quintal (100 kg). It is estimated that 5 quintals of feed barley are required to produce one quintal of eggs, and the duty on five quintals was 6.50 marks. Thus a foreign egg producer had an immediate advantage of 4.50 marks per quintal over the German egg-farmer. Very much the same situation applied in other branches, such as pig-farming. Thus the Bülow tariffs not only favoured agriculture but also favoured a specific sector within agriculture. The tariffs were not in the interest of agriculture as a whole, as the agrarians had argued, nor did they strengthen the independence of the German market from foreign producers. The Junkers were clearly favoured, the amount of rye exported increased, and Germany became more dependent than ever on the import of products of animal husbandry, with the exception of meat. The industrialists, although they were far from happy with the new treaties, were prepared to live with them and agreed that there was something to be said for stable commercial relations with Germany's major trading partners for the next twelve years. It was the German consumer who had to bear the brunt of the treaties, and the rising cost of living that resulted from them was the cause of bitter criticism and provided useful ammunition for the opposition parties.

With the trade agreements safely negotiated it was plain that a clear break had been made with the Caprivi era. In spite of their reservations most of the agrarians were satisfied with the treaties and grudgingly accepted that Bülow had done his best for them. They were encouraged by the complaints of export industry that the tariffs were too high, particularly with Russia and the United States, and that in some instances they were prohibitive. Heavy industry was able to profit from the treaties by cartelisation and monopolisation and price-fixing to overcome increased wage demands. By selling high on the domestic market and low abroad by cutting profit margins on foreign sales, heavy industry was able to increase sales and profits and the alliance with the agrarians could be maintained. Only in the case of the United States did agrarians, heavy industrialists and export industrialists combine in their condemnations of American protectionism, but the protectionists in Germany had no effective weapons to use against the even more successful application of a protectionist policy in the United States.

After the difficult period of the Caprivi tariffs and the world-wide depression of agricultural prices, the Bülow tariff and trade agreements brought almost instant relief to the agrarians. They had not been able to get the Reichstag's approval of the Kanitz proposal for a state import monopoly which would guarantee high prices for agricultural produce, for the Reichstag majority was in no mood in 1894 to give the agrarians a hand-out of 500 million marks, which was Gustav Schmoller's calculation of the cost of the proposals. But they had managed to get a system of export premiums which enabled Germany to become the world's second-largest rye-exporting country along with tariffs and treaties which forced up the price of food to the point that Lujo Brentano calculated that the average worker had to work for 13 to 18 days in order to pay for the increased price of his food.

Part of the reason for the increases in grain prices was that prices were rising on the world market. Substantial population increases in the United States pushed up the price of North American grain, and the failure of the Russian harvest from 1905 to 1908 drove up the price of Russian grain. As a result, world prices went up well beyond the level foreseen in the Bülow rates so that the tariff was an extra burden on the consumer rather than a means of ensuring that the farmers obtained an economic price for their produce. Protection thus became a system of direct subsidies to a privileged class who had managed to avoid the 'economic fight to the death' that Max Weber had predicted in 1895 by getting prices far in excess of those which would have been adequate to ensure an economic return. Higher prices for agricultural produce led to a rapid increase in the value of land. In the decade from 1897 to 1907 land prices in Prussia rose between 30 and 50 per cent. The most rapid increase was in the period immediately after the Bülow tariffs, there having been almost no movement at all in the early part of the decade. The rush to sell land at steadily rising prices immediately after the tariffs were settled led to an increase in indebtedness, so that the tariffs, far from relieving what was generally considered to be one of the most serious weaknesses of German agriculture, made it worse.

For the Junkers the tariffs were a tremendous success. Germany produced 33 per cent more rye between 1900 and 1913. The agrarians were able to increase the productivity of their land by using improved methods of crop rotation and by drawing on the ample supply of cheap foreign labour. Grain, potatoes and sugar-beet crops constantly improved in quantity and quality, but these crops were hardly those required of an advanced industrial society and the continued emphasis on these traditional commodities was a serious hindrance to the badly needed structural change of German agriculture. The deliberate protection of the interests of the Prussian land-owning aristocracy resulted in the majority of the population being fed with foreign produce, for Germany did not produce sufficient dairy products, fruit, vegetables and meat. Other important materials, such as leather, wool, wood,and vegetable oils, also had to be imported in large quantities.

The question of the future of German agriculture was clearly a major problem that should have been faced in Wilhelmine Germany. None would dispute that the country needed a healthy agricultural sector. Conservatives demanded that rural society should be preserved because of its social and political virtues which were under constant attack by the advance of industrial society. Industrialists realised that a healthy rural economy was necessary for there to be a healthy market for industrial goods. Southern Italy and rural Russia were examples of the dampening economic effect of a depressed agricultural sector. There can also be little doubt, given that in economic terms agricultural self-sufficiency was neither desirable nor possible, that Germany would have fared much better by relying on the cheap importation of foreign grains and concentrating on more specialised agriculture. Where this was tried, and the pig-breeding of northern Germany is a good example, the results were remarkable. As it was, Germany increased the production of grains like rye in an impressive manner, but it was exported to countries that specialised in dairy produce and meat production and thus made the necessary changes in German agriculture all the more difficult. With the growth of industrialisation and the increased prosperity of the country, and as the world economy pulled out of the slump, the situation grew worse. Demand for rye bread and flour and also for potatoes dropped, whereas demand for dairy products and meat grew. Germany produced agricultural goods of low-income elasticity of demand and thus could expect little growth of demand in times of expansion. Thus the determination of the agrarians to continue with the mass production of rye and potatoes became increasingly hard to justify. Protected by the tariffs and the law on entailed estates (*Fideikommiss*), the aristocrats were a heavy burden on the economy, an anachronism both politically and economically in the age of industrialisation. Yet their power was such that the Bülow tariff was to be revived in 1925 and remained in force under the Nazis, for all the talk of a 'national revolution'.

The debate over German agriculture in this period was not conducted in terms of what might be considered best for the economy as a whole but rather as a choice between agriculture and industry. The agrarians dressed up their selfish demands in the ideological trappings of autarky, but in fact the amount of agricultural produce imported grew rapidly in the pre-war years, and had it not been for the fortunate fact that the war broke out in August rather than a month later when the grain crop would have been exported, Germany would have faced an even more severe food crisis during the war. Agrarian ideology became increasingly extremist and irrational and spiced with imperialist and expansionist ideas. The continuation of these ideas throughout the first half of the twentieth century was to be a heavy burden on the German people, and their abandonment after 1945 helped to bring an exceptional level of prosperity to both the German states.

Weltpolitik versus Mitteleuropa

Meanwhile the announcement of the Anglo-French *entente* on 8 April 1904 was taken by Holstein to be the end of 'world politics', for as he put it in a letter to his cousin Ida Stülpnagel, 'against England and France an overseas policy is not possible.' The Reichstag elections of 1903 had shown that the electorate clearly rejected the trade agreements, prompting the 'Kaiser's friend' Eulenburg to ask Bülow if all that could be done was to wait for civil war against the fourth estate. Now the *Entente Cordiale* had delivered a further blow at the social imperialist policies of the German government. Although at this stage there was certainly no panic in Berlin, particularly as the Franco-Russian alliance was greatly weakened as a result of the Russo-Japanese war, the German Foreign Office was determined to resist the intended acquisition of Morocco by France. A trial of strength with France was thus imminent either by mounting diplomatic pressure or, as some hotheads in the military wanted, by war. At the same time Krupp was demanding action against France and specifically against Schneider-Creusot, which was becoming increasingly active in Morocco.

In spite of Krupp's complaints there were very few German interests in Morocco to defend. Direct investments were calculated at 5 million francs at a time when French investments were about 70 million. German banks showed no interest whatever in Morocco. The Foreign Office had actively discouraged German businessmen from becoming involved in Morocco so as to avoid friction with France and Britain. Now the Germans had to show that vital interests were at stake. Germany moved slowly and cautiously so that it became increasingly difficult to convince the world that German interests in Morocco were so vital. At first an agreement was reached with Britain over Egypt, but it took time to mobilise heavy industry. Tentative efforts were made to reach an agreement with Russia but they soon proved fruitless, and it was not until March 1905 that the Kaiser, pushed into action by Bülow and Holstein, arrived in Morocco, sitting on an unfamiliar horse of dubious temperament, exposing his withered arm to view and surrounded, he feared, by Spanish anarchists.

Although the crisis had prompted the dismissal of Delcassé, which was certainly a major success for German policy, the Tangier visit was a dismal failure. With the end of the Russo-Japanese war the situation in the east changed radically. German attempts to destroy the Entente by hinting that England was asking France to do her fighting for her backfired, and Germany had to accept an invitation to an international conference at which she was totally isolated and where she suffered a defeat which Holstein, although soured by his recent dismissal, had some justification in comparing to Tilsit and Olmütz. In this situation it is hardly surprising that ideas for a *Mitteleuropa*, particularly those of the forceful economist Julius Wolf and his Middle-European Economic Association, enjoyed renewed popularity.

Faced with the prospect of increasing competition with the great economic powers, such as the United States, Britain and France, it was argued that a central European union was essential. To an increasing number of Germans *Weltpolitik* had produced little in the way of concrete economic advantage and was degenerating into an empty prestige policy. As Tschirschky, the State Secretary for Foreign Affairs, wrote to Bülow in September 1907:

> Considering that the European base of the high pyramid of our world-wide commercial activities is not broad enough, the time has come to broaden it. In my opinion the task of our policy should be to achieve this, as far as possible by peaceful means.

He considered that the Germans were busy 'laying eggs in others' nests for want of any good nests of our own'. Such views were by no means eccentric, but were shared by many others, including the Kaiser and Bülow.

Most of these German eggs were relatively modest. German economic interests in South America were of minor importance apart from three banks and a branch plant of the AEG in Buenos Aires. The situation in east Asia was no better. In Africa the Germans concentrated on speculative mining shares and real-estate ventures. In the Congo, where German investments were higher than elsewhere, the Germans only invested about 25 million francs out of a total of approximately 500 million francs of foreign investment.

Part of the blame for the shortage of capital, which lay at the heart of Germany's problems, was laid on the Stock Exchange Act of 1896 which the Kaiser was pleased to describe as 'idiotic'. Max Weber was articulating a widely held opinion when he blamed the stock exchange regulations and the stamp duties for the poor performance of the German exchanges and for the exodus of German capital in search of more lucrative investment possibilities abroad. It is unlikely that the effects of the Bill were quite as dramatic as its critics claimed, although it certainly had the effect of encouraging investment abroad. The reform of the regulations in 1908 was a rather modest affair. The agrarians were able to retain the prohibition of trading in futures on grain and flour, and the concessions which were made were partly offset by an increase in the stamp tax. In spite of these jeremiads German industry continued to do well, even during the recession years from 1901 to 1904. Government bonds fell constantly, but industrial shares held their price and the economy continued to expand.

In colonial areas such as south-west Africa, where attempts were made to exploit the economic potential of the country, the results were disappointing. The expropriation of land for railway-building and the outright theft of cattle by the colonists prompted the Herero rebellion of 1904. German troops were sent to south-west Africa, 80,000 Africans were killed and the General Staff proudly reported that the Hereros had ceased to exist as an independent tribe. But such violent policies could never provide the markets that were needed for Germany to solve the problems of an expanding industrial power in a neo-mercantilist world. The relative failure of 'world politics' in economic terms led to an increasing emphasis on *Mitteleuropa*, but at the same time loud demands for the abolition of most-favoured-nation clauses in the trade agreements and for higher industrial tariffs suggested that Germany was about to retreat behind tariff barriers and that the system could only be stabilised by further window-dressing and social imperialist manoeuvrings rather than by the expansion of foreign trade.

Taxation

It was possible to satisfy at least partially the sectional interests of specific groups by means of tariff adjustments and trade agreements, but it soon became clear that the Bülow tariffs had failed to solve the major economic problems of the German Reich. With the rise of what Schumpeter called the 'taxation state' (*Steuerstaat*) further instruments of manipulation and control were available. The German taxation system had traditionally been grossly unfair, placing the major tax burden on lower-income groups and strengthening the economic and social *status quo*. Until 1861 the aristocracy had paid no tax on their estates (*Rittergüter*), the old tax system based on classes was not abolished until 1873 and an income tax on income above 900 marks per annum first instituted in 1883. Progressive taxation was regarded as the first step towards socialism so that the main source of revenue was from regressive indirect taxes which weighed heaviest on the poor. Even the much-vaunted tax reform of Miquel of 1893, although establishing an income tax with the dizzy maximum of 4 per cent, in effect restored the tax privileges of the land-owning aristocracy by handing the revenues of the income tax (*Ertragssteuer*) over to the communes where it was used by the agrarians. Thus the taxation mechanism, far from redistributing the wealth of the country so as to achieve some modicum of social justice, in practice handed much of the tax money back to those from whom it was taken, and thus for all the demagogic talk of far-reaching reform, the new taxation system further reinforced existing conditions. From the 1890s almost half of the income of the Reich came from the agricultural tariffs. The state was financed in large measure by the high price of food, a policy which directly profited the agrarians at a very high social cost.

With the mounting costs of the government, particularly with the naval arms race and the dreadnought programme after 1908, additional sources of revenue were badly needed. Most forms of direct taxation could only be imposed by the federal states and payments to the Reich government from these sources made by the 'matricular contributions'. Direct taxes were opposed by conservatives who rallied to the call of their most colourful spokesman, von Oldenburg-Januschau, that the taxes of the wealthy (*Besitzenden*) should not be handed over to a Reichstag of the poor (*Besitzlosen*). Furthermore, the whole question of direct taxation was bound up with the issue of states' rights, and the selfish states could pose as the champions of free enterprise against the socialist demands of the Reichstag for more taxation, more centralisation and a degree of redistribution. Bülow's attempts to reform the finances of the country to meet the tremendous increases in expenditure, particularly by the military, plunged the country into yet another domestic political crisis and were a major cause of the dismissal of the Chancellor.

Bülow's initial proposals included increases in indirect taxes, particularly on wines, spirits and beer, an increase in the matricular contributions and also in death duties. The proposal that death duties should be paid on money left to wives and to children was vehemently opposed by the agrarians who demanded, and got, the Chancellor's dismissal. Bülow's successor, Bethmann Hollweg, realised that revenues would have to be increased but he also knew that this was not possible without the support of the conservatives and the centre party, the alliance of the 'saints and the knights' that had replaced the Bülow bloc. The result was a tax reform which hurt the consumers, the industrialists and the bankers, and which favoured the agrarians once again.

Among the new measures were a stamp duty on cheques and an increased tax on bills and securities, though not on the seriously depressed government bonds. This resulted in a tax on joint-stock companies which forced some companies to reconstitute themselves in forms less suited to their operations. A fixed tax was also levied on income from dividends and interest from industrial shares. Bankers protested that the German banks had lost the 1.4 per cent margin over French banks, being the difference between French and German stamp duties on foreign securities, and that the banks would be unable to compete on foreign markets. The Chancellor agreed with these objections, but claimed that he was unable to do anything to ease the situation. In fact the numbers of shares issued were not affected by these measures, and the dire predictions of the banks proved to be unfounded. Even more outspoken was the protest of the social democrats, who found considerable popular support for demonstrations against the anti-social nature of the tax reform. The agrarians and their centre party allies were expecting the protest of the socialists against the 'black and blue alliance', but they were surprised and alarmed by the violence of the reaction of the bankers and the industrialists. Both the *Zentralverband* and the *Bund der Industriellen* complained that the tax burden on industry was already excessive and called for a reduction of government expenditure on the social services and a reduction in the freight rates on the state railways. The industrialists were determined to play a more active political role, and the *Zentralverband* proposed the establishment of an election fund that would be used to promote candidates who were known to favour the aims of industry and who would help prevent a repetition of the fiasco of the finance reform of 1909.

Complaints by industrialists during the debates over the tax reform should not lead one to imagine that industry was groaning under the heavy burden of a welfare state. Government expenditure had grown enormously from about 500 million marks in 1880 (2.6 per cent of GNP) to about 3.5 billion marks in 1913 (5.8 per cent of GNP). Although certain programmes such as the invalid insurance account for part of this increase, the major reason was the increase in military spending. The size of the army rose 87 per cent between 1880 and 1913, but the cost rose 360 per cent. The naval programme was a further heavy burden. Year for year, the military consumed about 75 per cent of the Reich's revenues, leaving little for education, health, welfare and the administration of the government services. Heavy expenditure on the military directly profited many sectors of industry and indirectly stimulated others, so that much of the tax that industry paid came back again in the form of government contracts. *Per capita* taxation was increasing, from 9.86 marks in 1875 to 32.97 marks in 1913, but this burden was remarkably evenly distributed. As a result the tax structure of the country strengthened the disparities of wealth and income.

This unjust tax structure strengthened the tendency towards an increasingly uneven distribution of wealth. Although Germany's gross national product increased by 58 per cent between 1870 and 1900, and although about one-third of the population worked in industry, the share of the industrial workers in the gross national product dropped by 55 per cent during these thirty years. This tendency for the workers' share of national income to drop, in spite of increases in real wages, continued up to the outbreak of the war. Thus the condition of the German working class improved, but the disparities between the rich and the poor grew even wider. The industrial sector grew faster than agriculture, there were growing disparities in the wage levels in both sectors and there was an over-all tendency for capital to concentrate. As the state was either reluctant or unable to intervene with a fiscal policy that would counteract these tendencies, the result was a striking example of relative impoverishment of the working class. Between 1890 and the outbreak of the war the real wages of the workers and lower employees rose by about 1 per cent per annum, but in the same period national income rose almost threefold, from 18 billion marks to 50 billion marks.

The Politics of Wilhelmine Imperialism

With the failure of Germany's policy in Morocco, even though some modest economic advances were made, increasing emphasis was placed on the Balkans. Germany's interests in the Balkans were twofold: here was the point where her major ally Austria-Hungary was menaced by an increasingly strident nationalism which threatened the continued existence of the multinational empire and could all too easily lead to a confrontation with Russia; and second, Germany had considerable financial interests in the area, particularly after the Deutsche Bank bought up the Hirsch railway empire in Turkey and when the German armaments industry began to sell extensively to Turkey. Turkey and Asia Minor offered attractive prospects for German capital. Paul

Rohrbach, in his book *Die Bagdadbahn* (1911), painted in vivid colours a picture of the mineral wealth of the area with its deposits of chrome, copper, lead and above all oil, and called for an aggressive German policy to secure this wealth for the Reich. In a world divided by tariff barriers and with the growing concern for adequate supplies of raw materials, the Balkans and Asia Minor were seen as possible sources of minerals, cotton and agricultural produce. It was also an area of immense strategic importance. Control of the straits could be used to hold Russia in check and would seriously weaken Britain's position in the eastern Mediterranean. With Turkey in a state of advanced decay, nothing seemed to stand in the way of German ambitions, and as early as 1898 the Pan-Germans' newspaper *Alldeutsche Blätter* called for a policy of: 'Full steam ahead towards the Euphrates and the Tigris and on to the Persian Gulf, so that the land route to India can be placed in the hands to which it rightfully belongs – warlike and hard-working German hands.' Last, there was the prospect of extensive railway-building which could bring enormous military and economic benefits.

Marschall von Bieberstein, who had been Secretary of State for Foreign Affairs, was appointed Ambassador to Turkey in 1897 rather than to the vacant position of Ambassador to Washington, thus stressing the importance of Turkey to Germany. In the following year William II made his second journey to the Orient. The Pan-Germans were delighted with the voyage of the German Kaiser to the Near East and their papers were filled with ecstatic articles on the German mission and the possibility of colonies in the area. The reaction of the French and Russian press was predictably violent, prompting the Foreign Office to attempt to explain the voyage as being a purely private pilgrimage by the Christian Kaiser to the Holy Places. This excuse was singularly unconvincing. The active influence of the German army in Turkey began with the activities of the military attaché Captain Morgen at the beginning of the century and the Turkish army was then advised by Goltz Pascha, who had considerable knowledge of Turkey from his days as a military attaché and who was a vigorous and inventive officer. With the German military advisers went massive arms sales and huge profits for the arms manufacturers. Krupp managed to sell guns that cost 12,000 marks for 160,000 marks apiece, and by the outbreak of the First World War Turkey owed Germany 500 million marks.

Colonial efforts, particularly in Africa, were opposed not only by the social democrats but also by the Catholic centre party. They were enthusiastically endorsed by the industrialists. With the anti-colonialist front of socialists and Catholics, the industrialists became increasingly concerned about their lack of support in the Reichstag. Seeing their position eroding, they decided to patch up their differences with the national liberals, the party of Ernst Bassermann and Gustav Stresemann, a party which stood for the interests of light industry as opposed to the big conglomerates of Rhine and Ruhr and which, much to the alarm of the latter, favoured a modicum of social reform and believed that the workers should have the right to organise. The 'Bülow bloc' of 1907 saw the formation of a new alliance of national liberals and the other liberal parties with the conservatives to form a powerful coalition of industry, agriculture and banking which pursued a vigorous imperialist policy. The success of the new bloc at the polls in 1907 was dramatic. Bülow unleashed a massive attack on the social democrats, accusing them of undermining authority, property, religion and the Fatherland and thus giving encouragement to the ultras on the extreme right. With the emphasis on Germany's imperial mission playing a key role in the campaign, the election became known as the 'Hottentot election'.

The election is also significant in that for the first time industry paid large contributions to an electoral fund designed to help candidates defeat the social democrats and the centre party candidates. Hundreds of thousands of marks were contributed by organisations like the *Zentralverband*, the *Stahl Deutscher – und Eisenindustrieller* and the *Bergbauliche Verein* as well as the big banks and large industry. In as much as the number of social-democratic mandates was reduced from 81 to 43, the election was a tremendous success to the industrialists, but at the same time their bloc tactics benefited the agrarians, many of whom were violently opposed to the aims of industry, although prepared to join with them in a crusade against socialism and the tiresome Catholics. Albert Ballin, the Hamburg shipping magnate, complained that:

> Our agriculture is in the happy position of being able to send many influential representatives to the Reichstag. Shipping does not have a single representative there, and members from big industry, high finance and commerce can all drive home in a single carriage.

Industry was thus disappointed by the outcome of the election in that its influence in the Reichstag scarcely increased.

The defeat of the social democrats in the Hottentot elections was not simply a result of the bloc tactics, but also of the distribution of seats. The socialists were actually able to increase the total number of votes cast for the party from 3 million to 3.3 million, in spite of the onslaught on the party and the intimidation tactics of many employers. Their percentage share of the vote dropped from 30 to 29 per cent, which was hardly a shattering defeat. The lesson that the industrialists drew from this was that although the existing electoral system was manifestly unjust and favoured the agrarians, it did keep out the socialists and therefore had to be supported at all costs.

With the collapse of the Bülow bloc over the proposed tax reforms and the formation of the 'black and blue' alliance which brought the centre party back out of the political wilderness, the industrialists decided to pool their resources to combat the new coalition. The result was the *Hansa Bund,* formed in June 1909, which was made up of representatives from industry, commerce and banking as well as small entrepreneurs and artisans. This diversity was, however, a source of weakness rather than strength. Heavy industry joined so that the organisation would not be dominated by the exporting industries and because it was in a fit of temporary pique after the failure of the Bülow bloc. The small fry that had joined the *Hansa Bund* demanded reforms of the franchise and thus came directly in conflict with the heavy industrialists who already had serious reservations about an organisation which included representatives of the employees. Quarrels between the heavy industrialists and the other members of the *Hansa Bund* about the franchise, customs policies, taxation, electoral tactics and social policy grew increasingly frequent and acrimonious. The agrarians were alarmed that the *Hansa Bund* was working for the revival of Caprivi's tariff system and warned the heavy industrialists of the dire consequences of a radical breach in the conservative forces. But the agrarians' concerns were ill-founded. The heavy industrialists had never intended an alternative to the old alliance of the 'productive estates' against social democracy. By 1911 they had broken with the *Hansa Bund* and returned to the fold when the majority of the *Hansa Bund* had the temerity to suggest that the social democrats must be 'accepted and given a role in the life of the state'. The chairman of the *Hansa Bund* who had made this frightful suggestion had his invitation to meet the Kaiser at the Kiel regatta instantly withdrawn.

The heavy industrialists withdrew from the Hansa Bund on the very same day that the German warship *Panther* steamed into the harbour at Agadir, thus provoking the second Morocco crisis. The object of this provocation was to give a clear demonstration of strength to the political right at home and also to soften up the French to make them prepared for concessions. German heavy industry was interested in Morocco as a source of ore, particularly at a time when men like Emil Kirdorf were beginning to become concerned that German ore supplies were rapidly becoming depleted: but industry was also interested in the 'Panther spring' in that it seemed to promise a 'national' election that would strengthen their political position at home. Some industrialists were prepared to negotiate with the French and to co-operate with them to exploit the resources of Morocco in joint undertakings. Others, like the Mannesmann brothers, wanted direct German annexations of west Morocco and were not content with mere mining rights. These views were enthusiastically supported by the chairman of the Pan-German League, Heinrich Class, whose pamphlet, *A German West Morocco*, sold 60,000 copies within three months, and also by politicians such as Gustav Stresemann and Ernst Bassermann. Although there is no evidence to prove that the plan to send the *Panther* to Agadir was influenced by the Mannesmann brothers or their supporters, it is nevertheless a striking fact that the Reich government could hardly have chosen a better spot at far as the Mannesmanns and the Pan-Germans were concerned. When the rumour that Germany was looking for compensation outside Morocco became increasingly persistent, for Kiderlen was suggesting the French Congo as a suitable compensation for the renunciation of German rights in Morocco, heavy industry protested vehemently. The government was bombarded with memoranda demanding secure supplies of ore, and an energetic policy towards Morocco even at the risk of war. But the government and the Kaiser were not prepared to run the risk of a war with England and France over Morocco and prepared to negotiate with the French. The resulting Morocco treaty of 4 November 1911 was regarded by the industrialists and the nationalists in Germany as a terrible humiliation, soon to be christened the 'second Olmütz'. In return for recognising the French protectorate over Morocco the Germans were allowed equal economic rights in the country and were given a swampy area of the French Congo which was infested with sleeping sickness. There was no enthusiasm at all about the 'sleepy Congo', even among the colonial enthusiasts. The French press mocked 'Guillaume le Timide', who had been so easily forced to back down, thus making the German Kaiser determined not to give way in future. For the army von Moltke, the chief of the general staff, complained that if Germany walked away from the Morocco affair with its tail between its legs it might just as well abolish the army and become a protectorate of Japan. The Pan-Germans, right-wing conservatives and industrialists around Kirdorf and Beukenberg clamoured for an uncompromising foreign policy, and the Crown Prince conspicuously associated himself with this group. The Chancellor, Bethmann Hollweg, regarded this policy as 'irresponsible playing with war', and in spite of Tirpitz's demands for a new naval Bill, was determined to continue the attempt to find some area of agreement with the British.

The Army and the Navy

A new naval Bill was a matter of critical concern to many industrialists. Shipyards had been expanded in 1908 to meet the increased demand, but without a new naval Bill in 1911 orders from the navy would drop by half, placing the shipbuilding industry in a critical situation. Bethmann's policy of coming to some sort of arrangement with the British was thus in direct conflict with the exigencies of the armaments industry, and heavy industry financed a massive campaign to step up naval building and thus also to close off Germany's foreign policy options. The Kaiser, smarting perhaps under the French taunts, supported Tirpitz's arguments that if the naval building programme was not stepped up the shipyards would be ruined and the workers become unemployed, and suggested that England would sooner or later be forced to come to terms with Germany because the financial strain of the arms race would be so great. The major problem seemed to be how to find the money to pay for the new ships. There had been a dramatic cost inflation in shipbuilding since 1898, caused in part by the considerable technological advances that had been made, particularly in gunnery, and Tirpitz found a formidable adversary in Wermuth, the State Secretary of the Reich Treasury, who insisted that the naval building programme would have to be funded by increased taxation and not on a loan, as Tirpitz had suggested. This at once raised the spectre of a financial reform, for death duties seemed to be the most suitable source of new revenue, and this in turn would obviously be fiercely resisted by the conservatives. As there was an election soon to be fought, it was clearly not the moment to demand heavy increases in taxation. These increases would have to be very considerable if Tirpitz were to get his way, for the army was also demanding substantial increases, demands which seemed to many to be wholly justified given the increased emphasis on Germany's position on the Continent after the Morocco fiasco.

The result of the complex negotiations over the naval and army estimates in 1911 and 1912 was a series of compromises which failed to satisfy any of the parties involved and which greatly reduced the flexibility of German policy both at home and abroad. The new naval Bill made any understanding with Britain unlikely and the Haldane mission of 1912 was such a failure that Zimmermann at the Foreign Office felt that war with France was now almost inevitable. Although the German navy almost managed to reach the 2:3 ratio with the Royal Navy for which Tirpitz had been striving, this did not give Germany a fleet that could be used to persuade or even threaten the British, and at the same time it placed an intolerable strain on the German economy. Tirpitz's grand scheme of using the naval building programme as a means of domestic political control had failed miserably, and the cost of the navy was such that tax reforms were suggested that would have precipitated a crisis even more severe than that which had brought down Bülow. As it was, economies had to be made in many areas so that the Reich's social policies had to be further curtailed. Militarily the fleet proved to be almost useless, for after the initial indecisive engagement at the battle of Jutland, it retired to port to become a centre of unrest and discontent that was to erupt into open mutiny in November 1918. Most serious of all, the determination to press ahead with the naval programme made any arrangement with Britain impossible and strengthened the determination of the Triple Entente to contain and resist Germany.

At first it seemed that the mounting cost of the navy might be met by careful housekeeping in the Treasury, but with the prospect of a considerable increase in the size of the army it soon became obvious that additional sources of revenue would have to be tapped. In June 1912 the Reichstag approved a resolution proposed by Erzberger and Bassermann that some form of new tax on property (*Besitz*) would be proposed to the Reichstag by the end of April 1913 at the latest. In the course of discussions with the Treasury, the Chancellor agreed that this tax would have to be either in the form of death duties or a wealth tax, and felt that the most acceptable form would be some type of capital gains tax. The main opposition to this plan came from the German states, for it was seen as a further attack on the states' right to levy direct taxation and thus on the states themselves. From Saxony came the perfectly justified accusation that the government would not extend death duties to include spouses and children for the simple reason that they feared the loss of the support of the 'black and blue', of the centre party and the conservatives.

Bethmann soon found himself awkwardly stuck between the states and the Reichstag majority. The Prussian Ministry of State rejected the idea of a capital gains tax. The conservative and centre party leaders showed no enthusiasm whatever for an extension of death duties. The suggestion that a once-and-for-all tax should be levied to raise almost one billion marks that were needed to meet the additional costs of the army estimates for 1913 was more favourably received, and no one challenged the need for this expenditure on the army. The Chancellor had no difficulty in convincing the politicians and representatives of the states that Germany's military position had worsened. German policy had suffered a severe reverse in the Balkans. Austria would have to involve a large portion of its armed forces in the Balkans in the event of a future war now that Turkey had been so severely weakened. Russia had recovered from the effects of its defeat by Japan. France had introduced a three-year service, thus greatly strengthening the army. Belgian forces could no longer be simply ignored, and the attitude of England was still uncertain, in spite of persistent German efforts to co-operate. In these circumstances there were few who were prepared to deny the need to spend more than 2 per cent of GNP on additional armaments, an enormous sum, but one that was deemed necessary given the obvious and dramatic decline of Germany's military position relative to that of the Entente.

With the exception of some complaints about the number of cavalry regiments and the increase in the number of adjutants for the ruling houses of Germany, there was little opposition to the army increases in the Reichstag except from the social democrats. There were, however, hectic debates about the form of the new taxes to meet the increased costs. Bethmann skilfully used this to convince the federal states that unless they accepted the idea of a capital gains tax the entire army increase would have to be abandoned and the states would have to bear the responsibility for leaving Germany defenceless against her enemies. The states gave way under this pressure, but the whole scheme backfired when the Reichstag voted in favour of a motion proposed by the social democrats that the ruling houses should also be taxed. It needed the threat of an instant dissolution of the Reichstag to convince the national liberals to abandon this plan and the Reichstag voted against the proposal in a second reading. The capital gains tax passed by 280 to 63 (most of the opposition were, predictably, conservatives) and 29 abstentions, most of them from the centre party.

Bethmann had steered the largest increase in the army that had ever been suggested safely through the Reichstag, and had managed to finance that increase in a manner which best suited his own position, although he had had to make some concessions along the way. But he had not been able to win the support of the conservatives for the new taxes. To the conservatives and to many industrialists the new taxes were an indication that the Reichstag was beginning an onslaught on property, and they drew the conclusion that capital would have to close ranks against the insolent and unjustified attacks of the democratic forces. In the summer of 1913 there were loud and persistent attacks on the Chancellor from the agrarians and the industrialists who accused him, in Bueck's unattractive German, of 'undermining the power of the propertied' (*Auspowerung des Besitzes*). Bethmann could not do without the support of the conservatives and was forced to do everything possible to conciliate them. In the Reichstag they were a small party, but they still had the ear of the Kaiser, controlled the Prussian Ministry of State, the Prussian upper house and the bureaucracy, and had a powerful faction in the lower house in Prussia. Bethmann had got his taxes, but the conservatives were determined to make him pay for them.

The discussions over financing the army and navy increases happened at a time of acute capital shortage in Germany. Although discount rates were about 1.5 per cent higher in Germany than in France, French short-term funds did not reappear on the German market after the Agadir crisis. Uncertainty over the Balkan crisis made investors nervous and some funds were hastily withdrawn. In the autumn of 1913 the Russian government withdrew almost two-thirds of its investments in Germany in order to pay back the interest on loans from France, leaving about 300 million francs still invested in Germany. By the autumn of 1913 the economy was in a recession which intensified in the following year, so that economists were justified in talking of a depression. The discount rate of the Reichsbank fell from 6 per cent in October 1913 to 4 per cent by February of the following year. It became difficult even to place the shares of prestige projects such as the Baghdad railway. Helfferich and Gwinner, on behalf of the Deutsche Bank, called for a loan of 250 million francs, and warned the Foreign Office that if they did not get the money they would abandon the Baghdad railway project which would be a terrible setback for German policy in Turkey, and an admission to the rest of the world that Germany lacked the financial resources to build the railway. At the same time Krupp and the Dresdner Bank were calling for a massive loan for the Turkish government so that they would buy armaments from Krupp rather than Schneider-Creusot. Helfferich warned Zimmermann that a loan for Krupp would oblige the Baghdad railway to 'pack up and go home'. The result was a victory for the Deutsche Bank over Krupp. The government decided that the issue of German prestige that was so closely tied to the Baghdad railway was more important than a shot in the arm for the German armaments industry which was suffering the effects of the recession and of stagnating exports.

Mounting international tensions, the enormous increases in the size of armies and navies and the shortage of capital made the question of the economic and financial preparation for war a matter of some concern. The General Staff was convinced that General Schlieffen had provided them with an infallible recipe for a short and victorious war, but some officers were less sanguine, and the bankers remembered the fiasco of 1870 and were determined that the Reichsbank should have adequate gold reserves to cover the cost of the initial days of the war. In 1906 mark notes in 20- and 50-mark denominations were introduced to increase the gold reserves of the bank, although only 300 million marks' worth of these notes were issued. The cheque law of 1908 tried to encourage Germans to use cheques rather than cash payments, but this measure met with little success, for many businessmen remained somewhat suspicious of transactions by cheque.

There was considerable uncertainty about the likely cost of a future war. Estimates ranged between 4.68 billion marks to 7 billion marks per year. But few believed that a war could possibly last very long, and thus the estimates tended to be optimistically low. In 1912 the Reichstag announced that it intended to keep a minimum of one billion marks in reserve to meet part of the estimated requirement for 2,833 million marks for the first thirty days of the war. Largely as a result of the Balkan wars, the Reichsbank decided to increase its gold reserves still further. By June 1914 they had reached 1,631 million marks.

The Reichsbank had done about as much as was possible under the circumstances and its director, Havenstein, was probably justified, although a trifle complacent, in being satisfied with his work when he reviewed the situation in September 1914. Other departments did very little. There was general agreement that Germany would not be blockaded in the event of a war, and any suggestions that the country might soon run dangerously short of food supplies were dismissed as infantile. Those who demanded a second look at Germany's food supply situation implied that the import certificates would have to go, that the agrarians could no longer be feather-bedded, and that the commercial treaties would have to be reviewed. This in turn would threaten the continued existence of the *Sammlung* and give rise to new political alignments involving radical changes in the political structure of the country. To many in positions of power and influence, the suggestion that the 'state supporting parties' should be delivered this death-blow after they had suffered severe set-backs in the 1912 elections was a notion too absurd and subversive to be even entertained. In 1913 the German Agricultural Council (*Landwirtschaftsrat*) smugly announced that Germany would soon be in a position of complete self-sufficiency in cereals. In fact, although yields per acre had increased considerably, Germany was only able to meet just over half her domestic requirement for cereals. It was indeed fortunate that the war started just before the harvest, for otherwise there would have been a chronic shortage of grain.

The Heightening of Social Tensions

Such discussions as there were about the economic preparation for war tended to concentrate on the particular interests of individual groups. Industrialists called for sterner measures against strikes, particularly as there had been no diminution of strike activity during the recession as there had been in the past. Others demanded less welfare measures, which, they complained, were ruining the competitiveness and the efficiency of German industry. From 1911 industry became somewhat pessimistic about Germany's future export prospects and hoped for increased orders from the military to make up any loss of exports. Bombastic appeals for the defence of the Fatherland 'to the last penny and the last drop of blood' came from the Chambers of Commerce and from industrialists whose patriotic fervour matched their desire to fill their order books. With the recession in 1913 these demands became even more strident and were coupled with requests to strengthen the cartels, cut back government expenditure on the social services and for legislation against the socialists and the liberals. Industry was beginning to think in terms of another great depression and longed for a revival of Bismarck's repressive and ill-fated anti-socialist laws. Middle-of-the-road politicians like Bassermann or the 'Red prince' Heinrich zu Schoenaich-Carolath were appalled at such talk, which they feared would lead to a violent polarisation of German society and possibly to a revolution.

The greater the emphasis the industrialists placed on the need for preparation for war, the more inclined they were to accept the agrarians' self-serving arguments in favour of autarky. This meant accepting high food prices which could either be countered by repressive measures against any further wage demands by the workers or, as some industrialists did, by fattening one's own cattle on unused land around the Westphalian factories. In one instance a company supplied its workers with meat at 25 per cent below the average retail price so as to counter any demands for higher wages and further to control the work-force by this paternalist policy.

Although the finishing industries continued in their fundamentally hostile attitude towards the policies of the agrarians and heavy industry there were those, the most prominent among them being Gustav Stresemann, who argued in favour of a certain 'opening to the right' and who warned that a reduction in the German agricultural tariffs would not automatically make the position of export industry any better, for Germany's trading partners would not necessarily lower their tariffs in response. Exports had increased by 31 per cent between 1907 and the end of 1912, whereas imports had only risen by 22 per cent during this period. Three-quarters of foreign sales had been to European countries, and much of the increase was only possible by price-cutting and the drastic reduction of profit margins. Some saw this as proof of the *Mitteleuropa* ideology, others argued that it demonstrated the need for secure markets overseas, for a powerful navy, for *Weltpolitik* and for *Weltwirtschaft*. By 1914 the arguments within industry over free trade or protection were far less intense, and it was left to the social democrats and progressives to argue the case for most-favoured-nation clauses and for the reduction of the tariffs. Delbrück's announcement to the Reichstag in January 1914, which excited so much comment at the time, that the government was not contemplating any modifications of the Bülow tariff was a neutral statement which was designed to appeal to all but the extreme hard-liners on the right or the economic liberals on the left. The government was trying to steer a passage between the demands for the protection of domestic production and the need to increase Germany's share of world trade, and hoped to be able to do so by sticking to the Bülow tariffs as far as possible. The renegotiations of the treaties were likely to be extremely difficult, particularly as Russia still resented the manner in which the Germans had taken advantage of their weak position after the war with Japan. Isolated voices from the light industrial camp continued to speak out against the high agricultural tariffs and denounced those who demanded a 'battle tariff' against Germany's economic rivals, but the vote in the Prussian house of representatives in March 1914 showed a clear majority in favour of a strict application of the Bülow tariffs. The agrarians and the heavy industrialists were always concerned about the attitude the *Bund der Industriellen* and the *Hansa Bund* would take towards the trade treaties when they were renewed in 1971, yet in spite of attacks from this quarter about excessive agricultural tariffs and the deliberate provocation of Russia, there is evidence that suggests that light industry would never have risked an outright confrontation with the cartel.

Much of the uncertainty and tension among the industrialists was due to the immediate consequences of the recession from late 1913 rather than concern over the renegotiations of the trade treaties. The German capital market had hardly recovered from the Agadir crisis when it was hit again by the uncertainties resulting from the Balkan wars and by the enormous capital requirements for the armaments programme. Industry was forced to cut prices and tried to overcome its problems by increasing production leading to serious problems of over-production in some sectors and further price-cuts. With the Reichsbank following a policy of deliberate restraint interest rates rose sharply. Industry found that capital was hard to obtain and unusually expensive. Exports could only be kept up by selling at dumping prices made possible by bank credits that were increasingly difficult to secure. The electrical and chemical industries managed to do surprisingly well, but metals, mining, textiles and even shipping did very poorly. Unemployment became a serious problem, but the government flatly refused a suggestion by the social-democratic party that unemployment insurance should be instigated. With loud demands for drastic cuts in government spending on the social services, new and expensive programmes could not even be discussed. With sharply rising prices, particularly for food and rent, and a stagnant economy, real wages fell in 1913–14. The economics editor of the *Frankfurter Zeitung*, Arthur Feiler, wrote:

> Thus social tensions grow: the wide gulf between heavy industry and finishing industry, between the beneficiaries of our economic policy and those who are hurt by it, between the propertied and the propertyless, between capital and labour. There is the marked tendency that this division will become greater in the course of the recession.

Limits to German Expansion

Worsening relations with Russia, which were apparent in the preliminary discussions over the future of the trade treaties, were greatly intensified by the German activities in Turkey after the Balkan wars. The wretched performance of the Turkish army was an embarrassing reflection on the quality of the German military advisers under Goltz Pascha and was a poor advertisement for Krupp's guns. The fact that the Turks had ignored Goltz's advice to maintain a strong defensive position and to avoid offensive actions was not an excuse that would satisfy world opinion, even though it gave some cold comfort to the General Staff in Berlin. The Germans were very concerned to restore their prestige and influence in Turkey, and the Turks to improve their army after its humiliating defeat. The Turkish army had been trained by German officers for thirty years and was so thoroughly infused with the German military spirit that even those who were lukewarm in their enthusiasm for Germany agreed that it would be impossible to change traditional methods at so late a stage and in so critical a situation. The Turks therefore asked the Germans to undertake a complete reorganisation of the army, and the Germans were quick to realise that through a German-trained and -controlled army the German government would be able to exercise a considerable degree of control over the Turkish government. A military mission under General Otto Liman von Sanders was sent to Turkey with specific instructions from the Kaiser to 'Germanise' the Turkish army, and to keep a close watch on Turkish foreign policy. The Kaiser told the mission, 'You are the pioneers of the future partition of Turkey', and to ease the task Liman was given one million marks per year for bribes. The mission was soon to consist of 42 carefully selected officers who formed quite a contrast to the motley lot under Goltz's command, most of whom had been men who for one reason or another had become unpopular at home. Liman was given considerable powers in Turkey. He was given command of all war academies and training centres, his officers were placed in key positions in the Turkish army, and he was given the right to inspect any unit or fortress whenever he wished. He concentrated on strengthening the fortifications and the artillery on the straits, and in spite of Turkish fears of the repercussions from Russia all the artillery on the Bosphorus was placed under the control of a German artillery specialist. In May 1914 the Bavarian Major Kübel was sent to Turkey and was appointed head of the railway section of the Turkish war ministry. His task was to see that the Turkish railway system was ready for war within six months. Kübel demanded 100 million marks for a thorough reform of the railway system, but he soon found himself locked in battle with the Deutsche Bank, who warned that if such sums were spent on the railways in Asia Minor there would be no funds available for the Baghdad railway, which needed another 500 million marks for its completion. The Deutsche Bank complained that Kübel was acting like a bull in a china shop, destroying the delicate diplomatic preparations that had been needed to get the powers to accept the Baghdad railway and endangering a project with which German prestige was so closely connected. Major Kübel was dismissed shortly after Gwinner and Helfferich had written to the Kaiser on behalf of the Deutsche Bank. The Baghdad railway was considered to be too serious a matter to be placed in jeopardy by an over-zealous and tactless officer.

There was of course much more than prestige and the patriotic sacrifices of the Deutsche Bank involved in Turkey. Massive arms shipments were highly lucrative. Railway-building, armaments for the Turkish army and navy, and heavy artillery for the fortresses on the straits brought colossal sums to German industry.

The political price that was paid for this success was very high. The Russian military attaché in Constantinople, Leontiev, was quick to realise that the German aim was to prepare the Turkish army to fight on their side in an eventual European war, and thus that more than the Balkans was at stake. The French saw that the Liman von Sanders affair could be used to break any remaining ties between Berlin and Petersburg. Sasonov saw the affair as a test case for the Entente, all the more so because the British with their naval mission and the delivery of British-built ships to the Turkish navy were up to the same tricks as the Germans. This in turn raised German hopes that England could be prised away from the Entente, for the Russians were distressed at the British dock treaty with Turkey. The result of a complex round of negotiations was an uneasy compromise that left the Russians bitter and understandably concerned at the powerful German position on the straits which had not been changed by the feeble expedient of posting Liman away from Constantinople. The Kaiser scribbled in a marginal note that the Liman von Sanders affair had done nothing to worsen relations with Russia. The historical record suggests the opposite.

The failure of German policy in the Balkans, the success of the liberal and socialist parties in the Reichstag elections of 1912, and the growing awareness of the relative decline of German military strength all helped to create an increasingly ugly and belligerent climate of opinion among influential circles in Germany. Heinrich Class's widely read and frequently discussed book, *If I were Kaiser – By a German*, which was written immediately after the 1912 elections, sums up these attitudes, although in somewhat drastic language. Class called for a major reform of the constitution of the Reich. A new franchise, similar to that in Prussia, would have to be introduced for the Reichstag elections, with those paying higher taxes getting more votes so that the trend towards democracy and socialism could be halted. With this 'parliament of the best people' it would be possible to have a constitutional monarchy and responsible Ministers. Social democracy would have to be rendered harmless by a revival of the anti-socialist laws and the exile of its 'Jewish leadership'. 'Positive social reform' could be begun which would help the 'valuable sectors of the community' favouring the small farmer and the energetic small producer. A middle-class policy would replace a social policy aimed at relieving the distress of the poor and helpless. This policy would be carried out in the context of a vigorous imperialist policy which would give to the nation a sense of national purpose and unity and overcome the divisions within German society which were threatening to tear it apart. Politically the strengthening of the right-wing parties into a firm coalition was needed to counteract the liberal policies of the 'Jewish associates' of Bassermann, Stresemann and Paasche and the 'Jew Riesser', all of whom had destroyed the national liberal party, the party of 'Bennigsen, Miquel, Treitschke, Sybel and Gneist'.

Although the book was published anonymously, the Pan-German League tried very hard to persuade leading industrialists to subsidise the publication of the book. Their reactions to these requests gives a very interesting picture of the political thinking of the industrialists in 1912. On the whole there was little support for Class's violent anti-Semitism. Class's confidant, Stössel, reported from Essen that the industrialists were not friendly towards the Jews but that they had to tread carefully because they relied on the support of the banks. It was taken as proof by the Pan-Germans of the pernicious influence of the Jews in German life that even the great industrial magnates of Rhineland-Westphalia feared them. The industrialists also felt that the political leadership was lacking to implement such far-reaching reforms, however desirable they might be in theory. But the industrialists were in full agreement with the outline of Class's scheme. The newspapers which reflected the attitudes of the industrialists, such as the *Post*, which was financed by Hugenberg and Stinnes, Krupp's *Berliner Neueste Nachrichten* and the *Deutsche Volkswirtschaftliche Correspondenz*, which was the organ of heavy industry, all carried articles developing a number of themes in Class's book. All these papers demanded territorial expansion and talked in terms of the war that was needed to secure Germany as a world power. They denounced the social policy of the Bismarck Reich and demanded the violent suppression of social democracy. There were calls for a strong man who would carry out a *coup d'état* against the constitution. Class was thus much more than an extremist on the lunatic fringe, he was articulating ideas that were widely held among the industrialists, even though the language he used was sometimes considered a trifle excessive. It is thus hardly surprising that political economists in the German liberal tradition like Max Weber, Lujo Brentano and Gustav Schmoller were increasingly alarmed at the radicalism of the industrialists and agrarians, whose wild demands for drastic measures were based on a lack of understanding of the social-democratic party and of its position in the country. They were quick to point out that the radical rhetoric of certain socialist theoreticians should not be mistaken for the feeling of the party as a whole, and that the massive strength of the state apparatus was enough to hold the party in check.

When the *Berliner Neueste Nachrichten* announced in July 1913 that 'Germany's European jacket is getting too tight', it was expressing widely felt feelings that even the particularly aggressive and ruthless economic policy of imperial Germany in Europe had little room left for manoeuvre. Even in countries like Serbia, whose interests ran counter to those of Germany's greatest ally, the Germans were actively engaged in strengthening their economic position. Germany would not abandon Austria in the Bosnian crisis, but neither would it break off economic relations with Serbia. German capital was actively engaged in the *Banque Franco-Serbe*. The Serbian loan of 1909 was partly placed in the Berlin stock exchange, and in return the Serbs agreed to order 25 per cent of their armaments in Germany, armaments which sooner or later were likely to be used against Austria. In 1913 Austria began to think in terms of a customs union with Serbia, but such schemes foundered not only on the understandable reluctance of the Serbs but also because of the determination of German interests not to be pushed aside. Germany and Austria also found themselves locked in controversy over the Serbian railway, with Austria anxious to come to terms with France so as to be able to gain access to the Paris capital market.

Germany was never able seriously to challenge the dominant position of France in Serbia. In Rumania the position was reversed. Although Rumania had tried to place a 250 million franc loan in 1913 in Paris, the French demanded terms that were unacceptable. Rumania was therefore obliged to beg the Germans for help, and although it proved exceedingly difficult to raise the money in Berlin, for the Rumanians had already placed a 150 million franc loan in the spring in Germany, the German government had no choice but to agree for fear of losing a valuable ally whose oil deposits they were determined to control. Yet in spite of massive German investments in Rumania and the vigorous policy of Germany industry towards that country, it still leaned politically towards the Entente. Friction with Austria-Hungary over Transylvania (Siebenbürgen) was a constant problem and the Kaiser's requests for concessions from the Hungarian government were largely ignored. In the long run it is doubtful if Germany could have continued to supply the loans that Rumania needed, and Rumanian businessmen looked to Paris for an alternative source of capital. Austria-Hungary was unwilling to make the concessions, Germany lacked the funds, and to many it seemed only a matter of time before Rumania would sever its relations with the Triple Alliance.

Although German capital dominated the state loans in Rumania without being able to hold Rumania to the alliance, in Bulgaria, where French capital dominated, the Germans were politically more successful. In 1913 the Bulgarians were desperately in need of a major loan, and the Austrian and German governments hoped that this could be placed in Germany so as to end Bulgaria's dependence on Paris and bring the country closer to the Triple Alliance. The German banks, however, protested that capital was too scarce for a successful loan to Bulgaria and that Germany would find it exceedingly difficult to meet its commitments to those countries where German interests were firmly established. German capital was heavily involved in Turkey, but Turkey in return placed huge orders with German firms and the Deutsche Bank feared that this undertaking, in which German prestige was so closely involved, would be endangered by further demands on the Berlin capital market. It was not until July 1914 that the German government agreed to a loan to Bulgaria which was handled by a German bank consortium in which the Deutsche Bank was not represented. A substantial part of the 500 million franc loan was earmarked for orders from German firms and for the modernisation of the lignite industry and the railways in which German interests would also be involved. Germany jumped in when France had been unable to provide the funds Bulgaria needed, in spite of Russian insistence that the loan was politically vital. Germany could scarcely afford the loan, but it was hoped that it would help German industry overcome some of the problems of the recession by unloading some of its excess production.

The effect of these activities was that Germany gradually squeezed Austria-Hungary out of its traditional markets in the Balkans. With its relatively underdeveloped industry and shortage of capital, Austria was no match for Germany, and many Austrians became increasingly resentful of the way in which Germany exploited every weakness and every setback in its ally's policy for its own immediate gain. In 1913 39 per cent of Austrian exports went to Germany and 39.3 per cent of its imports came from Germany. After the second Morocco crisis, when French capital was withdrawn from Austria, the country was almost entirely dependent on German capital at a time when the obvious shortcomings of the Austrian army had become painfully apparent in the Balkan crisis of 1912–13 and a major rearmament programme had to be undertaken. By contrast, Germany sent 11.6 per cent of its exports to Austria, less than it exported to England, and imported 7.8 per cent of its goods from the Danubian monarchy which put Austria in fourth place among the nations trading with Germany. In other words, Austria needed Germany desperately, and Germany could afford to use the alliance with Austria to its advantage. It is hardly surprising in these circumstances that a significant group of Austrians, chief among them Andrassy and Apponyi, began to think in terms of abandoning the alliance with Germany and seeking an arrangement with France, a suggestion which had considerable appeal in business circles which looked upon Germany more as a rival than a partner and which eagerly looked to the prospect of access to the Paris capital market. Germany was forced to counter this movement with massive injections of capital. Between April 1913 and April 1914 Germany lent Austria 971.6 million marks, much of which was spent on rearmament. These loans placed a further strain on the capital resources of the country and were deeply resented by the Reichsbank, but the German Foreign Office insisted that without these loans the Triple Alliance could well fall apart.

Economic Relations with Western Europe

There was a considerable degree of friction and rivalry between Germany and its greatest ally, but there was also a certain amount of economic co-operation with its rivals in the west, particularly with France. In many ways Germany appeared to be in an excellent position to challenge the great industrial states in the new imperialism of the monopoly stage of capitalism. Major technological advances in the newest branches of industry, a high degree of organisation in cartels, syndicates and trusts, and a close merging of industrial and banking capital in corporation capitalism placed Germany among the most advanced and developed industrial economies. But Germany's late arrival among the great powers and the exceptional rapidity of its growth placed a tremendous strain on its capital resources, so that demand for capital exceeded its formation. Demand for capital at home was usually met because with rising prices and attractive returns, investors preferred to share in Germany's industrial growth rather than risk their money abroad. Owing to these structural peculiarities of the German economy, which were compounded by the rivalries between light industry, the agrarians and the heavy industrialists, and exacerbated by uncertainties in the direction of foreign policy, *Weltpolitik* had an extremely contradictory basis. It is hardly surprising therefore that between 1904 and 1914, when British foreign investments doubled, Germany hardly increased its investments abroad, and two-thirds of that investment was in Europe rather than overseas.

Caprivi's policy, which had favoured industry, was anti-colonial and pro-European, and for all its shortcomings was more in accord with the needs and capabilities of Germany than was the *Sammlung*, *Weltpolitik*, the naval programme and the new tariffs of the late 1890s. But even Caprivi's talk of a possible European customs union had alarmed its neighbours and raised the spectre of a German-dominated Europe. Yet for all these suspicions the importance of German trade overcame many traditional animosities, and in the case of Belgium there were cordial relations between the conservative ruling elite and the German government right up to 1914.

One-third of Germany's seaborne trade went through the ports of Antwerp and Rotterdam. Antwerp was particularly attractive to the Germans. It is closer to an industrial centre like Essen than Rotterdam, Emden, Bremen or Hamburg. Railway tariffs to both Antwerp and Rotterdam were most favourable and German shipping lines were given preferential treatment in Antwerp. From the 1880s a number of German firms were established in Antwerp, although in Rotterdam, where the old family firms exercised a tight control on the commercial life of the city, the foreign intruders were excluded. Belgian heavy industry worked closely with German heavy industry and undertook a number of joint projects in France and Luxembourg. The French viewed these projects with some alarm, and with their vision of the domination of Belgian industry by German interests denounced German policy as 'economic pan-Germanism'. German firms were established in France to jump the tariff, take advantage of cheap labour and secure plentiful and inexpensive raw materials. This was particularly true of the big chemical firms. BASF established a subsidiary at Neuville-sur-Saône as early as 1875, Hoechst followed in 1881 with a factory at Creil. Bayer built a factory near Roubaix and Agfa at St Fons. With the relative backwardness of French industry by the turn of the century these German firms thrived in France, while the French were unable to retaliate in the same manner. French investments in Germany were considerable, indeed they were almost as high as German investments in France, but they did not lead to the control of German enterprises nor to the building of subsidiaries of French firms, with the exception of the glass industry, when St Gobain tried to break the German-controlled bottle-glass cartel by building a factory in Westphalia. There were other smaller French firms in Germany such as silver-plating in Karlsruhe (Christoffle and Company), buttons in Baden and cognac in Mainz.

In heavy industry relations between Germany, France and Belgium were of considerable importance. The Ruhr found it increasingly difficult to meet its requirements for ore as German deposits dwindled and the price of lower-quality ores was high. The French suffered from a shortage of coal in part because of a deliberate policy by the French mines to restrict production to ensure high prices. There was thus a common interest in coming to some arrangement. With the discovery of the ore deposits in Briey in the 1890s, France had ore to offer that could be exchanged for German coal. Yet there was considerable opposition to any such arrangement. Both the agrarians and the finishing industries attacked the Rhineland-Westphalian Coal Syndicate and its price policy, even going as far as to demand the nationalisation of the industry and to call for an export duty on coal. The syndicate had no desire to sell abroad any more than was necessary, for prices were usually lower and their main reason for selling abroad was to avoid letting foreign markets fall exclusively into the hands of the British. It was also very difficult for the French to buy German mines, for there was a very close association between the coal-mines and the smelting works and the cartel regulation was that no mine owned by a smelter could be sold to anyone outside the cartel. By 1905 there was only one major coal-mining company, Harpen, that was not controlled by the pig-iron and steel companies. The French were able to gain control of some mines on the left bank of the Rhine, but Belgium and Holland seemed to offer better prospects as they were not overshadowed by the mounting political tensions that constantly hampered any understanding between German and French industry.

The Ruhr coke-producers were able to dominate the market in the industrially important region of eastern and north-eastern France. British coal from Wales continued to supply the needs of north-western France, but the freight rates were too high for it to challenge the Germans in the east, and British and French coking coal was of inferior quality. French attempts to break this German monopoly met with little success, for Belgian and French producers were willing to join a powerful grouping which they knew they could not beat, so that the Germans dominated the eastern market until the outbreak of the war.

The German industrialists were concerned to secure adequate supplies of ore in the future, particularly when there were signs that ore exports from Sweden might well be restricted at some point in the not too distant future. They therefore invested heavily in French ore fields so that future supplies might be secured. About one-third of the Meurthe-et-Moselle ore fields were in German hands by 1906. By 1910 three-quarters of the Normandy ore district was under German control. This investment in French ore fields was the greatest foreign investment of German industry in the years before the First World War. The cost of exploiting new deposits coupled with the high freight rates made the ore fields economically unattractive except as reserves for future use. With long-term contracts with Sweden, which guaranteed supplies at about 30 per cent below the world market price, there was no immediate hurry. Some of these contracts ran out in 1912, others ran as long as 1917, and after a moment of uncertainty the Swedish government decided to allow an increase in ore exports and what amounted to a subsidy to the mining companies. On the other hand, the Germans were quick to see the advantages of a 'penetration pacifique' of the French market. Assisted by lower freight rates on ore imports from France, the Germans began to exploit their ore fields which were used to supply their new smelters in Lorraine. In return the French were positively encouraged by industrialists like Peter Klöckner, a rising star in Westphalia, to invest in coal-mines on the west bank of the Rhine. It was argued that the more the French invested in Germany the less likely the Germans would be to suffer reprisals from nationalist elements in France against their holdings in the French ore fields. Active joint enterprises were thus considered to be the best possible insurance against the French ultra-right and the socialists, who were becoming increasingly concerned with German activities in such a key industry.

With the superior strength of German industry there would be little doubt that any *ententes* with French and Belgian firms would be dominated by the Germans. The arrangements that did in fact exist were so complex that they confused contemporaries and in most cases elude even the most determined and assiduous historians. The aims of such arrangements were quite clear – to satisfy the French without giving them too much power or influence, and ultimately to tighten the bonds between German and French industry to the advantage of the former. In the mind of Otto Weber, the Foreign Office's expert on heavy industry, writing in 1911, these arrangements offered the exhilarating prospect 'of taking up arms at the head of the heavy industries of Continental Europe united under the direction of Germany, Belgium and France, in the decisive battle for the world market with the as yet unvanquished North America'. Others were less optimistic. By 1910 the French Ambassador in Berlin, Cambon, was convinced that the question of iron ore would lead to war between France and Germany. Three years later a group of German industrialists told the Italian trade Minister, Nitti, that war with France would be necessary to secure the ore deposits of French Lorraine. The question therefore seemed to be whether the French would agree to a series of co-operative ventures in which the Germans were likely to be the greatest beneficiaries, or whether Germany's appetite for ore would lead to war. No one seemed to suggest that the existing relationships between the two countries were likely to continue.

France badly needed German coal and coke, and Germany was concerned about reserves of ore, but it was French capital that most interested the Germans. Up to 1911 French bankers were heavily engaged in lending to Germany either directly or to finance projects throughout the world. Germany was able to borrow this money without losing her independence, but this need for foreign capital caused by the shortage of capital at home, partly because of the deliberate policy of the agrarians to restrict the activities of the stock market, was a serious limitation on *Weltpolitik*. The alternative *Mitteleuropa* policy was equally unrealistic, for it was no longer possible to come to terms with Russia or France, and the attempt to break the *ententes* by bully-boy tactics only served to strengthen them.

Although exports increased significantly, particularly to France, efforts to unload excess capacities were frustrated by the agrarians. Reform of the Bülow tariff, preferential tariffs on the railways, canal-building to open up the ports were all partly or wholly frustrated by the agrarians and their supporters. With the Reich's foreign policy stymied at every turn, with mounting domestic political tensions and the pressing problem of excess production, there was a general frustration that gave credence to those who argued that Germany needed a war. This dangerous mixture of fatalism and hubris infected government circles to an increasing degree after the Agadir crisis.

British co-operation with the Baghdad railway, after the French had pulled out of the project in 1913, and the Anglo-German agreement over the Portuguese colonies suggested to some that Germany should be encouraged in its overseas projects so as to avoid a European war. Grey and Cambon realised the problem, but their solution was unrealistic. The domestic capital requirements of the Reich were growing largely because of enormously increased military expenditure, government bonds were seriously depressed and there was such a shortage of capital that foreign investments had to be drastically restricted. *Weltpolitik* had insufficient capital resources to back it; it was based on the often contradictory alliance of rye and iron, and failed miserably as a social imperialist policy. The alternative to *Weltpolitik* as a means of Caesaristic rule was *Mitteleuropa*, an alliance of the European states under German domination locked in an economic battle for world domination with the United States. But German policy during the Agadir crisis had given the European states an indication of the reality behind the calls for European co-operation and Haldane warned the Germans in 1912 that the British government would not tolerate the domination of Europe by one power. The frustration of Germany at every turn was grist to the Pan-German mill and from 1912 the material, financial and psychological preparations for war began in earnest.

War

Contemporary observers were also aware of the forces that were bringing Europe into closer economic union. International cartels were growing in strength and importance and seemed to be binding Europe closer together so as better to meet the American challenge. But enthusiasm for European integration was largely confined to Germany. Given the disparities in economic growth, levels of development and power, the greater the degree of economic interdependence the stronger Germany's position became, for it was by far the most powerful industrial state on the Continent. Stinnes told Class in 1911 that given another three or four years of peace Germany would be 'the undisputed master of Europe'. Max Warburg made a similar remark to the Emperor just one week before the murder at Sarajevo. But the international cartels and trusts did not always function smoothly. They tended to concentrate on the exploitation of third markets rather than on attempting any real integration of the national economies. They were often fragile and contradictory, acting on the spur of the moment for some temporary purpose.

In both France and Germany there was discussion about the relative strength of Germany and Russia. The question was whether or not the potential and the vast size of Russia and its resources were sufficient to counteract the undisputed economic and military might of Germany. Would Russia be strong enough to hold Germany in check, or would Germany's rate of growth outstrip that of Russia? The answer to these questions seemed gloomy. The French government assumed that the Germans would be prepared to risk a European war for fear of Russia's future strength. It was precisely such fears that were among the key determining factors in the attitude of the German government in the July crisis of 1914. Bethmann Hollweg attempted to localise the war in 1914 and keep Britain neutral, but this attempt failed, partly because Germany's military planning necessitated an attack on France in the event of a war with Russia, and partly because Britain was not prepared to accept German domination of the Continent. Germany was prepared to risk a war for the possibility of a future indirect threat from Russia. In these terms war was not necessary in 1914 and it is stretching the meaning of words to inadmissible limits to describe the war as 'preventive', as has been the case in most of the literature in Germany on the outbreak of the war.

The question of Germany's war aims, which has been so fiercely debated in recent years, dramatically demonstrates the immoderate expansionist tendencies of German industry in 1914, tendencies which were deeply rooted in the past and which were not merely temporary and unthinking reactions to an immediate situation. Heavy industry demanded the ore basin of Longwy-Briey, the coal of north-western France and Belgium, and either the outright annexation of Belgium or its indirect domination. The result of such a policy would have been temporarily to destroy France as an industrial power and Continental rival to Germany. Most of France's iron and steel works would have been lost, along with 80 per cent of its blast furnaces and 85 per cent of its ore production. These demands were made in August and September of 1914, and were thus not a response to the need for a massive increase in war production, and thus of iron and steel, for the necessity did not become apparent until the spring of the following year. Nor can they be excused as compensation for the loss of property in those parts of France and her colonial possessions that were not occupied by the German army, nor by the spurious argument that large parts of the Longwy-Briey ore fields were controlled by German interests before the war. Even in the later stages of the war the French ore fields were of little significance. The ore was of poor quality, and high-grade steels could be more easily produced from scrap metal, using the Siemens-Martin process.

The clear distinction found in much of the literature between heavy industry, with its emphasis on direct annexations, and the export industries, commercial interests and banks, with a more flexible and indirect approach, does not bear up under close examination. There were proponents of both direct and indirect annexations in both camps, men frequently changed their minds and in some cases even suggested a settlement with France that would enable the creation of an alliance of Germany, France and England aimed against Russia. Some argued that France would have to be crushed once and for all, others that a punitive peace would simply lead to further wars.

Bethmann Hollweg attempted to steer his way between the *Mitteleuropa* enthusiasts and the extreme annexationists to find, in his words, the 'diagonal' between these two positions so that the political truce of August 1914 could be preserved and a broad national front be found and maintained to support the war effort. *Mitteleuropa* would be a German-dominated customs area rather than a close political federation of dependent states. This was exceptionally hard to reconcile with the idea of a 'federation of Germanic peoples' supported by many heavy industrialists which involved the annexation of Belgium, Luxemburg and the French ore fields as well as the Belgian Congo. Bethmann let the Pan-Germans know in November 1914 that as far as he was concerned:

> The aim of this war is not the restoration of the European balance of power, but rather the final destruction of that which has been described as the European balance of power and the foundation of the German domination of Europe.

But the annexationists were not convinced by such talk. To them

Bethmann's policies involved an opening to the left and relied on the support of bourgeois liberals and the right wing of the social democrats. That was enough for the agrarians, heavy industrialists and pan-Germans to denounce the Chancellor for being in bed with the socialists, for destroying the cartel of the productive classes, and for breaking with the traditions of German economic policy. Such criticisms were partly justified. *Mitteleuropa* as a customs union would spell the end of the Bülow tariffs and would be based on the most-favoured-nation clauses and the beggar-thy-neighbour policies which the 'productive classes' detested and which would need the support of the right wing of the social democratic party to be successful. The 'state preserving classes' were convinced that Bethmann's policy would spell the end of the 'solidarity protectionism' of the pre-war era and were determined to resist any shifts in the political basis of government support. In July 1916 these forces united in the Independent Committee for a German Peace (*Unabhängige Ausschuss*) chaired by Dietrich Schäfer, a prominent historian and publicist. The committee had representatives from all the great interest groups of industry, trade and agriculture and played an enormously important role in removing the 'gutless Chancellor' (in Schäfer's words) in July 1917.

The cartel was given a new lease of life with its attacks on Bethmann Hollweg's war aims policy, on his willingness to make certain political concessions to the left-of-centre parties, and on the suggestions that he might be contemplating some fundamental political and social reforms. A successful *fronde* against the Chancellor, the formation of a new political party, the *Vaterlandspartei* and its close associations with the High Command under Hindenburg and Ludendorff seemed to promise a spectacular future. But their excessive war aims and their repressive domestic political ideas could only be realised in the event of a successful war, and as the chances of success receded, these demands became increasingly strident and irrational. Even in defeat they were to live on to be revived in a new and hideous form.

Conclusion

Political democracy is not the necessary consequence of industrialisation, nor is it an adequate guarantee of wisdom and humanity. It is, however, the political system most likely to overcome, at least partially, the worst consequences of the economic inequalities and social injustices of industrialisation, and provides the best preconditions for increased social mobility, political participation and eventual equality. The liberal democratic welfare state, for all its obvious shortcomings and imperfections, is able to keep social conflicts within reasonable bounds and to provide the framework for further democratisation. Germany had made extraordinary progress since the mid-century to become the leading industrial nation in Europe, and yet politically, in spite of the apparently modern constitution of 1871, the country was seriously backward. An agricultural society had become an industrial society and there had been a dramatic movement away from the land to urban areas, and yet upward social mobility was hindered by a rigid caste system where birth, education, wealth and even religion counted for more than ability.

With the rise of social democracy, the universal suffrage of the Reichstag elections became increasingly menacing to the system. Bismarck had hoped that by enfranchising conservative peasants he might be able to neutralise parliamentary democracy and convert it into a form of plebiscitory authoritarian rule. With the rapid advance of industrialisation the working class became increasingly important and threatened to dominate the Reichstag. The frustrated reaction to this inevitable process was anti-socialist legislation, and when that too failed, a state of latent civil war existed in which the ruling class retreated to its power bases in the army, the bureaucracy and the Prussian Parliament, with its anachronistic three-class electoral system. This system could be held together by force and by the attempt to create an ideological consensus by stressing the community of interest of the *Volk*, by insisting that the state transcended the conflicts of class and party, and by the emphasis on authority and obedience as ends in themselves. The pre-industrial elites were able to maintain their position in society, in politics and in the economic life of the country. In the short term they were remarkably successful. For all the outspoken criticism of the abuses and shortcomings of the system, the vast majority of Germans did not find the situation intolerable and social frustrations and impatience were kept within bounds. Yet at the same time it became increasingly difficult to paper over the divisions within society, and the remedies suggested became ever more drastic. Under the strain of a near-total war the system began to collapse, but even in the crisis of defeat the old elites were able to retrieve many of their privileges and much of their influence. The golden opportunity for fundamental reform was lost.

The economic history of Germany in the nineteenth century is a history of extraordinary success. So too is that of the elites who were able to maintain their position for so long under conditions which hardly seemed favourable. Yet the price that was paid was terribly high. Rather than risk fundamental reform and modernisation, making the concessions which had to be made if social conflicts were to be regulated, it was considered better to risk a war. The gamble failed, but only partially. Old social and economic structures survived, and even politically the reform was incomplete. It is at this level that the much-debated question of the continuity of German history should be discussed, and it is for this reason that the development of the German economy in the nineteenth century provides the key to the understanding of the problems of the present day and the more recent past.

BIBLIOGRAPHY

Abel, Wilhelm. 'Handwerksgeschichte in neuer Sicht', *Göttinger handwerkswirtschaftliche Studien*, vol. 16, Göttingen, 1970

——*Bevölkerungsentwicklung*. Munich, 1950

——*Geschichte der Deutschen Landwirtschaft*. Stuttgart, 1967

——*Der Pauperismus in Deutschland am Vorabend der industriellen Revolution*. Dortmund, 1966

Abraham, K. *Der Strukturwandel im Handwerk in der ersten Hälfte des 19. Jahrhunderts und seine Bedeutung für die Berufserziehung*. Cologne, 1955

Adelmann, G. *Der gewerblich-industrielle Zustand der Rheinprovinz im Jahre 1836*. Bonn, 1967

——*Die soziale Betriebsverfassung des Ruhrbergbaus vom Anfang des 19. Jahrhunderts bis zum Ersten Weltkrieg*. Bonn, 1962

Adler, G. *Ueber die Epochen der deutschen Handwerkerpolitik*. Jena, 1903

Andre, Doris. *Indikatoren des technischen Fortschritts. Eine Analyse der Wirtschaftsentwicklung in Deutschland von 1850–1913*. Göttingen, 1971

Assmann, Klaus. *Zustand und Entwicklung des städtischen Handwerks in der ersten Hälfte des 19. Jahrhunderts*. Göttingen, 1971

Baar, Lothar. *Die Berliner Industrie in der industriellen Revolution*. Berlin, 1966

Ballin, Paul. *Der Haushalt der arbeitenden Klassen. Eine sozialistische Untersuchung*. Berlin, 1883

Barkin, Kenneth D. *The Controversy over German Industrialization, 1890–1902*. Chicago, 1970

Bartel, H. and Engelberg, E. *Die Grosspreussisch-militäristische Reichsgründung 1871*. 2 vols., Berlin, 1971

Baumont, Maurice. *La grosse industrie allemande et le charbon*. Paris, 1928

——*La grosse industrie allemande et le liquidité*. Paris, 1928

Beau, Horst. *Das Leistungswissen des frühindustriellen Unternehmertums in Rheinland und Westfalen*. Cologne, 1959

Bechtel, Heinrich. *Wirtschafts- und Sozialgeschichte Deutschlands*. Munich, 1967

Beck, L. *Die Geschichte des Eisens in technischer und kulturgeschicht-*

licher Beziehung, 4 Abteilung: Das XIX Jahrhundert von 1801–1860. Brunswick, 1899

Beckerath, H. von. *Der moderne Industrialismus*. Berlin, 1930

Beer, J.J. *The Emergence of the German Dye Industry*. Urbana, 1959

Benaerts, Pierre. *Les Origines de la grande industrie allemande*. Paris, 1933

Berdrow, W. *Alfred Krupp*. 2 vols., Berlin, 1927

Bergengrün, A. *Staatsminister August Freiherr von der Heydt*. Leipzig, 1908.

——— *David Hansemann*. Berlin, 1901

Berger, L. *Der alte Harkort*. Leipzig, 1902

Berghahn, Volker P. *Der Tirpitzplan. Genesis und Verfall einer innenpolitischen Krisenstrategie unter Wilhelm II*. Düsseldorf, 1971

Bergmann, Jürgen. *Das Berliner Handwerk in den Frühphasen der Industrialisierung*. Berlin, 1973

Berthold, Karl. *Untersuchungen über den Stand der Maschinenindustrie in Deutschland*. Jena, 1915

Beutin, Ludwig. *Einführung in der Wirtschaftsgeschichte*. Berlin, 1958

Bienenkopf, G. *100 Jahre Deutsche Eisenbahnen*. Berlin, 1938

Bloemers, K. *William Thomas Mulvany 1806–1865. Ein Beitrag zur Geschichte der rheinisch-westfälischen Grossindustrie*. Essen, 1922

Blondel, Georges. *L'essor industriel et commercial du peuple allemand*. Paris, 1899

Böhm, Ekkehard. *Ueberseehandel und Flottenbau*. Düsseldorf, 1972

Böhme, H. *Deutschlands Weg zur Grossmacht, Studien zur Verhältnis von Wirtschaft und Staat während der Reichsgründungszeit 1848–1881*. Cologne, 1966

——— *Prologemena zu einer Sozial- und Wirtschaftsgeschichte Deutschlands im 19. und 20. Jahrhundert*. Frankfurt, 1968

——— *Probleme der Reichsgründungszeit 1848–1879*. Cologne, 1968

Borchardt, Knut. *The Industrial Revolution in Germany*. London, 1972

——— 'Zur Frage des Kapitalmangels in der ersten Hälfte des 19. Jahrhunderts in Deutschland', *Jahrbuch für Nationalökonomie und Statistik*, 173 (1961)

Born, K.E. *Moderne deutsche Wirtschaftsgeschichte*. Cologne, 1966

Bosselmann, Kurt. *Die Entwicklung des deutschen Aktienwesens im 19. Jahrhundert*. Berlin, 1939

Brepohl, Wilhelm. *Industrievolk im Wandel von der agraren zur industriellen Daseinsform, dargestellt am Ruhrgebiet*. Tübingen, 1957

Brodnitz, G. 'Recent Works on German Economic History 1900–1927',

Economic History Review, 1, 1927–8
Bruck, W.F. *Social and Economic History of Germany from William II to Hitler, 1888–1938*. Oxford, 1938
Bry, Gerhard. *Wages in Germany*. Princeton, 1960
Buchholz, E.W. *Ländliche Bevölkerung an der Schwelle des Industriezeitalters*. Stuttgart, 1966
Buck, Herbert, *Zur Geschichte der Produktionskräfte und Produktionsverhältnisse in Preussen 1810–1933. Spezialinventur des Bestandes des Preussischen Ministeriums für Handel und Gewerbe*. Berlin, 1960
Büsch, Otto (ed.). *Untersuchungen zur Geschichte der frühen Industrialisierung, vornehmlich im Wirtschaftsraum Berlin–Brandenburg*. Berlin, 1971
——*Militärsystem und Sozialleben im alten Preussen 1713–1807*. Berlin, 1962
——*Industrialisierung und Geschichtswissenschaft. Ein Beitrag zur Thematik und Methodologie der historischen Industrialisierungsforschung*. Berlin, 1969
Buss, G. *Die Berliner Börse 1685–1913*. Berlin, 1913
Cameron, Rondo E. 'Some French Contributions to the Industrial Development of Germany 1840–1870', *Journal of Economic History*, 16 (1956)
——*Banking in the Early Stages of Industrialisation*. New York, 1967
Clapham, J.H. *The Economic Development of France and Germany*. Cambridge, 1936
Clow, A. and N.L. *The Chemical Revolution*. London, 1952
Cohnstadt, W. *Die Agrarfrage in der deutschen Sozialdemokratie von Karl Marx bis zum Breslauer Parteitag*. Berlin, 1903
Conze, W. (ed.). *Staat und Gesellschaft im deutschen Vormärz 1815–1848*. Stuttgart, 1962
—— 'Die Wirkungen der liberalen Agrarreform auf die Volksordnung in Mitteleuropa im 19. Jahrhundert', *Vierteljahrschrift für Sozial- und Wirtschaftsgeschichte*, Band 38, Heft 1, Wiesbaden (1949)
Dabritz, Walter. *David Hansemann und Adolf Hansemann*. Krefeld, 1954
—— *Gründung und Anfänge der Diskontogesellschaft*. Munich, 1931
Desai, Ashok V. *Real Wages in Germany 1871–1913*. Oxford, 1968
Dieterici, C.F.W. *Der Volkswohlstand im Preussischen Staate*. Berlin, 1846
Ehrenberg, Richard. *Grosse Vermögen, ihre Entstehung und ihre Bedeutung*, Band I, Jena, 1925
Ehrlicher, Werner. *Kompendium der Volkswirtschaftslehre*. 2 vols.,

Göttingen, 1967

Eichholtz, D. 'Junker und Bourgeoisie vor 1848 in der preussischen Eisenbahngeschichte', *Deutsche Akademie der Wissenschaften zu Berlin, Schriften des Instituts für Geschichte*, Reihe I, Band II, Berlin, 1962

Elias, Norbert, *Die höfische Gesellschaft*. Neuwied, 1969

Elm, Ludwig. *Zwischen Fortschritt und Reaktion*. Berlin, 1968

Engel, Ernst. *Das Zeitalter des Dampfes*. Berlin, 1880

Fabiunke, G. *Zur historischen Rolle des deutschen Nationalökonomen Friedrich List (1786–1846)*. Berlin, 1955

Facius, F. *Wirtschaft und Staat. Die Entwicklung der Staatlichen Wirtschaftsverwaltung in Deutschland vom 17. Jahrhundert bis 1945*. Boppard, 1959

Feis, Herbert. *Europe the World's Banker*. New Haven, 1930

Fester, Gustav. *Die Entwicklung der technischen Chemie*. Berlin, 1923

Finck von Finckenstein, H.W. Graf. *Die Entwicklung der Landwirtschaft in Preussen und Deutschland 1800–1930*. Würzburg, 1960

Fischer, Wolfram. *Wirtschafts- und Sozialgeschichtliche Probleme der frühen Industrialisierung*. Berlin, 1968

——— *Wirtschaft und Gesellschaft im Zeitalter der Industrialisierung*. Göttingen, 1972

Fischer, Wolfram and Bajor, Georg. *Die Soziale Frage: Neuere Studien zur Lage der Fabrikarbeiter in den Frühphasen der Industrialisierung*. Stuttgart, 1967

Forberger, R. *Die Manufakturen in Sachsen vom Ende des 16. bis zum Anfang des 19. Jahrhunderts*. Berlin, 1958

Fricke, Albert. *Die Anfänge des Eisenbahnwesens in Preussen*. Leipzig, 1912

Gehrig, H. *Friedrich List und Deutschlands politisch- ökonomische Einheit*. Leipzig, 1956

Gerloff, Wilhelm. *Die Finanz- und Zollpolitik des deutschen Reiches*. Jena, 1913

Gerschenkron, Alexander. *Bread and Democracy in Germany*. Berkeley, 1943

Giersiepen, E. and Lösche, D. *Beiträge zur deutschen Wirtschafts- und Sozialgeschichte des 18. und 19. Jahrhunderts*. Berlin, 1962

Glagau, Otto. *Der Börsen- und Gründungsschwindel in Berlin*. Leipzig, 1876

Göhre, Paul and Fischer, Karl. *Denkwürdigkeiten und Erinnerungen eines Arbeiters*. 2 vols., Leipzig, 1903–4

Goldschmidt, F. and P. *Das Leben des Staatsrats Kunth*. Berlin, 1881

Gollwitzer, H. *Die Standesherren.* Berlin, 1957
Goltz, T. von der. *Geschichte der deutschen Landwirtschaft.* 2 vols., Stuttgart, 1902
Grunberg, C. *Die Bauernbefreiung und die Auflösung des gutsherrlich-bäuerlichen Verhältnisses in Böhmen, Mähren und Schlesien.* 2 vols., Leipzig, 1893–4
Guillen, Pierre. *L'allemagne et le maroc de 1870 à 1905.* Paris, 1967
Gurland, A.R.L. *Wirtschaft und Gesellschaft im übergang zum Zeitalter der Industrie.* Berlin, 1960
Haber, L.F. *The Chemical Industry during the Nineteenth Century.* Oxford, 1958
Hagen, R. *Die erste deutsche Eisenbahn.* Berlin, 1886
Hallgarten, G. and Radkau, J. *Deutsche Industrie und Politik von Bismarck bis Heute.* Frankfurt, 1974
Hallgarten, George W.F. *Imperialismus vor 1914.* 2 vols., Munich, 1963
Hamerow, Theodore S. *Restoration, Revolution, Reaction Economics and Politics in Germany 1815–1871.* Princeton, 1958
Handwörterbuch der Staatswissenschaften. Jena, 1924
Hansen, J. *Die Rheinprovinz 1815–1915.* Bonn, 1917
——— *Gustav von Mevissen.* Berlin, 1906
Hausherr, Hans. *Wirtschaftsgeschichte der Neuzeit.* Cologne, 1960
Haushofer, Heinz. *Die deutsche Landwirtschaft im technischen Zeitalter.* Stuttgart, 1963
Heffter, Heinrich. *Die deutsche Selbstverwaltung im 19. Jahrhundert.* Stuttgart, 1969
Helfferich, Karl. *Deutschlands Volkswohlstand 1888–1913.* Berlin, 1915
Hellwig, Hans. *Die Preussische Staatsbank.* Berlin, 1922
Henderson, W.O. *The Zollverein.* London, 1939
——— *The State and the Industrial Revolution in Prussia 1740–1870.* Liverpool, 1958
——— *Britain and Industrial Europe 1750–1870.* Leicester, 1965
——— *The Rise of German Industrial Power 1834–1914.* Berkeley, 1975
——— 'Prince Smith and Free Trade in Germany', *Economic History Review,* 2 (1950)
Hoffmann, W. *Das deutsche Volkseinkommen 1850–1950.* Tübingen, 1959
——— *Stadien und Typen der Industrialisierung.* Jena, 1931
Hoffmann, W.G. *Das Wachstum der deutschen Wirtschaft seit der Mitte des 19. Jahrhunderts.* Berlin, 1965
Huber, Franz C. *Deutschland als Industriestaat.* Stuttgart, 1901

Hübener, E. *Die deutsche Eisenindustrie, ihre Grundlagen, ihre Organisation und ihre Politik*. Leipzig, 1913

Hue, O. *Die Bergarbeiter*. Stuttgart, 1913

Jaeger, Hans. *Unternehmer in der deutschen Politik*. Bonn, 1967

Jantke, Carl and Hilger, Dietrich (eds.). *Die Eigentumslosen. Der deutsche Pauperismus und die Emanzipationskrise in Darstellungen und Deutungen der Zeitgenössischen Literatur.* Freiburg–Munich, 1965

Jantke, Carl. *Der vierte Stand*. Freiburg, 1953

Kaeble, Hartmut. *Industrielle Interessenpolitik in der wilhelminischen Gesellschaft*. Berlin, 1970

—— *Berliner Unternehmer während der frühen Industrialisierung. Herkunft sozialer Status und politischer Einfluss*. Berlin, 1972

Kautsky, K. *Die Agrarfrage*. Berlin, 1899

Kehr, Eckart. *Der Primat der Innenpolitik*. Berlin, 1965

Kermann, Joachim. *Die Manufakturen im Rheinland 1750–1833*. Bonn, 1972

Kisch, H. 'The Textile Industries in Silesia and the Rhineland. A Comparative Study of Industrialisation', *Journal of Economic History*, 19 (1959)

Klein, Ernst. *Geschichte der öffentlichen Finanzen in Deutschland 1500–1870*. Wiesbaden, 1974.

—— *Von der Reform zur Restauration*. Berlin, 1965

Knapp, G.F. *Die Bauernbefreiung und der Ursprung der Landarbeiter in den älteren Theilen Preussens*, vol. I, Munich, 1927

Kocka, Jürgen. *Unternehmerverwaltung und Angestelltenschaft am Beispiel Siemens 1847–1914*. Stuttgart, 1969

Koppe, I.G. *Kurze Darstellung der Landwirtschaftliche Verhältnisse in der Mark Brandenburg*. Berlin, 1839

Kosselleck, R. *Preussen zwischen Reform und Revolution, 1791–1848*. Stuttgart, 1967

Krätschele, Hermann. *Carl Peters 1856–1918*. Berlin, 1959

Krönagel, E. *Die industriellen Unternehmungen der königlich preussischen Seehandlung*. Berlin, 1845

Krug, L. *Betrachtungen über den Nationalreichtum des preussischen Staats und über den Wohlstand seiner Bewohner*. Berlin, 1805

Krüger, H. *Zur Geschichte der Manufakturen und der Manufakturarbeiten in Preussen. Die mittleren Provinzen in der 2. Hälfte des 19. Jahrhunderts*. Berlin, 1958

Krzymowski, R. *Geschichte der deutschen Landwirtschaft*. Berlin, 1961

Kuczynski, Jürgen. *Studien zur Geschichte des Kapitalismus*. Berlin, 1957

Kuczynski, Jürgen. *Darstellung der Lage der Arbeiter in Deutschland von 1739 bis 1849*. Berlin, 1961

——*Darstellung der Lage der Arbeiter in Deutschland von 1849 bis 1870*. Berlin, 1962

Kuczynski, R.R. *Der Zug nach der Stadt*. Stuttgart, 1897

Kumpf-Korfes, Siegrid. *Bismarcks 'Draht nach Russland'*. Berlin, 1968

Lambi, Ivo. *Free Trade and Protection in Germany*. Wiesbaden, 1963

Lenz, F. *Friedrich List*. Berlin, 1936

Lippmann, E.V. *Die Entwicklung der deutschen Zuckerindustrie von 1850 bis 1900*. Leipzig, 1900

List, Friedrich. *Das nationale System der politischen Oekonomie*. Jena, 1920

Lochmüller, W. *Zur Entwicklung der Baumwollindustrie in Deutschland*. Leipzig, 1906

Lütge, F. *Geschichte der deutschen Agrarverfassung*. Stuttgart, 1963

——*Deutsche Sozial- und Wirtschaftsgeschichte*. Berlin, 1960

——'Ueber die Auswirkung der Bauernbefreiung in Deutschland', *Jahrbücher für Nationalökonomie und Statistik*, vol. 157, Jena, 1943

——*Studien zur Sozial- und Wirtschaftsgeschichte*. Berlin, 1963

Martin, Paul C. 'Die Entstehung des preussischen Aktiengesetzes von 1843', *Vierteljahrschrift für Sozial- und Wirtschaftsgeschichte*, 56 (1969)

Maschke, E. *Grundzüge der deutschen Kartellgeschichte*. Dortmund, 1964

Matschoss, Conrad. *Die Entwicklung der Dampfmaschine*. 2 vols., Berlin, 1908

——*Ein Jahrhundert deutscher Maschinenbau, von der mechanischen Werkstättc bis zur deutschen Maschinenfabrik 1819–1919*. Berlin, 1919

——*Preussens Gewerbeordnung und ihre grossen Männer*. Berlin, 1921

Mauersberg, Hans. *Deutsche Industrien im Zeitgeschehen eines Jahrhunderts*. Stuttgart, 1966

Mayer, G. *Die Freihandelslehre in Deutschland*. Jena, 1927

Meyer, A. von. *Geschichte und Geographie der deutschen Eisenbahnen*. Berlin, 1891

Michel, Ernst. *Sozialgeschichte der industriellen Arbeitswelt*. Frankfurt, 1953

Mieck, Ilja. *Preussische Gewerbepolitik in Berlin 1806–1844*. Berlin, 1965

Mietzen, August. *Der Boden und die landwirtschaftlichen Verhältnisse*

des preussischen Staates. Vol. I, Berlin, 1868
Mottek, H., Blumberg, H., Wutzmer, H. and Becker, W. *Studien zur Geschichte der industriellen Revolution in Deutschland.* Berlin, 1960
Mottek, H. *Wirtschaftsgeschichte Deutschlands.* Vols. 1 and 2, Berlin, 1959 and 1964
Olhausen, H.P. *Friedrich List und der deutsche Handels- und Gewerbeverein.* Jena, 1933
Oncken, H. and Saemisch, F.E.M. *Vorgeschichte und Begründung des deutschen Zollvereins, 1815–1834.* 3 vols., Berlin, 1934
Pöls, W., Ritter, G.A. and Kocka, J. *Deutsche Sozialgeschichte.* 2 vols., Munich, 1973
Poschinger, Heinrich von. *Bankwesen und Bankpolitik in Preussen.* 3 vols., Berlin, 1878
Pounds, Norman J.G. *The Ruhr.* New York, 1968
Reden, Friedrich Wilhelm von. *Erwerbs- und Verkehrsstatistik des Königstaates Preussen.* 3 vols., Darmstadt, 1853–4
Redlich, O.R., Dresen, A. and Petry, J. *Geschichte der Stadt Ratingen von den Anfängen 1815.* Ratingen, 1926
Reuter, O. *Die Manufaktur im fränkischen Raum.* Stuttgart, 1961
Riesser, J. *The German Great Banks and their Concentration.* Washington, 1911
Ritter, G.A. (ed.). *Enstehung und Wandel der modernen Gesellschaft. Festschrift für Hans Rosenberg zum 65. Geburtstag.* Berlin, 1970
Ritter, U.P. *Die Rolle des Staates in den Frühstadien der Industrialisierung.* Berlin, 1961
Rosenberg, Hans. *Grosse Depression und Bismarckzeit.* Berlin, 1967
——— *Die Weltwirtschaftskrise von 1857–59.* Stuttgart, 1934
——— *Politische Denkströmungen im deutschen Vormärz.* Göttingen, 1972
Rostow, W.W. (ed.). *The Economics of Take-off into Sustained Growth.* New York, 1963
Rothkegel, W. 'Die Bewegung der Kaufpreise für ländliche Besitzungen und die Entwicklung der Getreidepreise 1895–1909', *Schmollers Jahrbuch*, 34 (1910)
Rudhart, Hans. *Die Preussische Staatsbank (Seehandlung).* Leipzig, 1927
Sartorius von Waltershausen, A. *Deutsche Wirtschaftsgeschichte 1815–1914.* Jena, 1923
Sass, Friedrich, *Geschichte des deutschen Verbrennungsmotorenbaues von 1860 bis 1918.* Berlin, 1962
Saul, K. *Staat, Industrie, Arbeiterbewegung im Kaiserreich 1903–1914.*

Düsseldorf, 1974
Schmalenbach, E. von. *Die Aktiengesellschaft*. Cologne, 1950
Schmoller, Gustav. *Zur Geschichte der deutschen Kleingewerbe im 19. Jahrhundert*. Berlin, 1870
Schnabel, Franz. *Deutsche Geschichte im neunzehnten Jahrhundert*. 8 vols., Freiburg, 1964
Schrader, Paul. *Die Geschichte der königlich-preussischen Seehandlung*. Berlin, 1911
Schrieber, W. *Die preussischen Eisenbahnen und ihr verhältniss zum Staat 1834–1874*. Berlin, 1874
Schröder, E. *Krupp. Geschichte einer Unternehmerfamilie*. Göttingen, 1957
Schröter, A. and Becker, W. *Die Entwicklung der deutschen Maschinenbauindustrie in der industriellen Revolution*. Berlin, 1962
Schuchardt, J. 'Die Wirtschaftskrise vom Jahre 1866 in Deutschland', *Jahrbuch für Wirtschaftsgeschichte*, II (1962)
Schumpeter, J. *Theorie der wirtschaftlichen Entwicklung. Eine Untersuchung über Unternehmergewinn, Kapital, Kredit, Zins und den Konjunkturzyklus*. Berlin, 1952
Schumpeter, J.A. *Business Cycles*. 2 vols., London, 1939
Schwerin von Krosigk, Lutz Graf von. *Die grosse Zeit des Feuers, den Weg der deutschen Industrie*. 3 vols., Tübingen, 1957–9
Sheehan, James J. *The Career of Lujo Brentano*. Chicago, 1966
Skalweit, A. *Das Dorfhandwerk vor Aufhebung des Städtezwanges*. Frankfurt, no date
Slawinger, G. *Die Manufaktur in Kurbayern*. Stuttgart, 1966
Sombart, Werner, *Der Bourgeois. Zur Geschichte des modernen Wirtschaftsmenschen*. Munich, 1926
——— *Der moderne Kapitalismus*. 3 vols., Munich, 1916–28
——— *Die deutsche Volkswirtschaft im neunzehnten Jahrhundert und im Anfang des 20. Jahrhunderts*. Berlin, 1919
Spiethoff, Arthur. *Die Wirtschaftliche Wechsellagen*. Tübingen, 1955
Stadelmann, Rudolf. *Soziale und politische Geschichte der Revolution von 1848*. Darmstadt, 1970
Statistisches Jahrbuch für den Preussischen Staat, 7 Jahrgang 1909. Berlin, 1910
Stegmann, Dirk. *Die Erben Bismarcks*. Cologne, 1970
Stolper, Gustav. *Deutsche Wirtschaftsgeschichte seit 1870*. Tübingen, 1966
Thierfelder, Hildegard. *Rother als Finanzpolitiker unter Hardenberg*. Berlin, 1934

Tilly, Richard. *Financial Institutions and Industrialisation in the German Rhineland 1815–1870*. Madison, Wisconsin, 1966
Tipton, Frank B. *Regional Variations in the Economic Development of Germany During the 19th Century*. Middletown, 1976
Todt, Radandt. *Zur Frühgeschichte der Deutschen Gewerkschafts-Bewegung 1800–1849*. Berlin, 1950
Treue, Wilhelm. *Wirtschaftsgeschichte der Neuzeit*. Stuttgart, 1966
Treue, W., Ponicke, H. and Manegold, K.-H. *Quellen zur Geschichte der industriellen Revolution*. Göttingen, 1966
Treue, W. *Konzentration und Expansion als Kennzeichen der politischen und wirtschaftlichen Geschichte Deutschlands im 19. und 20. Jahrhunderts*. Dortmund, 1965
——— 'Wirtschaftszustände und Wirtschaftspolitik in Preussen 1815–1825', *Vierteljahrschrift für Wirtschaftsgeschichte*, Beiheft 31, 1937
Vagts, Alfred. *Deutschland und die Vereinigten Staaten in der Weltpolitik*. 2 vols., 1935
Veblen, Thorstein. *Imperial Germany and the Industrial Revolution*. New York, 1915
Verein fur Sozialpolitik, *Untersuchungen über die Lage des Handwerks in Deutschland*. 9 vols., Leipzig, 1895–7
Viebahn, Georg von. *Statistik des zollvereinten und nördlichen Deutschlands*, Band I. 2 vols., Berlin, 1858 and 1862
Vogel, Barbara. *Deutsche Russlandpolitik, das Scheitern der deutschen Weltpolitik unter Bülow 1900–1906*. Düsseldorf, 1973
Voigt, Fritz. *Die gestaltende Kraft der Verkehrsmittel im wirtschaftlichen Wachstumprozess*. Bielefeld, 1959
Wagenblass, Horst. *Der Eisenbahnbau und das Wachstum der deutschen Eisen- und Maschinenbauindustrie 1835 bis 1860*. Stuttgart, 1973
Wagenführ, Rolf. *Die Bedeutung des Aussenmarktes für die deutsche Industriewirtschaft*. Berlin and Hamburg, 1936
——— *Die Industriewirtschaft. Entwicklungstendenzen der deutschen und internationalen Industrieproduktion 1860 bis 1932*. Berlin, 1933
Wagner, Adolf. *Agrar- und Industriestaat*. Berlin, 1901
Weber, Adolf. *Der Kampf zwischen Kapital und Arbeit*. Tübingen, 1954
Weber, Max. *Wirtschaftsgeschichte*. Berlin, 1924
——— *Wirtschaft und Gesellschaft*. Berlin, 1956
——— 'Die Verhältnisse der Landarbeiter im ostelbischen Deutschlands', *Schriften des Vereins für Sozialpolitik*, 55, Leipzig, 1892
Wehler, H.-U. *Moderne Deutsche Sozialgeschichte*. Cologne, 1968
——— *Bismarck und der Imperialismus*. Cologne, 1969
——— *Krisenherde des Kaiserreichs 1871–1918*. Göttingen, 1970

Wehler, H.-U. *Das Deutsche Kaiserreich 1871–1918*. Göttingen, 1973
—— *Sozialgeschichte Heute. Festschrift für Hans Rosenberg zum 70. Geburtstag*. Göttingen, 1974
—— *Geschichte und Oekonomie*. Cologne, 1973
Wendel, H.C.M. *The Evolution of Industrial Freedom in Prussia 1845 to 1849*. New York, 1921
Wiedenfeld, Kurt. *Ein Jahrhundert rheinischer Montanindustrie 1815–1915*. Bonn, 1916
Winkler, H.A. (ed.). *Organisierter Kapitalismus*. Göttingen, 1974
Witt, P.-C. *Die Finanzpolitik des Deutschen Reichs von 1903 bis 1913*. Hamburg, 1970
Wunderlich, Frieda. *Farm Labour in Germany 1810–1945*. Princeton, 1961
Wurm, Franz F. *Wirtschaft und Gesellschaft in Deutschland 1848–1948*. Opladen, 1969
—— *Vom Hakenpflug zur Fabrik*. Frankfurt, 1966
Zorn, Wolfgang. 'Typen und Entwicklungskräfte deutschen Unternehmertums', *Vierteljahrsschrift für Sozial- und Wirtschaftsgeschichte*, Band 44, 1957
——'Wirtschafts- und sozialgeschichtiche Zusammenhänge der deutschen Reichsgründungszeit', *Historische Zeitschrift*, Band 197 (1963)
Zunkel, F. *Der rheinisch-westfälische Unternehmer 1834–1879*. Cologne, 1962

INDEX

For Product Safety Concerns and Information please contact our EU
representative GPSR@taylorandfrancis.com
Taylor & Francis Verlag GmbH, Kaufingerstraße 24, 80331 München, Germany

www.ingramcontent.com/pod-product-compliance
Ingram Content Group UK Ltd.
Pitfield, Milton Keynes, MK11 3LW, UK
UKHW021505240926
475702UK00035B/434

* 9 7 8 0 3 6 7 2 4 6 4 1 9 *